Tinsagu nu Hana ya
Chimisachi ni sumiti
Uyanu yuushi gutu ya
Chimu ni sumiri

Tin nuburi bushi ya
Yumiba yumarishiga
Uya nu yushi gutu ya
Yumi ya naran

Yuru harasu funi ya
Ninufaa bushi miati
Wan nacheeru uya ya
Wan du miati

Dye the tips of your fingernails
With the petals of the tinsagu blossom
Dye the teachings of your parents
Onto your heart

If you tried, you could
Count the stars in the sky
But you cannot count
What your parents teach you

A ship sailing at night
Gets its bearings from the North Star
My parents who gave me life
Get their bearings from me

TRANSLATION BY WESLEY IWAO UEUNTEN

Equestrienne

*This type of doll is called chinchin umagwaa,
named for the sound it makes (chinchin)
when pulled by its string (umagwaa means "small
horse" or "toy horse"). It was created by pasting paper
over a wooden mold, letting it dry, then painting it.
In this case, the wooden mold was superbly carved.
The doll resembles ancient Chinese funerary figurines
and is unusual in that it is wearinga hanagasa, a large
floral hat typically worn in Okinawan dance.*

*Papier-mâché. Made by Tomoshi Ryūwa.
Woodblock print by Ozaki Seiji.*

Frank Stewart

Katsunori Yamazato

EDITORS

Voices from Okinawa

Featuring Three Plays by Jon Shirota

UNIVERSITY
OF HAWAI'I
PRESS

HONOLULU

CONTENTS

Voices from Okinawa 🪀 **Featuring Three Plays by Jon Shirota**

Preface

Voices from Okinawa offers writings by Okinawan Americans who were born either in the United States, such as Jon Shirota, June Hiroko Arakawa, and Philip K. Ige, or in Okinawa, such as Seiyei Wakukawa and Mitsugu Sakihara. It has been a dream of the editors to compile such an anthology. *Voices* is the first publication of its kind, presenting authors from a region of the world that has yet to be fully acknowledged in American and international literature.

Some scholars and readers—but too few—have long been aware of the social and cultural atmosphere that is unique to literary works by Okinawan American writers. The best known of this literature is Jon Shirota's novel *Lucky Come Hawaii.* Widely read when first published by Bantam in 1965, the story was later adapted by Shirota as a play. It was produced in New York in 1990 by the Pan Asian Repertory Theatre, with a grant from the John F. Kennedy Center Foundation. The play was praised in the *New York Times* and continues to be produced in the U.S., along with Shirota's other plays about Okinawan immigrants and their descendants.

Lucky Come Hawaii is set on Maui and begins immediately before the Japanese attack on Pearl Harbor. Some of the male Okinawan characters express strong pro-Japanese nationalism as soon as they hear about the attack. They begin to think that Japan will take over all of Hawai'i and even hope that this will happen soon so that they—not well-placed haoles (Caucasians)—will be able to control Maui. They imagine that victorious Japanese soldiers will come to Maui, so that even Okinawans—marginalized and discriminated against by the Naichi (Japanese immigrants from Japan's main islands)—will be big shots. So thinks Kama Gusuda, an Issei (first-generation immigrant) from a small, impoverished village in the northern part of Okinawa. The reactions of the various characters to the war reveal where they came from and how they have been affected by immigrating to Hawai'i.

Shirota gives his Okinawan characters cultural and ethnic traits that distinguish them from other Japanese. The troubled relations between Okinawa and the rest of Japan have continued since 1879, when the Ryukyu Kingdom was annexed by the rising East Asian empire of the northern islands. Even after Okinawans settle in Hawaiʻi and the United States, they must struggle for an identity of their own, Japanese and yet undeniably Okinawan.

Despite the many cultural and linguistic distinctions, Okinawan writers have been seen as a small group within the larger category of Japanese American literature. Regarded as peripheral, these writers have generally been overlooked by scholars and editors. Why were Okinawan American writers not included in anthologies of Japanese American or Asian American writers?

In *Voices from Okinawa,* readers will discover the exuberance and excellence of Okinawan American literature, as well as its importance to world literature. Showcasing these works is a way of questioning the established "canon" of Asian American and Japanese American literature. We believe that as more Okinawan Americans are published, these literary categories will be seen from a new perspective: more inclusive, complex, and multilayered.

Okinawan American writing at present may be hidden deep in special collections and in public or private libraries. We look forward to presenting works by more Okinawan authors—both young and old—in the coming years.

The publication of *Voices from Okinawa* is made possible by a grant from the Ministry of Education, Culture, and Sciences of Japan. The University of the Ryukyus received a 2008 grant to do research on human migration, and we are grateful that the Pacific and North American Research Project generously provided the funds necessary for publishing this book.

Katsunori Yamazato

JON SHIROTA

Lucky Come Hawaii

Adapted from the 1965 novel of the same name, Lucky Come Hawaii *was produced in Los Angeles at the Inner City Cultural Center in 1990 and later by Kumu Kahua Theatre in Honolulu. In 1990, it was also produced in New York City by the Pan Asian Repertory Theatre with a production grant from the John F. Kennedy Center Fund for New American Plays.*

Introduction

Kapuna Valley is nestled between the lush, green, and majestic West Maui Mountains and the pounding, blue-green Pacific Ocean. The corrugated iron–roofed Gusuda home is at the bottom of a deep ravine, a stone's throw away from the Kapuna River. It is one of the few homes in the valley that is painted (the walls green, the roof red), and it is the only one with a telephone and an outhouse that has a flush toilet.

Except for a few moments in the living room and outdoors, the entire play takes place in the rather bare and confining dining room of the Gusuda home. Aside from a prominent Japanese flag on the wall Upstage, the room is not markedly Japanese, Hawaiian, or American. It actually is a combination of all three. The entrance to this goza-matted room is at Stage Right. At Center, beneath a naked lightbulb, is a long rectangular table with empty sardine-can ashtrays and a vase of fresh tropical flowers. Surrounding the table are old, hard-backed chairs. Through a lone window Upstage Center can be seen part of the West Maui Mountains. To the left of the window hangs a telephone of the late thirties, and to the right is an old, graying refrigerator. Upstage Left, beside the living-room door, is an antiquated chikonki (hand-winding phonograph). At Downstage Left is a door that leads into the kitchen. Except for the narration at the beginning and end, the time is December 1941.

Cast of Characters

Kama Gusuda, aged fifty-five. Okinawan pig farmer.
Tsuyu Gusuda, aged fifty. Wife of Kama Gusuda.
Kimiko Gusuda, aged eighteen. Nisei daughter of Kama and Tsuyu Gusuda.
Kenyei Shiroma, aged twenty-eight. Okinawan taro farmer.
Ishi, aged sixty-five. Narrator and retired Okinawan janitor.
Tengan, aged fifty. Okinawan fisherman.

1

Ikehara-san, aged sixty. Okinawan matchmaker.
Bob Weaver, aged thirty. White army sergeant.
Howard Specks, aged twenty-one. White army private.

Act One Scene One

As houselights dim and the stage remains dark, spotlight rises Downstage Center on Ishi, who is wearing a dark suit and hat and carrying a cane.

ISHI   [*To audience.*] Mensooree. Irasshai. Hele mai. Hele mai. Welcome. Welcome. Very glad you understand Okinawan-Japanese-Hawaiian-English. I come from Okinawa many years ago. Never go back, not once. Now, I go back. [*Shows passport.*] See. Passport. [*Beat.*] Oh, no, no. Not moving back; just visiting. Want to pay respect to anniversary of Grandfather's death. Ah, Grandfather. Great thinker. Just before I come Hawaii, you know what he say to me? "Always remember, Gensuke…" That me, Ishi Gensuke. [*Waves to audience.*] Ha-ro… "Whenever meeting stranger," Grandfather say to me, "find out right away if Okinawan or not Okinawan." Very good advice. But Grandfather, he don't know, sometimes don't have to ask if Okinawan or not Okinawan. Especially if stranger have blue eyes and red hair. Yes. I come Hawaii many years ago. So many memories. Some sad, some happy; some want to forget, some want to remember; some, even if want to forget, will always remember. [*Reminisces; smiling, shaking head.*] One memory can never forget. Come. Come to home of my good friend, Gusuda Kama. Number one pig farmer in all Maui.

Lights now rise in living room, Upstage Right, where Kimiko Gusuda is playing piano (Bach Minuet in G). She is dressed casually in jeans and aloha shirt. In a moment, light in living room dims, piano music diminishes, and light rises in dining room, where three "old-country" Japanese are seated at the table: Kama Gusuda, rather quiet, leathery-faced, smoking Bull Durham and sipping sake; Tsuyu Gusuda, soft-spoken, subservient, sitting quietly and listening attentively to the conversation; and Ikehara-san, a venerable Okinawan matchmaker and president of the prestigious Maui Okinawan Association. Ikehara-san is wearing a baggy old suit; the others are in casual old clothes. Seated Downstage Left, on the goza-matted floor, are Ishi, a janitor at Maui Pineapple Cannery, and Tengan, a fisherman. They are drinking sake and playing hanafuda cards for nickels and dimes, slamming their cards on the floor and cursing their bad luck.

ISHI   [*Picking up card from deck, slamming it down.*] Another no-good card!

TENGAN	[*Picking up card, slamming it down.*] Ah, shit-u! They're beginning to smell worse than you!
KAMA	Oi, you two! Be quiet! Can't you see we're discussing something very important?
ISHI	[*To Tengan.*] Kama must be drunk. Kimiko will never go along with the proposal.
TSUYU	Ikehara-san, please excuse those two. They don't know any better.
KAMA	If they weren't from the same village back home, I would never have them here.
IKEHARA-SAN	It's too bad you Ginoza people drink so much.
KAMA	[*Self-effacingly.*] Other villages were famous for their woodwork, their paintings, or their songs. We were famous for our drunkards.
IKEHARA-SAN	I understand there were no schools in your village.
KAMA	No. No, we didn't have any schools.
IKEHARA-SAN	We were a little more fortunate in our village. We not only had a school, but our schoolteachers were from Mainland Japan.
KAMA	Naichi schoolteachers! No wonder you Nago people speak good Japanese.
IKEHARA-SAN	I went as high as the sixth grade; and Kenyei, he went as high as the eighth grade.
KAMA	[*To Tsuyu.*] Kenyei was number one in his class. And when he joined the Imperial Army, he became a corporal in no time.
TSUYU	Is that right?
IKEHARA-SAN	Gusuda-san, I know this came as a surprise, but can we set the date for the wedding?
KAMA	Yes, of course.
IKEHARA-SAN	How about…say, in a month.
KAMA	In a month will be fine, Ikehara-san. It will give me time to prepare a big luau. I want everyone in Kapuna Valley to come: the Kanakas, the Porlegees, the Filipinos—just everyone.
IKEHARA-SAN	[*Rising.*] Then it's settled. The wedding will take place in a month.
KAMA	[*Rising respectfully.*] Yes. In a month. [*Offering sake.*] Let's drink to that.
IKEHARA-SAN	[*Accepting.*] Ah, arigato…It's going to be a fine wedding.

TENGAN	[*Quickly bringing his cup to refill.*] You might as well fill mine, too.
ISHI	Mine, too.
KAMA	[*Pours a few drops into their cups grudgingly.*] Yes. It will be a fine wedding.
IKEHARA-SAN	[*Toasting.*] Here's to the happy marriage of your daughter to my nephew. [*Facing the Japanese flag, they bow formally to it, then to each other. They drink. Tengan and Ishi look at each other, shrug, and return to their card game with their sake.*]
KAMA	My family is greatly honored, Ikehara-san.
IKEHARA-SAN	It is a great honor for my family, too, Gusuda-san. [*Stepping toward door.*] I'll be back next week to make more definite plans.
KAMA	Yes, please do that.
IKEHARA-SAN	Kenyei will be happy to know that everything went well here.
TSUYU	Be sure to tell him that he is always welcome here.
ISHI	[*To Tengan.*] How come she never tells us that?
KAMA	[*To Ishi and Tengan, urging them to bid Ikehara-san sayonara.*] Ishi…Tengan…
TENGAN	Sayonara, Ikehara-san.
ISHI	We hope to see you again soon, Ikehara-san.
TENGAN	[*To Ishi.*] Don't overdo it.
	Ikehara-san bids everyone sayonara, ad libbing, and exits.
KAMA	[*To Ishi and Tengan.*] You two shouldn't have said those things about Kenyei.
TENGAN	About Kenyei always banging his bicycle into a telephone pole?
ISHI	And always scolding the telephone pole?
KAMA	*Baka!*
TENGAN	[*Scornfully.*] That blind bat. He and that proud uncle of his are always reminding us how much schooling they have.
ISHI	They think they're the…Okinawan Confucius.
KAMA	[*Ridiculing.*] What do you know about Confucius?
ISHI	He's the smart Chinese who invented chop suey.
TENGAN	[*Kimiko steps in from living room and crosses toward refrigerator.*] Kimiko.
KIMIKO	Yes?

TENGAN	You better catch the next boat to Honolulu.
ISHI	Or to California.
KAMA	Tengan! Ishi!
KIMIKO	[*To Tsuyu.*] What are they talking about?
TSUYU	That was Ikehara-san who was here.
KIMIKO	Ikehara-san?
TENGAN	The matchmaker.
ISHI	Who wants you to marry Kenyei.
KIMIKO	What?!
KAMA	I've had enough of you two!
KIMIKO	That man was here to…match Kenyei and me?!
KAMA	He chose you from among all the Okinawan girls on Maui.
KIMIKO	Otosan!
TSUYU	You're a very lucky girl, Kimiko. You know who Kenyei is. When I came from Okinawa to marry your father, I didn't even know what he looked like.
ISHI	Good thing.
KIMIKO	I'm going to work at Kress Store for another six months, then I'm going to the university to become a music teacher. You know that.
TSUYU	You can still become a music teacher. Kenyei can buy you a piano in Tokyo.
KIMIKO	Tokyo?
KAMA	On your way to Okinawa.
KIMIKO	Okinawa?!
KAMA	We will all be going back soon.
TENGAN	Not me.
ISHI	Me, I'm going back just for a visit. I don't want to eat rotten potatoes three times a day for the rest of my life.
KAMA	Your mother and I are getting old, Kimiko. Is it too much to ask? To marry a good Okinawan boy so we can have grandchildren?
KIMIKO	Otosan, you want me to marry someone I…don't love? Someone I…don't think I can ever love?
KAMA	*Love?!* What does that have to do with marrying Kenyei?

KIMIKO	I…can hardly understand what he's saying half of the time.
KAMA	You'll get to understand him once you're married to him.
KIMIKO	[*To Tsuyu, desperately.*] Okasan, please…Explain to him.
KAMA	[*Exploding.*] You're going to marry Kenyei!
KIMIKO	No, I'm not!
KAMA	Yes, you are! [*There is knocking Upstage Right. Everyone turns toward door. More knocking. Finally, to Tsuyu.*] Go see who it is. *Kimiko rushes away in tears and exits.*
TSUYU	[*Walks to door, opens it.*] Oh, ha-ro, Bob-u… *Kama quickly steps up to Japanese flag on wall, takes down flag, and hides it.*
WEAVER	[*Offstage. Boisterously.*] Hi, Mrs. Gusuda. How are you this evening?
TSUYU	Okay. Okay. Come in. Come in.
WEAVER	[*Stepping in, apparently drunk, an ukulele in his big paw. Tall and heavyset, Weaver has on an aloha shirt that hangs over his khaki army trousers.*] Hi, everyone! [*Everyone responds, "Haro, Bob-u…"*] Hi, Mr. Gusuda.
KAMA	[*Pulling out of grave situation of moments ago.*] Ha-ro, Bob-u. Come. Come. Sit. Sit.
TENGAN	[*To Ishi.*] C'mon…[*They sit back down on floor to resume card game.*]
WEAVER	[*To Tsuyu, speaking carefully.*] I am glad you are learning to speak more and more English, Mrs. Gusuda. *Tsuyu looks at Kama questioningly.*
KAMA	Just say, "I am glad, too."
TSUYU	[*To Weaver, deliberately.*] I am glad, too.
WEAVER	That makes two of us.
TSUYU	I am glad, too.
KAMA	You already said that! Go get a clean cup for Bob-u.
TSUYU	[*Stepping Downstage Left toward kitchen, muttering.*] I am glad, too…
WEAVER	[*To Tengan and Ishi.*] How're you two gents doing? Any luck of the Irish?

TENGAN / ISHI	Too much pilikia. Too much pilikia.
KAMA	[*To Weaver.*] "Pilikia…" Kanaka talk: "no ruck of Irish."
WEAVER	I got it. Where's Kim tonight?
KAMA	Kimiko not feel too good.
WEAVER	Oh, sorry to hear that. You got yourself a fine girl, Mr. Gusuda. A mighty fine girl.
KAMA	[*Shaking head.*] Sometimes just like American gal…Too much paakiki head.
WEAVER	Yeah. Yeah. [*Indicating head.*] She sure got it up here alright. [*Repeating.*] Too much paakiki head. Too much paakiki head. I just hope my two girls turn out like her. [*Beat. Confidentially.*] Say, Mr. Gusuda, you think, maybe, I can get a gallon of sake in advance? You know… Christmas coming up and everything, I'm a little short on cash.
KAMA	Anytime, Bob-u. Anytime.
WEAVER	I'll bring you a case of beer next time I'm back. Okay?
KAMA	Okay. Okay.
WEAVER	Hey, Mr. Gusuda, you want to hear my latest island song?
KAMA	Go ahead, Bob-u. Sing. Sing.
WEAVER	[*Rises, strums a few chords on ukulele, then sings to tune of "When the Swallows Come Back to Capistrano."*] When the soldiers come back to Camp Paukokalu the Maui girls they all shake their big alu alu… *Rolls his big rear to "alu alu."*
KAMA	[*Bursts out laughing.*] "Big alu alu"… You big alu alu…
TENGAN / ISHI	[*Laughing.*] You one big alu-alu haole…
KAMA	This haole, he's almost as crazy as you two.
WEAVER	You really think it's great, eh?
KAMA	Numbah one. Numbah one.
WEAVER	[*To Tsuyu returning from kitchen.*] You like it, too, Mrs. Gusuda?
TSUYU	Numbah one. Numbah one.

Woman Playing Teeku

———————— ❧ ————————

*In the Ryukyus, women play handheld drums
(single-sided paarankuu or double-sided teeku) as
they dance and sing at such events as the women-only
outings held on the third day of the third month
of the lunar calendar (sangwachisannichi) or at the
bon festival (shichigwachieisaa) in the seventh month.
Their songs, yarashii and kweena, are sung for the
safe voyage and well being of travelers. Teeku are also
played at the ushideeku, an autumn harvest festival.
The jurigwaa ninjoo (female entertainer doll)
depicted here was likely sold at the yukkanufii festival
(held during the fourth month of the lunar calendar).
The strong, vibrant colors are characteristic
of the Southern Islands.*

*Paper-mâché. Made by Tomoshi Ryūwa.
Woodblock print by Ozaki Seiji.*

WEAVER	You betcha.
TSUYU	[*Pouring sake.*] Drink, Bob-u. Drink.
WEAVER	Thank you, Mrs. Gusuda. Thank you.
TSUYU	You betcha.
WEAVER	[*Toasting.*] Here's to you, Mr. Gusuda. And to you, Mrs. Gusuda. And to you two gents. [*Takes a long pull.*]
KAMA	You numbah one haole, Bob-u.
WEAVER	And you're number one Hawaiian, Mr. Gusuda.
KAMA	Okinawan-Hawaiian.
WEAVER	[*Mimicking.*] "Akisamiyo! What'samattah you, what'samattah me?"
	Everyone laughs.
KAMA	When wife, children come?
WEAVER	Oh, didn't I tell you? They're already in Honolulu. They're catching the boat Sunday night and will be here early Monday morning.
KAMA	Good. Good. [*To Tsuyu.*] His wife and children will be here Monday morning.
TSUYU	[*To Weaver.*] I am glad, too.
WEAVER	I haven't seen my wife and kids for over six months. Never been away from them this long before. Not even when I was stationed down in Panama.
KAMA	Pretty soon, all together again.
WEAVER	God, I hope so.
KAMA	Next month, you bring family to luau. Okay?
WEAVER	You're having a luau?
KAMA	Big one. No forget. You, family come.
WEAVER	We'll be here. You betcha. Well, I better get going. The boys back in camp—they're waiting for me.
KAMA	[*Offering gallon.*] Here, Bob-u. You take.
WEAVER	Thank you, Mr. Gusuda. Thank you. I won't forget to bring you that case of beer I owe you.
KAMA	Okay. Okay.

WEAVER	[*Picking up ukulele and speaking carefully.*] And thank you, Mrs. Gusuda. As always, I enjoyed your hospitality.
TSUYU	You betcha, Bob-u. You betcha.
WEAVER	[*At door.*] Goodnight, everyone.
	Everyone bows and bids Weaver goodnight. As the door closes behind him, he is singing his new song.
KAMA	[*Chuckling, stepping over to hidden flag.*] He's sure not like the Maui haoles who always have their noses in the air.
TSUYU	You think it was a good idea inviting him and his family to our luau?
KAMA	[*Retrieving flag.*] Of course.
TSUYU	What if there is no luau?
KAMA	A wedding without a luau?
TENGAN	There might not be a wedding.
ISHI	Not without Kimiko here.
KAMA	Baka! It's about time you two went home! [*To Tsuyu.*] Go and talk to that stubborn, paakiki-headed daughter of yours. Tell her I already make a yakusoku with Ikehara-san.
	As he hangs flag back on wall, lights slowly dim until BLACKOUT.

Scene Two

Early next morning. Tsuyu is Upstage Left in living room, listening to Hawaiian music on radio and preparing to iron week's laundry. Looking around, she sneaks out a pack of cigarettes, lights up, and smokes surreptitiously.

The Hawaiian music is abruptly cut off, and the announcer's voice comes on, urgent but not noticeably so: "We interrupt this program once again to bring you the following important message: enemy aircraft, now definitely identified as Japanese, are attacking Pearl Harbor and other military bases on Oahu…I repeat: enemy aircraft identified as Japanese are attacking Pearl Harbor and other military bases on the island. This is not a practice air raid. I repeat. This is not a practice air raid…"

Tsuyu, not understanding a word of the announcement, has already gone into living room to turn off the radio. Stepping back into dining room, she goes over to the old phonograph and plays an Okinawan record with the song "Tancha Meh." Feeling nostalgic, she cannot resist doing a few dance movements. Catching herself, she returns to her ironing board. In a moment, however, she is irresistibly drawn to the music and starts dancing again, this time with laundry basket. Kimiko enters unnoticed from living room. She watches her mother dancing, somewhat intrigued. Tsuyu suddenly senses someone is watching.

TSUYU	[*Self-consciously.*] Oh, it's you, Kimiko…
KIMIKO	I didn't know you could dance like that.
TSUYU	Oh, I did a little dancing in my day.
KIMIKO	In your village?
TSUYU	[*Ironing.*] During the festivals.
KIMIKO	[*Beat.*] You really want to move back to Okinawa, Okasan?
TSUYU	It's my home.
KIMIKO	What about me? My home is here.
TSUYU	Your home is wherever your husband wants to be.
KIMIKO	Okasan, you and Otosan can't be serious about…me and Kenyei.
TSUYU	A yakusoku made with someone like Ikehara-san can't be any more serious, Kimiko.
KIMIKO	What Kenyei wants is a…nice, quiet Okinawan girl.
TSUYU	You're not a nice, quiet Okinawan girl?!
KIMIKO	Okasan, please…Kenyei and I—we don't have anything in common.
TSUYU	You are both Okinawans. What could be more common than that?
KAMA	[*Offstage.*] Tsuyu! Tsuyu! [*Door Upstage Right flies open, and Kama rushes in, limping. He looks toward living room.*] Where's Kimiko?! [*Sees her.*] Why aren't you listening to the radio?!
KIMIKO	What happened? Why are you limping?
KAMA	They are attacking Pear-ru Har-bah!
KIMIKO	[*Skeptically.*] Who's attacking Pearl Harbor?
KAMA	Japanese airplanes!
KIMIKO	Aw, Otosan. Who told you that?
KAMA	Lin Wu, that's who!
TSUYU	And you said you and Lin Wu drink just coffee every morning.
KIMIKO	It must be just another air-raid practice. They're always having them over there.
KAMA	Kimiko! Go in the living room and turn on the radio!
TSUYU	Oi, Kama. Why don't you go lie down for a while?
KAMA	[*To Kimiko.*] Don't keep standing there! Go and turn on the radio!

KIMIKO	I'm telling you, Otosan. It's just another air-raid practice.
KAMA	Go!
KIMIKO	[*Resignedly.*] Aw, alright…[*Exits into living room.*]
KAMA	[*Rubbing his knee.*] That no-good sonnabitchee Chinese boy…
TSUYU	What sonnana Chinese boy?
KAMA	Lin Wu's boy. When I went to pick up the pig slop at their restaurant, the boy and his father were listening to the radio. The announcer kept saying, "This no practice. This real McCoy!"
TSUYU	And you fell?
KAMA	Tsuyu! All these years in Hawaii, and you still don't know that much English. Real McCoy! That means no bull sh—never mind. The war might be over by the time you understand.
TSUYU	What war?
KAMA	That's why the boy kicked me out of the kitchen!
	Tsuyu thinks this over.
KIMIKO	[*Rushing in.*] Otosan! They're attacking not only Pearl Harbor—Schofield Barracks and Kaneohe, too!
KAMA	See! What did I tell you?!
TSUYU	We're at war! [*Rushes over and takes down Japanese flag.*]
KAMA	They don't want all of America. Just Hawaii. [*To Kimiko.*] Get back in there and keep listening to the radio. If the announcer speaks in Japanese, it means the governor has surrendered.
KIMIKO	Otosan! You can get in big trouble for saying that.
KAMA	[*Pushing Kimiko.*] Get back in there!
KIMIKO	Okasan, you better talk to him. [*Exits.*]
TSUYU	Oi, Kama. Maybe Kimiko is right. If we are at war against Japan—
KAMA	Tsuyu! We—*we*—are at war against America! [*Walking up to phone.*] I'm calling the Japanese schoolteacher. He knows what to do at a time like this. [*Dials.*]
TSUYU	Watch out. There could be Japanese spying for America.
KAMA	[*Pause, then into phone.*] Ha-ro, Fukunaga-san? [*Bowing low.*] This is Gusuda Kama. Has the governor surrendered…?
TSUYU	Oi, Kama!
KAMA	You mean you haven't heard?! Hawaii is about to become a part of Japan!

TSUYU	Oi, Kama!
KAMA	[*Confidentially.*] Fukunaga-san, I can't explain over the telehone. There could be Japanese spying for America. Turn on your radio…Your radio, Fukunaga-san. Turn it on. [*With hand over mouthpiece, speaking to Tsuyu.*] The schoolteacher didn't know anything about it.
	Loud knock Upstage Right.
KENYEI	[*Offstage.*] Gusuda-san! Gusuda-san!
KAMA	[*To Tsuyu.*] It's Kenyei. Let him in.
	When Tsuyu opens door, Kenyei rushes in. He has a soiled towel around his neck. His face, hands, and bare feet are mud-stained, his knee-length taro-patch trousers wet.
KENYEI	[*Squinting. To Tsuyu.*] Gusuda-san! The radio—it keeps saying something about airplanes attacking Honolulu.
KAMA	You heard it, too, Kenyei?!
KENYEI	[*Squints again at Tsuyu; realizes he is not talking to Kama. Now stepping toward Kama.*] Gusuda-san! The radio—it keeps saying something about airplanes attacking Honolulu!
KAMA	You heard it over Radio Tokyo?
KENYEI	Over KGU.
KAMA	Radio Tokyo hasn't said anything about it?
KENYEI	Said what?
KAMA	Kenyei! Those are all Japanese airplanes.
KENYEI	Japanese airplanes? Yes, of course! They are all Japanese airplanes.
KAMA	Don't you think it means only one thing?
KENYEI	What?
KAMA	War!
KENYEI	Yes, of course! It can mean only one thing.
KAMA	What, Kenyei?
KENYEI	War!
KAMA	[*Speaking into phone and bowing.*] Yes, I'm still here, Fukunaga-san…Maui! You think Maui will be next?! Alright, Fukunaga-san. Alright…Yes, thank you. Thank you very much…Yes, all of us here in Kapuna will be waiting to hear from you. Sayonara. [*Bows deeply, then hangs up, muttering.*] Damn proud Naichi

	schoolteacher. Always drawing a line between us Okinawans and the non-Okinawan Japanese.
TSUYU	Didn't he thank you?
KAMA	Since when does a Naichi ever thank us Okinawans for anything?
KENYEI	What did he say?
KAMA	He said the governor knows better than to keep fighting.
KENYEI	[*No longer the meek, ingratiating taro grower, he is now Shiroma Kenyei, ex-soldier of the Imperial Army.*] I knew it. I just knew it!
KAMA	What, Kenyei?
TSUYU	[*Overlapping.*] You knew what, Kenyei?
KENYEI	They were coming!
KAMA / TSUYU	Who?
KENYEI	Japanese soldiers.
KAMA / TSUYU	Here?! They are coming here?!
KENYEI	[*Nodding stoically.*] They were on their way when I was in His Majesty's Army. All of the Pacific will one day belong to Japan, my captain told me.
KAMA	He might be in the Maui invasion?
KENYEI	Maui invasion?
KAMA	"They were coming." Isn't that what you just said?
KENYEI	Yes, of course! [*Pondering.*] "Whoever controls the water, controls the land." That's what my captain always said.
KAMA	[*To Tsuyu.*] Kenyei knows exactly what to do at times like this.
TSUYU	[*To Kenyei, alarmed.*] You're not thinking of poisoning the water tunnel!
KENYEI	I don't have to. As soon as the invasion starts, I'll run up to the mountain and shut off the water supply. [*To Kama.*] Gusuda-san, I want you to call the mayor and tell him to surrender or there won't be any more water.
KAMA	Hai, Kenyei.
KENYEI	[*Beat.*] At last, Hawaii becoming a part of Japan.
KAMA	We don't have to return to Okinawa anymore.
KENYEI	It'll be the same as being back there.

KIMIKO	[*Rushing in.*] Pearl Harbor and parts of downtown Honolulu are still on fire! They shot down several enemy airplanes, but the rest escaped.
KAMA	You and your mother better prepare to hide up in the mountains.
KIMIKO	Hide up in the mountains?
KAMA	The mayor—he's a typical hard-headed Porlegee. He might not surrender right away.
KIMIKO	[*Eyeing Kenyei.*] Who's been telling you these things?
KENYEI	Kimiko, things won't be the same here on Maui from now on. We'll have to start accepting many changes.
KIMIKO	Like what?!
KENYEI	The leaders of today will no longer be the leaders of tomorrow.
KAMA	You hear that? "The leaders of today will no longer be the leaders of tomorrow…" [*To Kenyei.*] What exactly does that mean, Kenyei?
KENYEI	It means that our ideas, our ways, our thoughts, they will all have to change.
KAMA	[*To Kimiko.*] You better start listening to Kenyei.
KIMIKO	He better stop spreading rumors.
KAMA	Kenyei is going to be an important man on Maui from now on. [*Kenyei raises his head.*] Why…he might even be the…next mayor of Maui.
KIMIKO	What?!
KAMA	Go back in there. General Tojo might be speaking to us any minute.
KIMIKO	What?!
KAMA	Stop saying, "What?! What?!" [*Pushes Kimiko.*]
KIMIKO	[*Exiting.*] I'm warning you, Otosan!
KENYEI	It would be better if Kimiko and I got married right away.
KAMA	Yes, of course. The sooner she learns how to conduct herself properly, the better it will be for you.
	There is an urgent knocking Upstage Right.
ISHI	[*Offstage.*] Oi, Kama! Kama! [*Enters before Tsuyu can open door.*] Did you hear?! The Chinese have attacked Pear-ru Har-bah!
KAMA	What?!

ISHI	That's what my neighbor, Johnny Halewa, said.
KAMA	[*Pinching Ishi's ear.*] You pupule jackass! They are Japanese airplanes!
ISHI	Japanese…?
KENYEI	China don't even have airplanes.
ISHI	How do you know? You don't even know what an airplane looks like.
KENYEI	[*Ignoring Ishi; rising.*] I better go home and listen to Radio Tokyo.
KAMA	[*Rising, bowing respectfully.*] Yes, Kenyei. Please do that. You have the only radio in Kapuna that's powerful enough to catch the Tokyo station.
KENYEI	[*At door.*] I'll be back tonight.
KAMA	We'll be waiting, Kenyei.
KENYEI	[*Exiting.*] Sayonara…
KAMA / TSUYU	[*Bowing low.*] Sayonara…
ISHI	[*To Kama.*] What was all that about? You never bowed to him before.
KAMA	You should have done it, too.
ISHI	Me? Bow to that…makapaa blind bat?
KAMA	He's going to be the next—never mind. You wouldn't know what I'm talking about. [*To Tsuyu.*] Oi, get the can of paint ready.
TSUYU	You're going to paint the house again?
KAMA	Just the roof.
TSUYU	You just painted it red.
ISHI	Can I have a cup of sake?
KAMA	[*Ignoring Ishi.*] How else can we let the Japanese soldiers know that this is a Japanese home?
TSUYU	[*Stares at Kama.*] You're going to…!
KAMA	All I'm going to do is leave a big red circle in the middle and paint the rest of the roof white.
ISHI	[*Looking around.*] Don't you have any sake left?
TSUYU	[*Ignoring Ishi, crosses into kitchen Upstage Left.*] What if American soldiers see the Rising Sun on our roof?!

KAMA	[*Following Tsuyu.*] We can always erase it.
TSUYU	What if we run out of paint?
KAMA	Tsuyu! Just do as I say!
ISHI	[*Now alone, finally finds sake jug under table. Pours himself a cupful and drinks thirstily. Deliberating.*] So…those sneaky Chinese were really Japanese…
	As he takes another drink, lights slowly dim until BLACKOUT.

Scene Three

Early that evening. Stage is dark.

WEAVER	[*Offstage.*] Yes, Major. We've made sure everyone on this end of the island is informed…Yes, sir. Complete blackout and no one permitted outside after dark.
	Lights rise on dining room. The window is blacked out with a blanket. A bare lightbulb is lit above the table. Now in army MP uniform with sergeant's stripes, Weaver is on phone while his companion, Specks, is standing rigidly against far wall, surveying the room suspiciously. Kimiko is checking the windows, making sure no light is leaking out. Tsuyu, seated quietly at table beside Kama, is not quite sure what Weaver is saying over the phone.
	The Gusudas? They're alright, sir…Well, they're not really Japanese—Oh, you're absolutely right, sir. You're never half-pregnant. But these people, sir, they speak a language all their own…No, sir. It's not Chinese…No, sir. It's not Filipino either…Outer Mongolian, sir? Well, you could be right…
TSUYU	[*To Kama.*] We're Outer Mongolians?
KAMA	Be quiet.
WEAVER	Oh, yes, sir. Very loyal. Very cooperative…Just a minute, sir. [*To Kama.*] Mr. Gusuda, you know anyone here in the valley who might be considered subversive?
KAMA	Oh, yes. Everybody.
WEAVER / SPECKS	Everybody?!
KIMIKO	Otosan! He's asking if you know anyone who is a spy.
KAMA	Spy?! Oh, no, no. Don' know spy.
KIMIKO	[*To Weaver.*] He thought you meant whether he knows anyone who can be trusted.

SPECKS	The sergeant and I don't trust anyone. Absolutely no one.
WEAVER	[*Into phone.*] Sir, these people—they're as American as apple pie and Coca-Cola.
TSUYU	[*To Kimiko.*] Coca-Cola? Do we still have any left?
KAMA	[*To Tsuyu.*] Shhh! You don't know what we're talking about.
WEAVER	They're actually from a place called Okinawa, sir…No, sir. They're not Okis…Mr. Gusuda, sir? He raises pigs.
SPECKS	[*Disdainfully to Kama.*] So you're a pig farmer.
KAMA	You, too?
SPECKS	Do I look like a pig farmer?
KAMA	Maybe, maybe not…
WEAVER	[*Into phone.*] Right, sir. I'll be more careful not to discuss security matters over the phone again…You bet, sir. Over and out—oh, sir! Sir! [*Hangs up, muttering.*] Dammit! I forgot to ask if he's heard about my wife and kids.
KAMA	Wife, children alright?
WEAVER	That's what I've been trying to find out since early this morning.
KAMA	No worry, Bob-u. Japanee airplane never hurt women, children.
WEAVER	They better not! Bunch of sneaky sonsofbitches!
SPECKS	You can't trust a single one of them, Sarge. Absolutely not one of them.
WEAVER	I guess you all know. The islands are now under martial law.
SPECKS	Which means the military has absolute jurisdiction over every one of you. Anything less than one-hundred-percent cooperation and you'll find yourselves in violation of martial law.
KAMA	Oh, we kokua. We kokua all time.
KIMIKO	"Kokua." That's "help" in Hawaiian.
SPECKS	Remember what the major said, Sarge. We can't take any one of them for granted.
WEAVER	[*Sarcastically.*] And what else did the major say, Specks?
SPECKS	They're all considered potential enemies. Every one of them.
WEAVER	[*Indicating Kimiko.*] Her, too?
SPECKS	She's a Jap, isn't she?

KIMIKO	I am an American!
SPECKS	You?
KIMIKO	Yes! Me!
WEAVER	Americans don't all look like you, Specks.
KIMIKO	Thank God for that.
WEAVER	[*To Specks.*] Get back to the jeep and wait for me.
SPECKS	You're gonna be alright?
WEAVER	Will you get going?!
SPECKS	[*At door.*] Be sure to holler if you need me. [*Exits.*]
WEAVER	[*Muttering.*] With all the MPs around, I gotta get stuck with that junior-college nitwit. [*To Kama.*] Look, we've been told that there might be subversive activities taking place on the island. If you hear or see anything suspicious going on, be sure to let us know. Okay?
KAMA	Okay, Bob-u. Okay. I hear, I let you know. I see, I let you know.
KIMIKO	[*To Weaver.*] Are we in any danger of an invasion?
WEAVER	We'll know before the night's over.
KAMA	Japanee soldier come tonight?
WEAVER	You think they will?
KAMA	Maybe. Ah, maybe not.
WEAVER	What we got to watch out for is certain elements on the island leading the enemy to strategic areas.
KAMA	No worry, Bob-u. No poison water tunnel.
WEAVER	Water tunnel?
TSUYU	Oi, Kama!
WEAVER	You've heard that someone might try to poison our water supply?
KIMIKO	What he's trying to say is…we should have guards at the water tunnels.
WEAVER	That's a great idea, Mr. Gusuda. Damn good idea. I'll tell the major about it. [*Beat.*] Well, I better get going.
KAMA	You come back, okay?
WEAVER	I will. I sure will. Goodnight. [*Exits as Kimiko, Kama, and Tsuyu say "goodnight."*]

KIMIKO	[*To Kama.*] You could've gotten yourself in big trouble, Otosan.
KAMA	With Bob-u?
KIMIKO	With the other MP.
TSUYU	I don't think he likes pig farmers, Kama.
KAMA	Once he gets used to the smell of pigs, he'll get to like me.
	Sudden knocking on door Upstage Right.
KENYEI	[*Offstage.*] Gusuda-san…Gusuda-san…
KAMA	It's Kenyei.
KIMIKO	He's not supposed to be out.
KAMA	Let him in.
TSUYU	[*Opens door.*] Come in, Kenyei. Come in.
KENYEI	[*Stepping in cautiously, looking around.*] They're gone?
KAMA	The MPs? They came to use the tele-hone. Sit down, Kenyei. Sit down. [*To Tsuyu.*] Where's the tea?
TSUYU	Yes, of course…[*Lifts teapot to pour.*]
KAMA	Tsuyu! Make fresh tea.
TSUYU	Oh, yes. Kenyei likes his tea nice and fresh.
KAMA	[*To Kenyei as Tsuyu takes teapot into kitchen.*] What have you heard over Radio Tokyo?
KENYEI	It fell.
KAMA	Honolulu?!
KENYEI	My antenna.
KAMA	[*Regards Kenyei sympathetically.*] I'll come over tomorrow and help you put it back up.
KENYEI	[*Beat.*] I finally figured out what they plan to do. [*Takes out map from pocket, lays it open on table, then brings out magnifying glass.*]
KIMIKO	What are you doing?!
KENYEI	It's a map of Hawaii.
KIMIKO	You two are going to get in big trouble!
KAMA	For looking at a map of Hawaii?
KIMIKO	For subversive activity!

KENYEI	All I want to do is show your father where we are.
KIMIKO	You are in America!
KENYEI	Not when we're surrounded by the Japanese navy.
KAMA	You really think so, Kenyei?
KENYEI	[*Nods knowingly, then indicates spot on map with magnifying glass.*] We're here. California is there. There are hundreds, maybe thousands of Japanese naval ships between us.
KAMA	[*To Kimiko.*] You hear that? It's like the Kapuna Bridge washed away. No one can get to the other side.
KIMIKO	I'm warning you, Otosan.
KENYEI	If the governor doesn't surrender right away, all of Hawaii will be out of food.
KAMA	I hope he's not a hard-headed Porlegee.
KENYEI	Without food and water, he'll have to surrender.
KAMA	Ah, Kenyei…About the water tunnel—I heard there might be American soldiers guarding it.
KENYEI	They know of my plan!
KAMA	The MP who was here—somehow, he knows.
KENYEI	Traitors! There must be Japanese traitors spying for America. [*Folds map, sticks it back into pocket.*] You can trust no one at a time like this.
KAMA	[*Regarding Kimiko.*] Not even your own family.
TSUYU	[*Returning with teapot, pours.*] Have some fresh Tokyo tea, Kenyei.
KENYEI	Ah, nothing like good old Tokyo tea…[*Sips.*]
TSUYU	We serve it only when we have a special guest.
KENYEI	[*Sipping again.*] Only a special guest deserves tea like this. [*To Kama.*] Do you know how many soldiers will be guarding the water tunnel?
KAMA	I have no idea, Kenyei.
KENYEI	Find out from the MP who was here.
KAMA	Bob-u?
KENYEI	Find out also how many soldiers they have at Camp Pauku-kalo, how many airplanes they have at the naval station, how many big guns they have at the harbor.

KAMA	Bob-u is a friend, Kenyei.
KENYEI	Keep making him feel welcome.
KAMA	And take advantage of him?
KENYEI	He is the enemy.
KIMIKO	Enemy? Bob Weaver?
KAMA	Kimiko. Be quiet.
KENYEI	I'm going to need your help, too, Kimiko.
KIMIKO	To do what?!
KENYEI	Represent me.
KIMIKO	Represent you?
KENYEI	A Japanese wife usually stays home, but until everything is settled, you will be representing me at many official functions.
KIMIKO	This has gone far enough!
KAMA / TSUYU	Kimiko!
KIMIKO	Of all things—a matchmaker! You could have saved yourself a lot of trouble if you had asked me yourself.
KENYEI	[*Flabbergasted.*] I…wasn't sure how you felt about me, Kimiko.
KIMIKO	Now you know.
KAMA	And you becoming the mayor has nothing to do with it.
TSUYU	Isn't that right, Kimiko?
KIMIKO	It's about time this was settled once and for all.
	Loud knocking on door Upstage Right.
TENGAN / ISHI	[*Offstage.*] Oi, Kama! [*Quite drunk, they stagger in.*]
KIMIKO	You're not supposed to be out.
TENGAN	[*Indicating Kenyei.*] If that blind bat is out, why can't we?
TSUYU	You two behave yourselves or I'm going to ask you to leave.
ISHI	Aw, Tsuyu, you really believe that blind bat is going to be the next mayor of Maui?
KENYEI	Pigs, that's what you are. Pigs!
TENGAN / ISHI	What?!

KENYEI	It's people like you who make the Naichis look down on us. They think all we do is make sake and get drunk.
TENGAN	That's better than making wars.
KENYEI	Be proud you are Japanese!
TENGAN	I am an Okinawan! I was minding my own business this morning when the MPs said I was a spy and took my boat away.
ISHI	He can't even read or write.
KENYEI	You'll get your boat back.
KAMA	Kenyei will see to it that you get it back.
TENGAN	Him?!
ISHI	[*Nudging Tengan.*] When he becomes mayor of Maui.
TENGAN	Mayor? He was a fake when he came from Okinawa, and that's what he's always going to be. A pig-headed, illegal fake.
KENYEI	[*Exploding.*] I was a squad leader and a karate instructor in the Imperial Army!
TENGAN / ISHI	Ha!
KENYEI	I'll show you! [*Steps to center, assumes a karate stance, then begins the Okinawan Te Karate movements, yelling, grunting, kicking, punching, etc., at times threatening Ishi and Tengan with near blows and causing them to fall off their chairs. Kama and Tsuyu encourage Kenyei with "ahs" and "ohs" while Kimiko looks on, amused. Breathing hard, Kenyei stops and bows low to no one in particular.*]
KAMA	That was great, Kenyei! Just great! The best kuusankuu I've ever seen. The best.
TSUYU	That was wonderful, Kenyei. Just wonderful.
ISHI	Ha! I've seen better.
TENGAN	Even I can do better.
KAMA	You?!
TENGAN	Sure!
KAMA	You can't even take a pee without wetting all over youself.
TENGAN	[*Crosses over to corner and picks up broom.*] Ishi. Come here. [*Wraps handkerchief around head.*]
ISHI	[*Holding broom.*] What're you gonna do? Dance with this broom?

Male and Female Dancers

———————— ❧ ————————

*The Ryukyus are extolled as the islands of song and
dance, with each village developing its own variations.
In addition, there is a national dramatic form,
kumiwudui, which derives from classical sources.
This female doll has the expressive hand movements
of such dances, and is regarded as a jurigwaa ninjoo
(female entertainer doll). Her clothing is made of
bingata, dyed fabric stenciled with traditional
Okinawan motifs. Male dolls from an earlier period
had their hair tied up in a knot, but more recent
Okinawan dolls, like this one, do not have the
topknot, reflecting changes in social customs.*

*Paper-mâché.
Woodblock print by Ozaki Seiji.*

TENGAN	Hold it steady. [*Ishi holds broom unsteadily. Tengan does his warm-up routine, then screams "Ahhh!" and strikes broom. Ishi staggers backward, and Tengan falls forward. Everyone bursts out laughing.*] You damn fool! I told you to hold it steady!
KENYEI	[*Stepping over to Ishi.*] Hold it any way you want. [*Kenyei raises two fingers dramatically to show what he intends to do. He smiles vainly to Kimiko. Taking a deep, convulsive breath, he screams "Ahhh!" and breaks the handle with a blow.*]
KAMA	[*Awed.*] That was great, Kenyei! Just great!
TSUYU	Such power, Kenyei! Such power!
ISHI	[*Inspecting split handle.*] He did it. With just his fingers.
TENGAN	I used to do it with my forehead.
KIMIKO	Now let's see one of you put the broom together. That's the only one we have.
KENYEI	I used to be better in the Imperial Army. Much better.
KAMA	[*To Ishi and Tengan.*] Now you two believe Kenyei?
KENYEI	I can break a chair with one blow. [*Ishi and Tengan look at each other.*] You want me to show you?
KIMIKO	You better not!
TENGAN / ISHI	That's alright, Kenyei. That's alright.
KAMA	Ishi! Tengan! Stand at attention whenever speaking to Corporal Shiroma Kenyei!
TENGAN	[*Reaching.*] I need a drink.
ISHI	Me, too.
KAMA	[*Quickly taking gallon jar away.*] Only soldiers who obey orders deserve a drink.
TENGAN / ISHI	[*Moaning.*] Aw, Kama.
KENYEI	Private Ishi! Private Tengan! Kiotsuke! [*Ishi and Tengan snap to attention, battling the liquor in them, as Kenyei inspects his troops.*] The first thing a soldier in the Imperial Army learns is discipline.
KAMA	[*To Ishi and Tengan.*] You hear that?! Discipline.
KENYEI	The next thing he learns is dedication.

KAMA	Dedication.
KENYEI	When the time comes, I'm going to need two volunteers to go up to the mountain. [*Ishi and Tengan look behind them, at each other.*] Japanese soldiers are always volunteering for dangerous missions.
TENGAN	It's going to be dangerous?
ISHI	I haven't even learned to salute yet.
TENGAN	I need a drink.
ISHI	Me, too.
KENYEI	Kora!
KAMA	[*Relenting.*] Oi, Kenyei. Let's rest a moment and make a toast.
ISHI	[*Rushing for cup.*] Let's make a big toast.
TENGAN	[*Also rushing for cup.*] An extra big one.
KAMA	[*Pours all around. Then, lifting cup high.*] To the next mayor of Maui: Shiroma Kenyei!
THE MEN	Banzai!
KIMIKO	Otosan!
TSUYU	[*Looking out window.*] Oi, Kama!
THE MEN	Banzai!
TSUYU	Kama!
KIMIKO	Stop it!
THE MEN	Banzai!
TSUYU	[*Reacting to what she sees out window.*] A jeep just came into our yard.
THE MEN	[*Spewing out liquor, scrambling for door.*] Jeep! MP jeep! Akisamiyo!
KAMA	Hurry! Hide in the bushes!
TSUYU	Kama!
KIMIKO	Otosan! You don't have to hide!
KAMA	[*Steps back into dining room, grins impishly.*] What makes you think I was going to hide? [*Kimiko and Tsuyu avoid his eyes, holding back giggles.*] Don't keep standing there. Clean up the table. It must be Bob-u coming back to use our tele-hone.

As Tsuyu and Kimiko rush over to clean table, giggling, lights begin to dim until CURTAIN.

Act Two

Scene One

A week later. Dusk. Tsuyu, alone in the dining room, is busy fitting, measuring, and placing a dark piece of cloth over the window.

KAMA	[*Entering from Upstage Right.*] Haven't you replaced the blanket yet?
TSUYU	[*Finishing.*] I'm almost done. How long more do we have to keep our windows blacked out?
KAMA	Until the Japanese army come.
TSUYU	It's already been a week since Kenyei said they would be here.
KAMA	Radio Tokyo must have sent him wrong signals.
ISHI	[*Entering with Tengan from Upstage Right.*] If you don't think he's going to be mayor, why were you polishing his bicycle the other day?
TENGAN	Me?! Polishing Kenyei's bicycle?!
KAMA	Oi, you two! Be quiet. The MPs will hear you.
TSUYU	Sit down. Have some sashimi.
	Ishi and Tengan sit at table, ad libbing.
KAMA	[*Beat. To Tsuyu.*] Did you talk to her again?
TSUYU	She's still against it.
KAMA	You know what's going to happen if she doesn't go through with the marriage? All the Okinawans on Maui will keep away from me. "Don't ever make a yakusoku with Gusuda Kama," they're going to say. "He's not a man of his word." Before long, I won't have any friends left.
TENGAN	I'll always be your friend, Kama.
ISHI	Me, too.
KAMA	[*Appraises Tengan and Ishi; mutters.*] Maybe it's better not to have any friends. [*To Tsuyu.*] It's all your fault! You should never have let her become so Americanized!
TENGAN	Kimiko is too good for that…Okinawan King Kamehameha.

ISHI	I hope the real Naichi soldiers don't treat us the way he does.
TENGAN	They're always looking down on us—those damn Naichis. Just because we're darker and a little more hairy than them.
ISHI	[*Sliding forearm beside Tengan's and comparing.*] You're dark and hairy even for an Okinawan, you know that?
	Sudden knocking on door Upstage Right.
KAMA	It's Kenyei. He must have something very important to tell us.
TSUYU	[*Rising.*] Just a minute, Kenyei.
	Another loud knock.
WEAVER	[*Offstage.*] Mr. Gusuda!
TENGAN / ISHI	[*Jumping up.*] Akisamiyo! MP!
TSUYU	[*To Ishi and Tengan.*] Go out the front door. Hurry!
KAMA	Hide in the bushes until I send him away.
WEAVER	[*Offstage.*] It's me, Bob Weaver.
	Tengan and Ishi rush out.
KAMA	[*Stalling.*] Who?
WEAVER	[*Offstage.*] Weaver.
KAMA	Weaver?
WEAVER	[*Offstage.*] Your friend, Bob Weaver.
KAMA	Oh. Bob-u. [*Opens door. Weaver stands there with case of beer on his shoulder.*] Ha-ro, Bob-u.
WEAVER	Anything wrong?
KAMA	Not sure. Not sure.
WEAVER	[*Stepping in.*] You did the right thing, Mr. Gusuda. I could've been a Japanese soldier.
KAMA	[*Amused.*] You? Japanee soldier?
WEAVER	I brought you the case of beer I owe you.
KAMA	Oh, thank you, Bob-u. Thank you.
WEAVER	One case of beer, one gallon of sake. Best exchange on the island, right?
KAMA	Drink beer, be American. Drink sake, be Japa—Okinawan.
WEAVER	You betcha. [*To Tsuyu.*] Hi, Mrs. Gusuda. I'm back.

TSUYU	Oh, no.
KAMA	She means, "Oh, yes." [*To Tsuyu.*] Don't keep standing there.
TSUYU	Ask him if he wants some soup.
KAMA	Bob-u want soup?
WEAVER	Soup? Homemade soup?
KAMA	Pig feet soup. Wife, she make plenty.
WEAVER	[*Grimacing but polite.*] Pig's feet soup? [*To Tsuyu.*] Ah, thank you, Mrs. Gusuda. But I…just don't feel like it right now.
TSUYU	[*To Kama.*] What did he say?
KAMA	He said he doesn't feel like he's one of us yet. Get him a clean cup.
TSUYU	Oh, yes. Clean cup…[*Hurries into kitchen.*]
WEAVER	[*Sitting.*] There's been talk that Japanese soldiers have parachuted on the island. You know anything about it?
KAMA	Japanee soldier already on Maui?!
WEAVER	You heard it, too?
KAMA	When?!
WEAVER	Who told you?!
KAMA	You! You not just tell me?
WEAVER	[*Studies Kama.*] You really don't know anything about it, do you?
KAMA	What?
WEAVER	Aw, never mind.
TSUYU	[*Returning from kitchen.*] Drink, Bob-u. Drink.
WEAVER	Thank you, Mrs. Gusuda.
TSUYU	You betcha. [*Pours for Weaver and Kama, then sits.*]
KAMA	When Bob-u wife, children come Maui?
WEAVER	They're not coming.
KAMA	No?
WEAVER	All military dependents are being shipped back to California.
KAMA	[*To Tsuyu.*] Bob-u's family are not coming.
TSUYU	They're not? [*To Weaver.*] Sonnanabitchee, Bob-u. Sonnana-bitchee…

WEAVER	It took me six months to get them here. Now…I won't even get to see them. [*Takes hefty gulp, then places cup before Tsuyu for more.*]
TSUYU	[*Pouring.*] Kama, tell him that it won't be long before he'll be together with his family again.
KAMA	War pretty soon pau, Bob-u. Finish.
WEAVER	You damn right. We're gonna wipe them out.
KAMA	Oh, yes.
WEAVER	Every one of them bastards.
KAMA	Oh, yes.
TSUYU	Oi, Kama, you should say "Oh, no" sometimes.
KAMA	"Oh, yes" sometimes means "Oh, no." [*Weaver takes another big gulp, then places cup before Tsuyu.*] Bob-u, not good get drunk.
WEAVER	After what we've been through since Sunday?
KAMA	I no want you tell me.
WEAVER	Tell you what, Mr. Gusuda?
KAMA	How many soldiers, Camp Paukukalo; how many airplanes, navy station…
WEAVER	You wanna know, I'll tell you.
KAMA	No, no. Don' wanna know.
WEAVER	We ain't got nothing, Mr. Gusuda. Nothing!
KAMA	Nothing?
WEAVER	Not a damn thing.
KAMA	When Japanee soldier come, better not fight back.
WEAVER	We can't just lie down and let them take over. Hell, no! [*Takes another pull.*] I don't think they're gonna land.
KAMA	No?
WEAVER	Not as long as they keep thinking the island is heavily fortified. [*Lifting cup and toasting.*] Let's keep hoping they'll never find out the fix we're in. Right? [*Kama hesitates to lift his cup.*] Right, Mr. Gusuda?
KAMA	Alright, Bob-u. Alright. Nobody find out.
WEAVER	[*Beat.*] You know, this stuff—it's the best thing to hit the islands.
KAMA	Oh, yes.

WEAVER	The people back in your village, they sure know how to make everyone happy.
KAMA	Sometimes too happy. Too happy.
WEAVER	But you like it better here, right?
KAMA	Oh, yes. Hawaii numbah one.
WEAVER	[*Eyeing gallon jars along walls.*] I see you've increased your sake production...For the luau?
KAMA	For soldiers, too.
WEAVER	You're inviting soldiers to the luau?
KAMA	Oh, yes.
WEAVER	That's great of you, Mr. Gusuda. Real great. The soldiers, they're gonna really appreciate it. [*Indicating paint on table.*] Planning on painting something?
KAMA	Oh, yes. Big flag on roof.
TSUYU	Oi, Kama...
WEAVER	That's a helluva idea, Mr. Gusuda. The good ol' Red, White, and Blue.
SPECKS	[*Offstage.*] Sarge! Hey, Sarge! [*Door flies open, and Specks rushes in, pistol in hand.*] They're out there!
WEAVER	Who?!
SPECKS	Jap spies!
WEAVER	[*Yanking out pistol.*] Out in the yard?!
SPECKS	They ran into the bushes when they saw me.
WEAVER	C'mon! [*Rushes out door with Specks.*]
SPECKS	[*Offstage.*] Watch it, Sarge! They could be dangerous!
KAMA	[*Lights begin to dim. Laughing.*] Dangerous? Ishi and Tengan?
SPECKS	[*Offstage.*] There! Over there, Sarge! Over there!
	Pistol shots. BANG! BANG! BANG!
WEAVER	[*Offstage.*] Hold your fire! That's Mr. Gusuda's pigs!
KAMA	[*Stops laughing.*] Pigs! [*Rushing toward door.*] They're shooting at my pigs!
	Lights keep dimming until BLACKOUT.

Scene Two

Dining room. Later that evening. Kenyei and Kama are going over map at table.

KAMA	[*Indicating map.*] What makes you so sure they'll be landing there at Waihee Beach, Kenyei?
KENYEI	I know how an admiral thinks.
KAMA	Admiral? I thought the army was led by a general. [*Kenyei gives Kama a harsh, disdainful look.*] Yes, of course. The Japanese army is led by an admiral…
TSUYU	Have some tea, Kenyei.
KENYEI	[*Puts away map.*] Those two drunkards. They disobeyed my orders to check the water tunnel. They must be punished.
KAMA	Yes, of course. No more sake for them the rest of the week.
KENYEI	[*Sips tea, frowns. To Tsuyu.*] This tea is cold!
KAMA	Kenyei likes his tea hot!
TSUYU	I'll make some right away. [*Crosses into kitchen.*]
KENYEI	That information I told you to get from the MP, you should have gotten it by now.
KAMA	The MP—he's very clever, Kenyei. He tells you something, then makes you promise not to repeat it.
KENYEI	Get that information! Our troops must know how well Maui is fortified.
KAMA	You have any idea when they will be here?
KENYEI	[*Confidentially.*] Tomorrow.
KAMA	Tomorrow?!
KENYEI	It's the "Seventh Day."
KAMA	The "Seventh Day"?
KENYEI	When I was in the Imperial Army, we were told that whenever we lose contact with our unit, we are to expect the unexpected.
KAMA	[*Mutters.*] Expect the unexpected…
KENYEI	What was last Sunday?
KAMA	December 7.
KENYEI	What is tomorrow?
KAMA	December…14.

KENYEI	Exactly seven days apart.
KAMA	You mean…?
	Kenyei nods assuringly.
KAMA / KENYEI	"The day to expect the unexpected."
KAMA	Will there be much fighting?
KENYEI	Maui will fall in no time.
KAMA	Some of these haole soldiers—they're good boys, Kenyei. Be sure they are not mistreated.
TSUYU	[*Entering with teapot.*] I made it nice and hot for you, Kenyei.
KAMA	[*To Tsuyu.*] Japanese soldiers are coming tomorrow.
TSUYU	Yes, I know. It's the "Seventh Day." You see, when Kenyei was in the Imperial Army—
KENYEI	[*Folding map.*] I told the Higas not to tell anyone!
	Knock at door Upstage Right.
KAMA	That must be Ishi and Tengan. They got away from the MPs.
WEAVER	[*Offstage.*] Mr. Gusuda!
KAMA	It's Bob-u!
KENYEI	The MP!
WEAVER	[*Offstage.*] Mr. Gusuda! It's me! Weaver!
KAMA	[*To Kenyei.*] Hide in the kitchen.
TSUYU	Hurry, Kenyei. Hide behind the rice bag.
KENYEI	[*Rushing into kitchen.*] Gusuda-san, get that information from him.
WEAVER	[*Offstage.*] Mr. Gusuda!
KAMA	[*Crossing to door.*] Okay, Bob-u. Okay. [*Opening door.*] You catch spy?
WEAVER	[*With Specks behind him.*] They got away.
KAMA	Good, good—ah, too bad, too bad, Bob-u. Come in. You, too, Howard-san. Come in.
	Specks looks around suspiciously.
WEAVER	Mr. Gusuda, Specks here thinks those "spies" he saw out there were trying to contact you.

KAMA	Me?
SPECKS	They were either waiting to come in here or waiting for you to go out there.
KAMA	What for?
SPECKS	That's what we want to know. [*Beat.*] Well?!
KAMA	You know, you tell me. I know, I tell you.
WEAVER	[*To Specks.*] You and your damn spies! We combed every inch of the bushes and couldn't find a single trace of them.
SPECKS	They must be hiding somewhere around here.
KAMA	Here?!
SPECKS	Right here in your home!
KAMA	[*Blocking kitchen door.*] No! Not in kitchen.
SPECKS	[*Stepping toward kitchen.*] That's a good place to begin…
WEAVER	Specks! You've gone far enough!
SPECKS	He's hiding them.
WEAVER	Mr. Gusuda?
SPECKS	A Jap's a Jap!
WEAVER	That's it! That's it, Specks. I've had it with you!
SPECKS	Sarge! You can't trust any of them.
WEAVER	[*Arms around Kama.*] He looks like the enemy? Huh? He looks like one of them? [*Kama raises head.*] Wasn't for him we would never have gotten the idea to paint the Stars and Stripes on our roofs. Isn't that right, Mr. Gusuda? [*Kama raises head even higher.*] You still wanna search the house, go ahead.
KAMA	Not behind rice bag!
WEAVER	Go on! The major will be glad to hear that you accused Mr. Gusuda of aiding the enemy.
SPECKS	The least we can do is interrogate him.
WEAVER	Go ahead. Interrogate him. [*Beat.*] Go on!
SPECKS	Mr. Gusuda, do you pledge allegiance to the flag of the United States of America?
	Kama, glassy eyed, looks at Weaver.
WEAVER	[*Coaching.*] Sure you do, Mr. Gusuda.

SPECKS	Sarge!
WEAVER	[*To Kama.*] You're glad you're living in this country—right, Mr. Gusuda?
KAMA	Oh, yes. Very lucky come Hawaii.
SPECKS	[*To Kama.*] Do you now know, or have you ever known, anyone who might be a spy, a saboteur, or an enemy agent who is seeking to overthrow the government of the United States of America?
KAMA	Oh, yes.
WEAVER	You do?!
KAMA	Oh, yes. Two.
WEAVER / SPECKS	Two?!
KAMA	Adolf Hitler and Benito Mussolini.
WEAVER	[*Smiles warmly at Kama.*] Any more questions, Private Specks?
SPECKS	I…don't think he understood me.
WEAVER	Sure he did. And so did she. Right, Mrs. Gusuda?
TSUYU	Dan tootin', Bob-u. Dan tootin'…
WEAVER	[*To Kama and Tsuyu.*] Sorry to have troubled you like this…
KAMA / TSUYU	No pilikia. No pilikia.
WEAVER	[*To Specks.*] C'mon. Let's get going.
KAMA	[*Walking to door with Weaver. Gravely.*] Bob-u, you duty tomorrow?
WEAVER	Tomorrow, the next day, and the next day…
KAMA	More better take tomorrow off.
WEAVER	Sure wish I could.
KAMA	[*Confidentially.*] Seventh day, Bob-u. Seventh day.
TSUYU	Oi, Kama!
WEAVER	Nice of you to remind me, Mr. Gusuda. But at times like this, we can't take any days off. Not even us good Christians.
SPECKS	What does he know about Christians?
WEAVER	Didn't you hear him? Work six days; rest on the seventh day.

Shirota . *Lucky Come Hawaii*   35

KAMA	Oh, yes. Go up mountains.
WEAVER	[*To Specks.*] Hear that? Go up to the mountains and get away from all you dogfaces. You can learn something from him, Specks.
SPECKS	Me, learn from him?!
WEAVER	They never learned you to listen between the lines in that junior college you went to, huh? Between the lines, Specks. Between the lines. [*At door.*] Goodnight, Mr. Gusuda, Mrs. Gusuda…
KAMA / TSUYU	Good-u night-u, Bob-u. Good-u night-u, Howard-san.
WEAVER	[*To Specks.*] Chrissake, Specks! Can't you at least say good-night to them?
SPECKS	[*Cursorily to Kama and Tsuyu.*] Goodnight…[*Exits with Weaver.*]
TSUYU	What's happened to Ishi and Tengan?
KAMA	Those two drunkards—they're probably passed out in the bushes.
KENYEI	[*Appearing stealthily from kitchen Downstage Left.*] Did you get the information?
TSUYU	[*Startled.*] Oh! It's you, Kenyei…
KENYEI	[*Scratching top of head. To Tsuyu.*] There's a big rat in your kitchen. It kept running over my head…
TSUYU	It's still there? [*Picking up broom and rushing into kitchen.*] I thought I got rid of it the other day.
KAMA	Kenyei, the MPs—they don't seem to know anything about the invasion tomorrow.
KENYEI	American soldiers—all they're interested in is sake, women, and parties.
KAMA	Not like Japanese soldiers, huh?
KENYEI	Japanese soldiers always put country before women.
TSUYU	[*Returning from kitchen with dishrag, which, under the circumstances, could be mistaken for a rat. Stepping beside Kenyei to wipe table.*] Awful rat…One of these days…[*Kenyei jumps up. So does Kama.*] What's wrong?
KAMA	Baka! [*Tsuyu commences to wipe table innocently as Kenyei studies dishrag in her hand. Living-room door opens, and Kimiko, dressed in shorts and aloha shirt, enters and steps over toward refrigerator.*] Kimiko! Can't you wear something more Japanese?

KENYEI	You should start wearing a kimono, Kimiko.
KIMIKO	Kimono?!
KENYEI	Wives of Japanese government officials all wear them.
KIMIKO	You and I better settle this once and for all!
KAMA	Yes, yes. Talk to Kenyei. [*To Tsuyu while stepping toward living room.*] Come, Tsuyu. They want to be alone.
TSUYU	[*To Kimiko.*] Be sure to boil more water when Kenyei's tea gets cold.
KIMIKO	[*Sitting beside Kenyei. Determined, yet managing to restrain herself as Kenyei moves closer while glancing at her longingly, admiringly.*] Kenyei…
KENYEI	[*Simultaneously.*] Kimiko…
KIMIKO	[*Beat.*] Kenyei, you and I…
KENYEI	[*Simultaneously.*] Kimiko, me and you…
KIMIKO	[*Beat.*] Kenyei, do you know why you and I, we hardly speak to each other?
KENYEI	I'm glad you're finally getting over your shyness, Kimiko.
KIMIKO	Shyness?! Kenyei, listen to me.
KENYEI	I always enjoy listening to you, Kimiko. Especially when you play the piano. You…inspire me to keep working on my poems.
KIMIKO	Your…poems?
KENYEI	Oh, yes. I've written many of them. I'm working on another right now. [*Reciting.*]

I keep longing for my home
In the hills where I was born
Why do I always want to roam
To places I have never gone

Having joined the tide
And sailed out into the sea
I yearn for a last ride
Into the hills I want to be

The skies are no longer stormy
The horizon…[*Falters.*]

I…haven't been able to finish it.

KIMIKO	Why…that's beautiful, Kenyei.

KENYEI	Someday, when I finish it, I'm going to dedicate it to you.
KIMIKO	Kenyei, I'm…just not the girl you think I am.
KENYEI	Oh, yes, you are.
KIMIKO	I don't deserve someone like you.
KENYEI	Yes, you do.
KIMIKO	Only a nice, understanding, and…sacrificing girl deserves someone like you. A girl like…Fusayo Higa.
KENYEI	Higa Fusayo?!
KIMIKO	She's…gentle, and quiet, and…very attractive.
KENYEI	She's fat, and bossy and…[rubbing forearm] very hairy!
KIMIKO	[Beat.] You think you know me because…you've known me since I was a little girl. You really don't know me.
KENYEI	Yes, I do.
KIMIKO	Kenyei, when you look out into the ocean, what do you see?
KENYEI	The…blue water?
KIMIKO	See what I mean?
KENYEI	The…waves?
KIMIKO	[Envisioning.] When I look out into the ocean, I see the horizon. And beyond the horizon, I see my dreams, my goals…
KENYEI	"And beyond the horizon, I see my dreams, my goals…" That's beautiful.
KIMIKO	I was never meant to be just a nice, quiet Japanese girl.
KENYEI	You will always be a beautiful chrysanthemum flower, Kimiko.
KIMIKO	I am not a chrysanthemum flower! Do you see me walking around like this [taking mincing, knock-kneed steps]?! Huh, do you? Do you see me laughing like this [covering her mouth with hand]?! I walk like this [head high and shoulders back, haughtily]. And when I laugh, I really laugh! [Laughs boisterously. Kenyei laughs, too.] And…I don't dance like this [daintily, demurely, takes a few Japanese dance steps]. When I dance, I really dance. [Dances hula, shaking her rear, then kicks legs up cancan style.]
KENYEI	[Applauding.] You look so cute doing that.
KIMIKO	[Flustered.] I'm…not a happy person, Kenyei. Deep inside, I'm very lonely.

KENYEI	I am, too. But, when I'm around you…
KIMIKO	I'm always searching.
KENYEI	We'll search together, you and me.
KIMIKO	I'm always looking for that…place where I can feel I belong.
KENYEI	We'll find that place together.
KIMIKO	[*Snapping out of it.*] Your friends back in Okinawa—what will they say about you wanting to marry someone like me?
KENYEI	[*Painfully.*] I…don't have any friends back there anymore. They…all started to ignore me when my eyes went bad and I was discharged from the army…But now, Kimiko, with Hawaii becoming a part of Japan, there's just no telling how high I'll rise. [*Excited.*] You and me—we can live wherever we want. Even in that big white Baldwin house up in Ulupalakua.
KIMIKO	Kenyei!
KENYEI	[*Almost submissively.*] I'll…even start wearing glasses, if that's what you want me to do.
KIMIKO	It's about time that you did.
KENYEI	You don't think I'll look less manly?
KIMIKO	Of course not.
KAMA	[*Entering from living room.*] Kenyei, it's almost time for the next Tokyo news.
KENYEI	[*Taking out pocket watch and holding close to eyes.*] Akisamiyo! I've already missed some of it. [*Rushing to door Upstage Right.*] I have to find out exactly when our troops are arriving.
KIMIKO	[*To Kenyei as he exits.*] You understand about us, don't you?
KAMA	[*Elated.*] I knew it! I just knew that once you and Kenyei had a nice talk, you'd marry him.
KIMIKO	Marry him?!
KAMA	You have an understanding—isn't that what you just said?
KIMIKO	Otosan! Can't you see? Kenyei and me—it's just impossible!
KAMA	You've changed your mind again?!
KIMIKO	Yes!—I mean no! I haven't changed my mind!
KAMA	[*Hands on hips.*] Then you will marry him?!
KIMIKO	[*Hands on hips, defiant.*] No! I'm not going to marry him.

Cat

---- ❧ ----

*Cat figurines are common in mainland Japan.
The most popular are the maneki neko,
believed to bring prosperity to businesses
(maneki means "beckoning" or "welcoming").
Other types are used solely as toys:
for example, the kuro neko (black cat)
made in Hizen Koga, Nagasaki Prefecture,
and the kubifuri neko (bobble-headed cat)
of Kaga Kanazawa, Ishikawa Prefecture.*

*The type of cat shown here is called
mayaagwaa and is used only as a toy.
Painted in colors such as yellow or purple,
it is sold during the yukkanufii festival
(held during the fourth month
of the lunar calendar).*

*Papier-mâché.
Woodblock print by Ozaki Seiji.*

KAMA	Yes, you are!
KIMIKO	No, I'm not!

As they stand there challenging each other, lights begin dimming until BLACKOUT.

Scene Three

Early next evening. At table, Tsuyu is standing behind Kama and rubbing his neck.

KAMA	[*Worrying.*] What will I tell Ikehara-san?
TSUYU	You'll think of something. You always do.
KAMA	[*Beat.*] She still refuses to come out of her bedroom?
TSUYU	She won't even talk to me.
KAMA	[*Rising, faces Kimiko's bedroom Upstage Right.*] Oi, Kimiko! If you don't want to marry Kenyei and become the Mrs. Roosevelt of Maui, that's alright. [*Beat.*] Ikehara-san, of course, will tell everyone on Maui not to have anything to do with our family. But that's alright. We don't care what anyone thinks of our family anyway. [*Beat.*] Your mother and I may have to move to the leper settlement on Molokai, but we won't mind it. [*Kama and Tsuyu look at each other, toward Kimiko's room, back at each other. Silence. Kama steps back to table, and Tsuyu resumes massage.*] That girl! How can she do this to me?
TENGAN	[*Entering from living room with Ishi, both limping exaggeratedly.*] Why don't you tell Ikehara-san the truth? Kimiko gets sick just looking at Kenyei.
ISHI	Me, too.
KAMA	Baka! Don't forget. Kenyei expects you to run up to the water tunnel as soon as the invasion starts.
ISHI	I don't think I can make it.
TENGAN	Why can't I stay behind and paint the roof?
KAMA	I'm the painter; you are the mountain climber. [*Sudden knocking on door Upstage Right. To Tsuyu.*] It's them!
TSUYU	[*Crosses to door, then opens it and bows.*] Ah, Ikehara-san…So good to see you back again.
IKEHARA-SAN	[*In suit and tie, steps in and bows.*] Nice to be back again, Gusuda-san.
TSUYU	Please. Come in. [*To Kenyei.*] Ah, you brought your radio with you, Kenyei.

Kenyei, carrying a small radio, follows his uncle in. His hair is parted in the middle and slicked with pomade. He has on a bulky, oversized jacket buttoned to the neck.

KENYEI   The invasion could start any minute.

KAMA   Ah, Ikehara-san...I'm glad you were able to come.

Ishi and Tengan look at each other.

IKEHARA-SAN   For a while I didn't think I could make it.

KAMA   Sit down. Please. Sit down. You, too, Kenyei.

KENYEI   Uncle is staying with me tonight.

KAMA   Good. Good idea. The MPs are arresting anyone caught outside after dark.

IKEHARA-SAN   Where's Kimiko?

KAMA   [*To Tsuyu.*] Where is she?

TSUYU   I'll go and call her. [*Exits.*]

KENYEI   We're a little early, Uncle.

IKEHARA-SAN   That's no excuse.

KAMA   This is a great day for her, Ikehara-san.

TENGAN   She was in tears when I saw her a moment ago.

IKEHARA-SAN   Good. Good. A true Japanese woman always cries when she is happy.

ISHI   Let's hope she doesn't get any happier.

IKEHARA-SAN   [*Beat.*] I was proud of you two, Ishi and Tengan, when I learned that you volunteered to go up to the mountain.

TENGAN   What do you plan to do when the invasion starts?

IKEHARA-SAN   Whatever is necessary.

TENGAN   Why don't I do that, and you climb the mountain?

KAMA   Tengan!

ISHI   I'd like to do whatever is necessary, too.

KENYEI   Shikkari shite! You are soldiers in His Majesty's Army.

IKEHARA-SAN   Kenyei is going to be the Emperor's representative on Maui after tonight. He will be receiving his orders directly from Tokyo.

KAMA   You hear that?! Kenyei is the next ambassador to Maui.

IKEHARA-SAN	[*Beat.*] What's taking them so long?
TENGAN	Kimiko stays in her bedroom whenever she's nervous.
ISHI	Sometimes for days.
IKEHARA-SAN	She has nervous breakdowns?!
KAMA	Oh, no. Nothing like that. She…just can't handle too much excitement.
TENGAN	What Kama is trying to say is, the marriage should be post-poned.
KENYEI / IKEHARA-SAN	Postponed?!
KAMA	Maybe…that would be better, Ikehara-san.
KENYEI / IKEHARA-SAN	For how long?!
KAMA	Until…Kimiko decides she really wants to marry Kenyei.
KENYEI	She has changed her mind?
IKEHARA-SAN	Gusuda Kama! I always believed you to be a man of your word.
KAMA	Please try to understand, Ikehara-san.
IKEHARA-SAN	Bring your daughter here! Right now! [*Kama lowers his head.*] You refuse to bring her here?!
KAMA	Ikehara-san, I think she's locked herself in her bedroom and… she refuses… [*Living-room door opens. Kimiko, dressed in a beautiful, formal kimono, enters. All eyes turn to her, transfixed. Tsuyu, beaming, follows Kimiko in. Kimiko, no longer a rebellious, Americanized girl, stands submissively, demurely, resignedly.*] As I was saying, Ikehara-san, we are very proud of our daughter. She would never do anything to dishonor her father and mother.
IKEHARA-SAN	[*Very impressed.*] Yes, Gusuda-san. You have a fine daughter. Very beautiful. Very Japanese. She and Kenyei will make a wonderful couple. [*Raising sake cup.*] Let's drink to them. [*Ishi and Tengan, having overcome their bewilderment at Kimiko's change of heart, quickly join in toast.*] Here's to the happy marriage of Kenyei, the Emperor's representative on Maui, and Kimiko, a fine Okinawan girl.

Kama and Ikehara-san roar, "Banzai! Banzai!" Before they can complete the third "Banzai!" there is a sudden, horrendous, earth-shaking bombardment. BOOM! BOOM! BOOM! The house rattles, the roof creaks, the floor vibrates ominously. Everyone stares at each other, horrified. BOOM! BOOM! BOOM!

KIMIKO	What's that?!
KENYEI	They're here!
IKEHARA-SAN	It's them!
	BOOM! BOOM! BOOM!
TSUYU	The house is falling!
TENGAN / ISHI	Akisamiyo!
KAMA	Tsuyu! Get the paint!
KIMIKO	Otosan! What's happening?!
KAMA	[*Grabbing can of paint.*] Where's the brush?!
KENYEI	Tengan! Ishi! Get ready to go up to the mountain!
TENGAN / ISHI	Right now?
	Everyone waits breathlessly for the next bombardment. Silence.
KAMA	What's happened?
IKEHARA-SAN	Why have they stopped?
KENYEI	[*Plugging radio into outlet.*] Radio Tokyo should tell us what's going on.
ISHI	Maybe they changed their mind.
TENGAN	Damn Naichis! They better not wreck my boat.
KENYEI	[*Finding the right station.*] There! Radio Tokyo. [*Static, then the clear sound of a staccato army march.*] The victory march!
	Loud, urgent knocking on door Upstage Right. Everyone stares at door.
ISHI	[*Beat.*] They're here already?
IKEHARA-SAN	[*Stepping toward door.*] Everyone! Put on your best manners. As president of the Okinawan Association, I will do the greeting.
WEAVER	[*Offstage.*] Mr. Gusuda!
IKEHARA-SAN	[*Backing away from door.*] Who's that?!
KAMA	MP!
IKEHARA-SAN / KENYEI	MP?!
TENGAN / ISHI	Again?!

WEAVER	[*Offstage.*] Mr. Gusuda! Open up!
KAMA	[*To men.*] Go out the front door. Hurry!
KENYEI	[*Rushing into living room with radio, the others following. To Kama.*] Find out where our troops have landed. [*Exits.*]
KIMIKO	[*Crosses to door Upstage Right, opens it.*] What was all that noise?
WEAVER	That's what I'm trying to find out. Okay I use your phone?
KAMA	Go. Go ahead. Find out.
WEAVER	[*At phone, dials. Beat.*] Dammit! Line's busy…[*Dials operator. Beat.*] Hello, operator. This is Sergeant Weaver from the military police. Get me through to my headquarters…Of course I heard it! Ma'am…Ma'am! Will you calm down, for Chrissake!
	Kenyei, Ikehara-san, Ishi, and Tengan walk backward from living room slowly, haplessly, hands over their heads. Specks appears, herding the four men with pistol.
SPECKS	Sarge! Hey, Sarge! Look what I got here.
WEAVER	[*Into phone.*] I'm here at the Gusudas in Kapuna Valley. Have my headquarters call me soon's you can. Got that? [*Hangs up.*]
SPECKS	I caught them sneaking out of here, Sarge. They look like the same bunch of spies I chased into the bushes a week ago.
KAMA	Spies?
WEAVER	[*Studying four men.*] I know those two. [*Indicates Ishi and Tengan.*]
SPECKS	You do?
WEAVER	They're friends of the Gusudas.
TENGAN / ISHI	Ha-ro, Bob-u.
WEAVER	Hi, guys.
SPECKS	What about them? [*Indicates Kenyei and Ikehara-san.*] They look like they just got off the boat.
KAMA	[*Indicating Ikehara-san.*] Him, president, Maui Okinawan Association.
SPECKS	[*To Kenyei.*] You! Tojo! Turn around.
KAMA	No! No Tojo. Him, Shiroma Kenyei.
TENGAN / ISHI	Next ambassador to Maui.

SPECKS	[*To Kenyei.*] I said turn around! [*Kenyei does not respond.*] What's the matter with you?!
KENYEI	You nuga? What'samattah you, what'samattah me? Pupule jackass.
SPECKS	What'd he say?
KAMA	You jackass.
SPECKS	He just insulted the United States Army, Sarge!
WEAVER	He just meant you.
SPECKS	[*To Kenyei.*] Turn around. Take off that jacket. [*Kenyei does not respond.*] Take off that jacket! [*When Kenyei still does not respond, Specks reaches over and attempts to take the jacket off. Kenyei, however, is determined to keep it on.*] Keep still! [*Kenyei struggles desperately. Specks manages to pull jacket off.*] Holy—! He's a Jap soldier!
	Kenyei stands stoically in his old, tattered, and ill-fitting Imperial Army uniform, his chest gleaming with row upon row of store-bought medals, his sleeves resplendent with endless stripes. Everyone except Ikehara-san is stunned. Ikehara-san moves away from Kenyei sheepishly.
KIMIKO	Ohmygod!
WEAVER	[*Yanking out pistol.*] I'll be a sonofabitch! Where'd he come from?!
KAMA	I…don' know.
SPECKS	He was here all the time!
KAMA	Kenyei, yes; soldier, no!
WEAVER	[*To Specks.*] Put the cuffs on him.
	Specks fumbles ineptly with handcuffs.
KIMIKO	Bob, he's not a Japanese soldier.
KAMA	Him friend, long time.
SPECKS	What did I tell you, Sarge: they're all a bunch of spies.
WEAVER	[*To Kimiko.*] That…uniform?
KIMIKO	Uniform? That's not a uniform. That's a…costume for an Okinawan dance.
KAMA	Yes, yes. Kenyei—him Okinawan dancer.
SPECKS	You expect us to believe that?!

KIMIKO	Those…medals and…those stripes—do they look real?
KAMA	Kress Store. Kress Store.
WEAVER	[*To Specks.*] For Chrissake! Don't you know how to use those cuffs? [*Phone rings.*] Must be for me. [*Answering.*] Hello…Yes, sir! I sure did try to contact you, sir…Sir…Sir! We just captured a Jap soldier.
SPECKS	[*To Kenyei while struggling to put handcuffs on him with one hand and while holding pistol in the other.*] Keep still! [*When Kenyei, standing ramrod straight, keeps resisting, Specks inadvertently hands pistol to Kama. Kama, shocked, stares at pistol in his hand, then quickly places it on table. He begins to work his way toward chikonki phonograph in corner.*] I said keep still!
WEAVER	[*Into phone.*] He looks like a heavily decorated officer, sir. A captain most likely.
SPECKS	He could be a general, Sarge.
	Kama winds phonograph and puts on record.
WEAVER	[*Into phone.*] He could be a general, sir. They must've landed him just before they started shelling. [*Staccato Okinawan music comes on.*] The Jap sub, sir. We heard it all the way here in the valley…
KAMA	Kenyei, do the kuusankuu dance…
	Kenyei, still stunned over his capture, keeps struggling to avoid being handcuffed.
WEAVER	[*Into phone.*] They were?! But…Yes, sir. Now that you mention it, sir…
KIMIKO	[*Realizing what Kama is up to, begins to dance to staccato music. To Kenyei.*] Kenyei, the kuusankuu dance…[*Dances closer to Kenyei.*] Kenyei, dance…
	The other Okinawans, realizing what is going on, begin to clap vigorously in time with music. Finally struggling free of Specks, Kenyei steps up to Kimiko and joins her in the kuusankuu karate dance.
WEAVER	[*Into phone.*] Yes, sir. We'll bring him in right away, sir. Over and out. [*Hangs up. To Specks.*] That was one of our own artilleries firing practice rounds into the channel.
	Kama, now standing beside Weaver, nudges him to join in the clapping as Kimiko and Kenyei continue dancing. Weaver is somewhat intrigued by the dancing, but hesitates to clap. Kimiko dances up to Specks, who is looking on scornfully. When she invites him to join in the dance, he turns his head away and retrieves pistol from table. Kimiko dances up to Weaver and invites him to join

her. He does not need much encouragement. He follows her Okinawan dance movements, then jitterbugs with her. Everyone except Specks enjoys the lively spectacle. Music finally stops. Older Okinawans break into hearty applause, eyeing MPs and hoping they have pulled it off. Kenyei acknowledges applause, bowing and glowing. Kama steps over to gallons of sake in corner.

SPECKS
Sarge! Who are you going to believe? Me or them? [*Weaver appraises Specks, the others.*] Sarge!

WEAVER
At ease, Specks. At ease. Can't you tell a dancer from an enemy soldier?

SPECKS
He was heading for the bushes with the others.

WEAVER
When you gotta go, you gotta go.

KAMA
[*Carrying two gallon jugs.*] Yes, yes. Gotta go, gotta go…[*Offering.*] Here, Bob-u…

WEAVER
Aw, Mr. Gusuda…After what we just put you through…

KAMA
Take, take…[*To Specks.*] Here, Howard-san…[*Specks turns away disdainfully.*]

WEAVER
What, you crazy, Specks?

KAMA
Take. Take.

OTHER OKINAWANS
Take. Take.

SPECKS
I don't drink. Even if I did, I certainly wouldn't drink that.

WEAVER
Then take it to the major.

SPECKS
The major? He drinks that?

WEAVER
Do hogs fart louder on hot days?!

KAMA
Make boss happy.

OTHER OKINAWANS
Make boss happy. Make boss happy.

WEAVER
The major might be willing to overlook that false report of yours, Specks.

SPECKS
False report?

WEAVER
On you capturing a Jap general.

SPECKS
[*Reconsidering.*] The major really likes it, huh?

WEAVER
For a whole gallon of this stuff, he might even give you that stripe you're always crying about.

SPECKS	[*Reaching eagerly.*] Well…I guess I owe it to the major…
	Everyone applauds.
WEAVER	[*To Specks.*] C'mon. Let's get moving. [*To everyone.*] We'll be seeing you…
SPECKS	[*Lifting gallon high.*] See you…
EVERYONE	See you. See you.
	Specks and Weaver exit. The men, now breathlessly silent, glance at one another sheepishly, then rush for drinks on table. They down drinks with grateful sighs.
IKEHARA-SAN	[*Still perplexed, Kenyei stands alone. Ikehara-san picks up jacket and throws it at him.*] You bobura pumpkin head!
KIMIKO	You could have all gone to jail! And you, Kenyei! Take that off! [*Kenyei meekly takes off shirt.*] Don't you ever wear that around here again! And you, Ikehara-san! Stop dreaming of Hawaii ever becoming a part of Japan!
KAMA / TSUYU	Kimiko!
KIMIKO	[*Shaking head and marching off into living room.*] So foolish! All of you!
IKEHARA-SAN	[*Recovering from tongue lashing. To Kama.*] Your daughter— she's…so sassy! She doesn't deserve Kenyei!
KENYEI	Yes, she does, Uncle!
KAMA	[*Gingerly.*] You and me, Ikehara-san, we made a yakusoku.
TENGAN / ISHI	[*Pressing.*] A yakusoku is a yakusoku…
IKEHARA-SAN	As president of the Okinawan Association, I cancel all yaku-sokus made between you and me, Gusuda Kama. Come, Kenyei, let's go. [*Agitated pounding of piano music—Tchaikovsky in D Major—comes from living room. Kenyei ignores his uncle and steps toward source of music.*] Kenyei! [*Torn between loyalty to uncle and love for Kimiko, Kenyei halts, then steps toward music again.*] Kenyei!
KENYEI	[*Halts, then finally capitulates.*] Hai, Uncle…[*Crossing toward door, looks longingly back, then bumps into Ikehara-san.*]
IKEHARA-SAN	Baka! Bobura! Pumpkin head!
KENYEI	[*Bowing low.*] Gomen nasai, Uncle. Gomen nasai…[*They exit.*]

TENGAN	[*Scornfully.*] Two Okinawan pigs!
ISHI	Kimiko should have let the MPs lock them up!
KAMA	That's enough! Ikehara-san is our president.
TENGAN / ISHI	Not mine.
TENGAN	C'mon, Ishi. Let's play cards.
ISHI	[*Crossing into living room with Tengan.*] Getting cheated by you is better than what we just went through.
KAMA	[*Beat. To Tsuyu, shaking head. Piano music now soft.*] That Kenyei…After all these years in Hawaii, that's all the English words he knows: "You pupule jackass…"
TSUYU	Won't everyone in Hawaii be speaking Japanese soon?
KAMA	It might take longer than I thought.
TSUYU	You think I should learn more English words?
KAMA	You should. Next time Bob-u comes here, don't keep repeating what he says. It's bad manners. Just say, "Excuse-u me, Bob-u."
TSUYU	What does that mean?
KAMA	It's a polite American way of saying, "Don't mind me. I'm acting a little foolish today."
TSUYU	[*Eyes Kama.*] "Excuse-u Kama, Bob-u. Excuse-u Kama today…"
KAMA	Baka…

Light dims in dining room and spotlight rises on Ishi Downstage.

ISHI	Ah, yes…So many memories…Days just like bird. Always flying forward, never backward. And, years like turtle. Never stop crawling. Always watching some things change, some things no change. And, some things, even if want change, will always be same. [*As he mentions their names, the actors appear, assuming semblance of their characters.*] Kenyei Shiroma, he still grow taro across river. Now, wear glasses. [*Kenyei puts on glasses.*] Ikehara-san, no longer president Maui Okinawan Association. [*Much older now, Ikehara-san is unaware of his surroundings. Kenyei guides him to look toward audience.*] Now, resident Maui old people home. Tengan, still fisherman. Still cheating me, cards. [*Tengan hides card in his pocket.*] Kimiko, very happy girl. Live Honolulu. Music teacher. Two nice children. [*Smiling graciously, Kimiko is now in comfortable aloha shirt and jeans.*] Kama and Tsuyu, very okay. [*Kama brings American flag out of drawer and*

pins on wall where Japanese flag was.] When Kimiko first marry haole boy, Kama very angry. Now, when half-haole grandchildren come Maui, he say, "Aw, whatdahell…" [*Tsuyu rubs Kama's shoulders.*] MP Howard-san, he go back school after war. Now, police captain, San Joe-say, California. [*Specks walks in with gallon of wine.*] He come back Maui one time. Bring Kama one gallon San Joe-say wine. Bob-u Weaver, retire from army. Now live Honolulu. He come Kapuna Valley all time. Still drink sake; still dance hula-hula. [*Weaver does a few hula movements.*] Me, Ishi Gensuke, little older, much wiser. [*Takes out passport.*] See. American passport. Oh, yeah. Now, American citizen. [*Beat.*] When I come back home, Hawaii, maybe you, me, we get together again. I tell you all about trip to Okinawa; you tell me all about new American president. Until then…[*Lights begin dimming.*] Mata mensooree…Sayonara…Aloha…See you…See you…

Lights continue dimming until BLACKOUT.

Curtain

Leilani's Hibiscus

Leilani's Hibiscus *was produced first by East West Players in Los Angeles in 1999 and later by Kumu Kahua Theatre in Honolulu in 2000. Katsunori Yamazato translated the play into Japanese, and this version was produced in Okinawa in 2001 and 2003, in Los Angeles in 2002, and in Tokyo in 2003.*

Introduction

During the opening of the twentieth century, thousands of contract laborers were imported from Okinawa to work in the sweltering sugarcane fields of Hawaii. The laborers' goal was to earn as much as they possibly could and return home wealthy. They learned, however, that a dollar a day was barely enough for their living expenses. They labored and slaved and persevered, the pot of gold at the end of the rainbow as elusive as ever. Some did go home with the little they managed to save. Those who remained sent for picture brides to start families, postponing the long-awaited journey back to their homeland. The rising and setting of the sun dragged on inexorably for years, then decades, then generations. Every family had a unique story to pass on to the next generation. This story is one of them.

Most of the play takes place at a gravesite on the island of Maui in summer 1960. The gravesite is on a sandy hillside overlooking the town of Wailuku and is overshadowed by the cloud-draped West Maui Mountains. At Upstage Left are two headstones on a slightly elevated platform, which is covered by grass and/or other green vegetation. At each of the headstones is an urn for senko (incense) and a vase for flowers. The inscriptions on the headstones read:

IN MEMORY OF	IN MEMORY OF
KAMA GUSUDA	TSUYU GUSUDA
JUNE 11, 1898	MAY 12, 1902
JULY 8, 1950	JULY 26, 1950

There is an old, weathered, wooden bench angled Upstage Right; beside it is a wooden box that an actor can stand on. Angled Downstage Left is another old wooden bench. The rest of the stage is bare. The Downstage area is open and unencumbered. The stage entrance is Downstage Right.

Ichiro Gusuda, Okinawan-American. Forty years old. Only son.

Kama Gusuda, pioneer Okinawan. Deceased at fifty-two years old. Father.

Kimiko Gusuda, Okinawan-American. Thirty-seven years old. Only daughter.

Tsuyu Gusuda, Okinawan. Deceased at forty-eight years old. Mother. Wife of Kama.

Yasuichi Gusuda, Okinawan. Fifty years old. Younger brother of Kama. Uncle of Ichiro and Kimiko.

Leilani Makaole, Native Hawaiian girl. Ages from seventeen to thirty-six years old.

Emma Wu, Okinawan-Hawaiian girl. Eighteen years old. Daughter of Leilani Makaole.

Act One

Scene One

House lights dim. In the darkness, before stage lights come on, we hear a samisen and someone singing an old, traditional Okinawan song, "Kajadifuu," a song of greeting and celebration. Stage lights come on gradually. Playing the samisen and singing nostalgically Downstage is Uncle Yasuichi Gusuda in khakis and white, open-collar shirt. Beside him is a package of senko. After a few more verses, Kama Gusuda and Tsuyu Gusuda slowly rise from their graves and dance to the ethereal music. Kama is wearing khaki trousers and an aloha shirt; Tsuyu, a simple Okinawan outfit. They are barefoot and speak only to each other throughout the play.

KAMA	Akisamiyo! It's him and that samisen of his.
TSUYU	It's the same one he brought when he first came to Maui.
KAMA	I suppose Maui wouldn't be the same for him without it.
TSUYU	He used to take it wherever he went, remember? Parties, luaus, family gatherings. Playing his samisen and singing were his only ways of expressing himself.
KAMA	He sure was a changed man when he left.
TSUYU	How long did he live with us?
KAMA	Oi, Basan. There's no excuse for not remembering what went on in our other life.
TSUYU	Listen to him. You can't even remember that song he just sang.
KAMA	It was "Tung-Tang-Tang."
TSUYU	It was "Kajadifuu," Ojiisan. It opened every celebration in Okinawa.
KAMA	He must be celebrating because I can't scold him anymore.

TSUYU	Bringing his samisen all the way from Okinawa and singing at our graves is his way of honoring us.
KAMA	Yeah. Ten years after we're gone.
UNCLE	[*Lights several senko sticks (mimed) and ceremoniously places them in Kama's urn, then Tsuyu's. Bows deeply and clasps his hands.*] Kama. Tsuyu. I hope you enjoyed some of the songs of our homeland. After all these years in Hawaii, you will at last be returning home. Your ashes will be placed in our new family tomb among the ashes of all our family members who have gone ahead of you. [*He resumes playing his samisen, softly, melodiously.*]
KAMA	So he finally built a new family tomb.
TSUYU	You really want him to take us back to Okinawa?
KAMA	It's our home, Basan.
TSUYU	We've spent most of our lives here.
KAMA	Still…
TSUYU	The children, what about them?
KAMA	Ichiro, I'm sure, will go along.
TSUYU	Kimiko, she always had a mind of her own.
KAMA	It's because you didn't teach her to be a nice, quiet Okinawan girl like you used to be.
TSUYU	Used to be?!
KAMA	You became a bossy old basan who never listens to her husband anymore.
TSUYU	And you became a stubborn old jisan who forgot how lucky you were I was willing to marry you.
KAMA	Ha. You were lucky I picked you from all the picture brides.
TSUYU	Listen to him. Just listen to him. A proud old rooster. [*Raising his head high, Kama playfully flaps his "wings." Tsuyu chuckles.*] You know, you've never told me. What did you really think of me when you first saw me getting off the boat?
KAMA	After all these years, you want to know what I thought of you then?
TSUYU	Oh, it really doesn't matter anymore.
KAMA	Then I won't tell you.
TSUYU	[*Disheartened.*] So you thought I was a yanakagi.

KAMA	I thought you were a churakagi.
TSUYU	Really? You really thought I was pretty?
KAMA	I didn't put you back on the boat, did I? [*Beat.*] What did you think of me?
TSUYU	Well…You could've at least taken a bath. [*Gestures something is smelly.*]
KAMA	I was busy working in the sugarcane field that day when Ige Kentaro came rushing on his wagon and said our brides had arrived.
TSUYU	You kept staring at me after I introduced myself.
KAMA	You were the first woman I had seen in a kimono since I left home.
TSUYU	I waited for you to say something.
KAMA	Your kimono…
TSUYU	That's all you noticed? My kimono?
KAMA	It was beautiful.
TSUYU	What about my hair, my eyes, my nose, my fair complexion…?
KAMA	[*Teasing.*] You really want to know?
TSUYU	Good? Bad?
KAMA	Excellent.
TSUYU	Why didn't you tell me that?
KAMA	You were already my wife.
	Uncle begins playing the samisen louder and starts singing nostalgically another traditional Okinawan song, "Fishibushi."
TSUYU	[*Listens a moment. Nostalgically.*] My favorite song…[*Recites in Okinawan what Uncle is singing, and Kama translates in English after each line.*] Satu tumiba nuyudi Iyadi iyumi uyadu Fuyu nu yu no yusiga Tageni katayabira.
KAMA	If I had known that you would be my favorite I would not have denied your request for a room While waiting for the long winter to pass Let's talk and listen to each other.

Fighting Chickens

———————————— ❊ ————————————

The toy depicted here is of a type called kubifuri
(bobble-headed). Until the Meiji period (1868–1912),
cockfights were held frequently, even in Naha.
In Shuri, the fighting chickens were called tauchii,
a derivation of the Chinese word for gamecocks.
The tradition of cockfighting continues
on certain islands today.

Papier-mâché.
Woodblock print by Ozaki Seiji.

TSUYU	It sure brings back memories of a young, innocent girl on a boat expecting her husband to be greeting her in a white suit and riding a white horse.
KAMA	Oi, Yasuichi! Sing another song.
TSUYU	He can't hear you.
KAMA	Oi, Yasuichi!
TSUYU	He's there; we're here.
KAMA	[*Picking up a pebble, throws it at Uncle. Uncle remains unfazed.*] I must've missed.
TSUYU	Oi, Jisan. We're not in the same world.
KAMA	[*Throws another pebble, and Uncle slaps his cheek.*] See. He felt that one.
	Uncle slaps his cheek again.
TSUYU	Mosquitoes, Jisan. Mosquitoes.
UNCLE	[*To headstones.*] Remember Kimo Makaole, our Hawaiian land-lord? I drove over to his home right after Ichiro and I arrived on an airplane yesterday.
KAMA	[*To Tsuyu.*] He went to see Kimo? What for?
TSUYU	He and Kimo were good friends.
UNCLE	"Pehea oe?" Kimo greeted me. "Hele mai. Hele mai." Just like the old days. "Come in. Come in."
KAMA	Yasuichi still remembers some Hawaiian words.
TSUYU	He practically became a Kanaka before he left.
UNCLE	Kimo is quite old now. But he's still healthy, still wise and friendly as ever.
KAMA	It's been almost twenty years since they last saw each other. Of course, Kimo's gotten older.
TSUYU	So has Yasuichi.
KAMA	And so has everyone else.
TSUYU	Not me. I don't look a day older than when we first met.
KAMA	As long as there's no mirrors around.
UNCLE	Kimo has over a dozen great-grandchildren now. He wasn't sure exactly how many.
KAMA	When we first met him, he didn't even have a grandchild.

UNCLE	The youngest of Kimo's seven children, Leilani—remember her?
KAMA	Leilani…?
TSUYU	She was the young girl always with Kimo after her mother died.
KAMA	Oh, that one. Always barefoot. Always singing and dancing at her father's luaus.
UNCLE	You used to think she was just another stupid, dark-skinned, and ill-mannered Kanaka girl.
KAMA	What's he talking about?
TSUYU	Let him finish.
UNCLE	When I first knew her, she was just a young Peahi schoolgirl. Then she blossomed into a mature young woman. She was fun to be with; always happy; always making me laugh; always wanting to do exciting things. And, she was not stupid; she was akamai.
	As he reminisces, Leilani at seventeen years old appears Downstage Right. She is in aloha shirt and shorts and has an ukulele. She is girlishly pretty and vivacious.
KAMA	I knew it. He didn't come back to Maui just to take our ashes back to Okinawa.
TSUYU	Oi, Jisan.
KAMA	And he didn't go over to Kimo's just for a visit.
TSUYU	Shhh…
LEILANI	[*To Uncle confidentially.*] You gonna pick me up same place tomorrow?
UNCLE	[*Responding dreamily.*] Tomorrow, no same place.
LEILANI	Then where?
UNCLE	Hana-Holokai Road.
LEILANI	I wait wait yesterday, corner of Hana and Peahi Road. Why you no pick me up?
UNCLE	Brother, Kama, he go with me. Kokua unload pineapple.
LEILANI	When you gonna tell him? Y'know, you and me, we…You know. We wanna get married.
UNCLE	I tell him. Someday.
KAMA	Marry?! A Kanaka girl?
LEILANI	If you no tell him now, I gonna tell him myself.

UNCLE	No!
LEILANI	Maybe, I tell Ichiro or Kimi. Then, they can tell their father and mother.
UNCLE	No. No.
LEILANI	Yes. Yes.
UNCLE	I tell myself.
LEILANI	When?
UNCLE	Now not right time.
LEILANI	I not gonna moe moe with you until we get married, you know that.
UNCLE	Just honi honi?
LEILANI	Not even that.
KAMA	"Honi honi." He became a Kanaka alright.
UNCLE	[*To Leilani.*] I go find 'nother Kanaka gal.
LEILANI	Go! Go find another girl.
UNCLE	No pilikia?
LEILANI	I no care! [*Slapping his arm.*] Go! Go!
UNCLE	Ouch! [*Backing away playfully.*] Ouch! Ouch!
LEILANI	[*Now chasing, swinging, as Uncle runs away.*] You no-good Japanee!
UNCLE	Okinawan! [*Letting her catch him, restrains her, then hugs her.*] Be nice gal…[*She struggles to free herself.*] Leilani…Be nice gal.
LEILANI	Why? Why be nice gal? You no like me no more.
UNCLE	Sure. Sure, I like you.
LEILANI	[*Wrapping her arms around him affectionately.*] You naughty Okinawan-Japanee…You're lucky I still see you.
UNCLE	Why? Why you see me?
LEILANI	Because…Oh, I don't know. Maybe, because, you and Papa get along great, and he's not lonely for Mama when you visit us.
UNCLE	On'y that?
LEILANI	Or, maybe, because you a'ways make me laugh, talkin' funny kine. Japanese, Okinawan, Hawaiian, English—all mix up.
UNCLE	You, too.

LEILANI	I no talk like you no understand me.
UNCLE	How you talk…school?
LEILANI	With my friends, pidgin English. With schoolteacher, good English.
UNCLE	Try. Try good English.
LEILANI	[*Dramatically.*] "Four score and seven years ago, our fathers brought forth on this continent, a new nation, conceived in Liberty, and dedicated to the proposition that all men are created equal…" You know what that means?
UNCLE	Ever'body same-u same-u.
LEILANI	You tell your brother that.
UNCLE	He know.
LEILANI	Then?
UNCLE	He tink Okinawan, Kanaka—no same-u same-u.
LEILANI	Who he tink him? One Okinawan god?
KAMA	[*To Tsuyu.*] In a way, I am a god. I can see and hear them; they can't hear or see me.
TSUYU	But I can!
LEILANI	[*To Uncle.*] I talked to Papa last night.
UNCLE	About you, me, marry?!
LEILANI	About why no start your own pineapple field.
UNCLE	Not ready yet.
LEILANI	You never gonna be ready, you keep saying that.
UNCLE	Must learn more from Kama first…Plowing, pula-pula planting, fertilizing. Also, business talk with Libby Cannery manager.
LEILANI	Papa can do that for you. He knows Mr. Gibson, the haole manager.
UNCLE	Papa, he okay, lease land to me?
LEILANI	You're his best friend.
UNCLE	You tell him: you, me, we marry?
LEILANI	[*Teasing.*] Of course.
UNCLE	You tell him that?!

LEILANI	Aw…Of course not.
UNCLE	Someday soon. You tell him.
LEILANI	That you wanna marry me?
UNCLE	[*Nodding.*] Also, you, me, we start our own pineapple field.
LEILANI	[*Hugging.*] Oh, Yasu…We'll have the biggest pineapple field in all Peahi.
UNCLE	All Maui.
LEILANI	And every year, after the season is all pau, we'll throw a big luau.
UNCLE	Kalua pig. Laulau. Andagi…
LEILANI	Everybody happy, singing, dancing…Like you and me right now. [*Stepping over for ukulele, strums a few chords.*] C'mon, Yasu. That happy song I taught you. [*Begins singing "Puamana," coaxing Uncle.*] C'mon, Yasu. [*Uncle finally joins her in duet.*] You sing more and more better nowadays. C'mon. Dance. The hula I showed you.
UNCLE	Aw…
LEILANI	[*Urging; strumming on.*] C'mon.
UNCLE	Next time.
LEILANI	Hawaiian style. You not only sing when you're happy, you dance, too. C'mon. Dance. [*Uncle finally gives in and begins dancing. He is quite good.*] You really becomin' one of us. Even lookin' like us.
UNCLE	Leilani a'ways make me very happy. Number one gal, Maui.
LEILANI	Just on Maui?
UNCLE	All Hawaii!
LEILANI	Oh, Yasu. You can be the sweetest man sometimes.
UNCLE	Leilani sweet all time. [*As they embrace and kiss, lights fade on them.*]
KAMA	[*To Tsuyu.*] You knew about him and the girl, didn't you?
TSUYU	He was happy, Kama.
KAMA	Getting involved with a wild native girl!
TSUYU	Getting involved in a romance with a pretty native girl. Like you used to be with me.
KAMA	Aw…

TSUYU	C'mon. Give me a kiss-u.
KAMA	Baka.
TSUYU	C'mon. It can't kill you.
UNCLE	[*Alone now. Lights rise on him.*] Leilani became very special to me. It was memories of the happy days we spent together that got me through the terrible days of the war.
	Stage lights keep dimming until BLACKOUT.

Scene Two

An hour later. Same scene. Kama and Tsuyu are by headstones where additional bouquets of flowers have been placed. Uncle is sitting on bench. Ichiro—in aloha shirt, khakis, and zoris—is Downstage Right with a bottle of sake and an ukulele. A little drunk, he pours himself a cupful and drinks.

UNCLE	That bottle of sake—I thought you went to get it for your father.
ICHIRO	Aw, Otosan doesn't mind sharing it with me.
UNCLE	How much did you pay for that?
ICHIRO	The sake?
UNCLE	The ukulele.
ICHIRO	Forty-five dollars.
UNCLE	That much? Back in my day, I could get it for five dollars.
ICHIRO	Back in your day, five dollars was a whole week's wages.
UNCLE	[*Beat.*] Are you sure you told Kimiko we're to meet here on Maui today?
ICHIRO	She knows.
UNCLE	Then why isn't she here?
ICHIRO	She's flying in all the way from Utah.
UNCLE	China?!
ICHIRO	Utah. America. Where the Mormons live. She became one of them.
UNCLE	A haole?
ICHIRO	Otosan and Okasan must've known better than to try and stop her.
UNCLE	She was always strong willed. Very independent. Even as a child. Don't forget now. We must take the ashes back with us.

ICHIRO	If Kimiko goes along.
UNCLE	You're the chonan.
ICHIRO	That stuff about being the oldest means nothing here in America.
UNCLE	[*Scornfully.*] You American-born Japanese…
KAMA	[*Apparently looking for something.*] Are you hiding my Bull-u Dur-ram-u bag again?
TSUYU	[*Innocently.*] Why would I do that?
KAMA	Basan…
TSUYU	Smoking is not good for you.
KAMA	What harm can it do me now?
UNCLE	[*To Ichiro.*] You should stop drinking and go visit some of your friends.
ICHIRO	They all went away. What about you? Any Okinawan friends still here?
UNCLE	A Hawaiian friend. You might remember him. Kimo Makaole.
ICHIRO	Mr. Makaole? His son, Ernest—we went to grade school together. Until he transferred to Kamehameha School in Honolulu.
UNCLE	I drove over to see Kimo yesterday. He asked about you and Kimiko.
ICHIRO	Why didn't you take me with you?
UNCLE	You were in the hotel bar feeling sorry for yourself.
ICHIRO	Aw…I missed Otosan and Okasan not being there at the airport. [*Beat.*] What did you and Mr. Makaole talk about, after all these years?
UNCLE	Old days. And what's happened since.
ICHIRO	Since you caught that last ship to Japan the year the war started?
UNCLE	Bad timing.
ICHIRO	I can still remember you playing your samisen in your bedroom night after night, and Otosan, whenever drunk, singing along at the kitchen table.
UNCLE	[*Begins singing an Okinawan drinking song, "Imu Nu Jidai." Ichiro joins him. When Kama joins in, Uncle stops. He looks behind him. Beat.*] No matter how much better life was here, Okinawa was always our home.

ICHIRO	[*Offering cup.*] Here.
UNCLE	I've had enough. [*Ichiro downs drink.*] You've had enough, too.
ICHIRO	[*Ignoring; toasting.*] Otosan and Okasan…Just when life was getting better for them…
KAMA	[*Reaching out.*] Oi, Ichiro, your mother and I are happy where we are.
ICHIRO	[*Suddenly turning to Uncle.*] Huh? You said something?
UNCLE	[*Staring.*] You better stop drinking.
ICHIRO	Yeah. I think I better.
UNCLE	[*Beat.*] I'm glad your father and mother didn't have to go through what we did during the war.
ICHIRO	You should have kept staying here instead of returning.
UNCLE	Your father wanted me to take Tokujiro's ashes back to Okinawa. It was the seventh anniversary of his death.
ICHIRO	That uncle—you never told me why he committed suicide.
UNCLE	It happened during the pineapple depression. When his debts began piling up, he started drinking more and more. Until one night…We found him hanging under a tree in his backyard.
ICHIRO	[*Drinks.*] Talk about family skeletons. Suicide, unauthorized removal of ashes…
UNCLE	I hope we don't have to sneak the ashes out of the country this time.
ICHIRO	I'll make the necessary arrangements after I talk it over with Kimiko. [*He sips again.*]
UNCLE	It's not going to make you feel less guilty—getting drunk.
ICHIRO	[*Beat.*] As long as I didn't see their graves…[*turns away from headstones*] I could still see them the way they used to be: happy, laughing, working together in the pineapple fields, feeding the chickens and pigs. Now…
UNCLE	I'm sure they're happy together even now.
KAMA	[*To Tsuyu.*] That's the smartest thing he said since coming here.
TSUYU	Why are you always criticizing your brother?
KAMA	He always made mistakes whenever I wasn't around.
TSUYU	Like getting involved with a young native girl?

KAMA	He should have known better.
ICHIRO	[*To Uncle.*] By the time I got Kimiko's letter, Otosan's funeral was over. And Okasan's…So soon afterward.
TSUYU	[*To Kama.*] I wish we could have been together once more. Ichiro, Kimiko, you and me. Just once more.
KAMA	In here [*touches his chest*] we will always be together.
ICHIRO	[*To Uncle.*] Sometimes, I can still hear us singing that children's song I learned in Japanese school. [*As he sings "Yuyake Koyake," Kama and Tsuyu join him.*]
	Yuyake koyake de hi ga kurete Yama no otera no kane ga naru Otete tsunai de mina kaero Karasu to issho ni kaerimasho.
KAMA	He sure was a smart boy, our Ichiro. He knew all the English alphabet and the Japanese alphabet even before he was in the second grade.
TSUYU	As he learned to read and write, so did we.
ICHIRO	[*To Uncle.*] I wanted my wife and son to meet Otosan and Oka-san. Find out what made them leave their mountain village in Okinawa and come to a place called Hawaii.
UNCLE	Kodomo no tame ni.
ICHIRO	Yeah. For the sake of their children. [*Toasting.*] Arigato, Otosan, Okasan. [*Pours another cupful.*]
UNCLE	That's enough, Ichiro.
ICHIRO	Aw, they won't mind. [*Sips.*] You know something, Uncle? Otosan and me, we hardly knew each other. I mean really knew each other. Someday, when my son is old enough, me and him, we're gonna sit down with a gallon of sake and…get to know each other. Not only as father and son. As friends.
UNCLE	You'll lose his respect.
ICHIRO	Not after I share with him all I've gone through. Growing up in Peahi, working my way through University of Hawaii, fighting in the war…Then, how I met his mother. I never told you, huh? Come to think of it, you and me, we always avoided talking about the war.
UNCLE	What's there to talk about? Your side won; my side lost.
KAMA	[*To Tsuyu.*] Akisamiyo!…They could have ended up shooting each other.

TSUYU	That's why they never talked about it.
UNCLE	[*To Ichiro.*] They sure fed us POWs well, the GIs. We used to think it was our last meal before they shot us.
ICHIRO	You were fed what us GIs didn't want.
UNCLE	[*Bowing mockingly.*] Tank you bery much…
ICHIRO	[*Bowing back mockingly.*] Do itashimashite…Things couldn't have been too bad for you—you being able to speak a little English.
UNCLE	I always impressed the GI guards with…[*Recites dramatically, with heavy accent.*] "Four scores, seven e-yas 'go, our fathers brought-u forth-u on tis continent-u…"
ICHIRO	Hey, that's pretty good. Who taught you that?
UNCLE	Somebody. [*Reminiscing.*] Somebody, long time ago, who wanted me to speak good English so we could understand each other better. [*Leilani appears, and Ichiro fades off. She is a year older now, her demeanor more mature. They are at a beach, a picnic basket beside them.*]
LEILANI	Go on, say it. "The beach is beautiful."
UNCLE	"Da bitch iz-u bea-u-ti-ful."
LEILANI	Not "bitch." "Beach."
UNCLE	Let's kau kau.
LEILANI	Not yet.
UNCLE	Bery hungry.
LEILANI	Not "bery." "Very."
UNCLE	[*Indicating picnic basket.*] What you bring?
LEILANI	Poi, lomilomi, dried squid.
UNCLE	Oh, bery good…Ah, *very* good.
LEILANI	That's better.
UNCLE	[*Reciting, trying to impress.*] "Da sky is-u clear; da ocean blue; da mountains, dey nice and…green."
LEILANI	[*Applauding.*] That's wonderful, Yasu.
UNCLE	Hawaii numbah one; Okinawa numbah two.
LEILANI	I'm glad you love it here.
UNCLE	Oh, very much. 'Specially flower Leilani like best.
LEILANI	Hibiscus?

UNCLE	In Okinawa, "akabana." Hawaii, much bigger, much more nice than Okinawa hibiscus. 'Specially on Leilani's hair.
LEILANI	I'm glad you think so. And I'm glad your English is getting better.
UNCLE	Leilani good teacher. Maybe, better, go university, become schoolteacher.
LEILANI	I don't like it over there in Honolulu. And I don't like long boat rides.
UNCLE	Me, too. But must. [*Leilani looks at him.*] Must go back Okinawa.
LEILANI	When?!
UNCLE	Soon.
LEILANI	And not come back?
UNCLE	Oh, yes.
LEILANI	Oh, yes, you're not coming back?
UNCLE	Oh, yes. Come back. Right 'way.
LEILANI	Then?
UNCLE	We get married.
LEILANI	No bull lie?
UNCLE	No bull lie.
LEILANI	Oh, Yasu! [*Hugs him.*] Now I'm hungry, too. [*Opening picnic basket, spreading out contents.*] C'mon. Lotsa kau kau.
UNCLE	[*Mimes dipping finger into poi bowl and eating.*] Kanaka style.
LEILANI	Hawaiian, Yasu. Hawaiian.
UNCLE	Oh, yeah. Hawaiian, not Kanaka.
LEILANI	And I'm your "kuuipo."
UNCLE	"Kuuipo"?
LEILANI	Your sweetheart. You wanna, you can call me "Ipo."
UNCLE	"Kuuipo" much better. [*Light begins fading on them.*]
ICHIRO	Hey, Uncle. Uncle!
LEILANI	[*Stepping away.*] Yasu…Yasu…
ICHIRO	Uncle! You alright?
UNCLE	[*Snapping out of it as Leilani exits.*] Huh? Oh, yeah. Yeah, I'm alright.

ICHIRO	Can't forget the war, eh?
UNCLE	You GIs shouldn't have destroyed our shrines and tombs.
ICHIRO	That's something they never told us about at MIS school: the shrines and tombs in Okinawa.
UNCLE	MIS?
ICHIRO	Military Intelligence Service. Where we studied Japanese.
UNCLE	Were there many Okinawan GIs in this school?
ICHIRO	Quite a few.
UNCLE	All willing to fight against their homeland?
ICHIRO	Like the old samurai story: if you're adopted into a family, you must be willing to fight for that family. Even against your own blood family.
UNCLE	Did you, yourself, kill many Okinawans?
ICHIRO	I tried to save as many as I could.
UNCLE	Save?
ICHIRO	By talking them out of committing suicide.
UNCLE	We were told American barbarians would rape the young girls and torture everyone else before killing them.
ICHIRO	Some of the girls, just fifteen and sixteen, were holding a grenade to their stomach and pulling the pin. Others were running away from us, screaming, crying, pleading. That's when I saw her.
UNCLE	Who?
ICHIRO	This young girl about to jump off the cliff. I kept talking to her, reaching for her hand; she kept crawling away. Just as she was about to jump off, I said, "I'm an Uchinanchu like you!" She looked at me. "My mother and father, they're from Ginoza Village." She thought I was lying, trying to trick her. [*Reaching out, sings "Densa Bushi."*]
TSUYU	He remembered that song I taught him.
	Uncle joins Ichiro, then takes over the singing.
ICHIRO	She finally gave me her hand. I took her away from the cliff.
UNCLE	What happened to her family?
ICHIRO	They had all jumped off the cliff: her father, her mother, her two older sisters, and a baby brother.

UNCLE	[*Mournfully.*] Akisamiyo...And the girl?
ICHIRO	That was Mayumi.
UNCLE	Your wife!
ICHIRO	"When you save someone's life, you become responsible for that person forever." Remember?
UNCLE	A lesson from our Chinese ancestors. [*Beat.*] It must've been right afterward that we ran into each other.
ICHIRO	I already knew.
UNCLE	That I was a POW?
ICHIRO	My duty, then, was to make sure the POWs were treated okay. When I came across your name in the Tengan camp, I came over as soon as I could.
UNCLE	[*Imitating.*] "Ojisan! Chaganju! It's me, Ichiro." Akisamiyo! Ichiro, a big shot in the American army.
ICHIRO	The guards—they must've treated you better after that.
UNCLE	Of course. I was an uncle of a general in the American army.
ICHIRO	A general?
UNCLE	It sounded better than a sergeant.
TSUYU	So that's why Ichiro didn't want to talk about the war when he came home.
KAMA	So many of our people died, Basan. So many.
TSUYU	All he said was he was going back to Okinawa as a civilian interpreter for the American government. Nothing about Mayumi.
KAMA	He was always that way, remember? Always quiet, always keeping things to himself.
TSUYU	Even about volunteering for the army.
KAMA	"If this is what you feel you must do," I told him, "shikkari shite. Do your very best."
TSUYU	Little did we think he would be fighting against his own people.
KAMA	War is war, Basan.
	Lights begin dimming.
TSUYU	We can only hope his children won't have to go through another one.
	Lights keep dimming until BLACKOUT.

Scene Three

Moments later. Kama and Tsuyu are Downstage Left. Ichiro, with ukulele, sips, then pours himself another cupful from half-empty bottle. Uncle, his samisen beside him, is looking on disapprovingly.

ICHIRO	If Kimiko isn't here in a few more minutes, let's drive down to the airport.
UNCLE	[*Wiping face with handkerchief.*] I'll wait here. It's too hot walking down the trail and coming back up again.
ICHIRO	[*Indicating mountain.*] We should be up there.
UNCLE	Haleakala. Always nice and cool. Once, when I was up there with Kimo, it actually snowed.
KAMA	[*Ichiro sips, frowning. Kama steps up to him.*] Warm sake. On a hot day like this. [*Blows into Ichiro's face.*]
ICHIRO	[*Reacting.*] Hey, that felt good.
UNCLE	What?
ICHIRO	The cool breeze.
UNCLE	You're drunk.
ICHIRO	Aw…Our Peahi days, I don't remember you ever drinking.
UNCLE	Those days, I practiced playing the samisen instead of drinking.
ICHIRO	You were the best samisen player around.
UNCLE	Not the best—just the loudest. I played the ukulele, too. [*Takes ukulele from Ichiro and begins strumming.*]
ICHIRO	Yeah. That's right. You'd play the ukulele, and Otosan would do the hula.
UNCLE	Your father used to be a pretty good hula dancer.
ICHIRO	Kimi and I used to be ashamed watching him dancing. Today, I do the same thing. Like father, like son. [*Dances few steps of hula.*]
KAMA	[*To Tsuyu.*] C'mon, Basan. Dance hula-hula with me. [*Shakes his rear in time with ukulele music.*]
TSUYU	Aw…[*Looking around self-consciously.*] The other spirits might see us.
KAMA	In this world we're our own boss. C'mon. [*Demonstrating.*] Shake your okole like this. [*Shakes rear. Tsuyu, feeling ridiculous, tries to follow.*] No, no. Not like that. Like this! [*A big shake. Continues dancing. Tsuyu gives her okole a big shake, too. Laughter.*]

	Beat.] Remember me saying, "When I die, I'm coming back for you"?
TSUYU	You were always talking about dying.
KAMA	It's something no one can escape from. It makes us all equal: the big-shot haoles, the cane-field workers; the Japanese, the Filipinos; even Okinawans and Kanakas.
TSUYU	I'm glad you came back for me.
KAMA	I didn't want you to go chasing after another man.
TSUYU	Aw…
ICHIRO	[*To Uncle.*] I remember you started going out at nights.
UNCLE	I…used to visit our neighbors.
ICHIRO	The Shimabukuros? Iges?
UNCLE	The Makaoles, too.
ICHIRO	I don't think Otosan wanted us to associate with Kanakas.
UNCLE	He always enjoyed going to Kimo's luaus.
ICHIRO	Mr. Makaole, he wasn't a Kanaka; he was a high-toned Hawaiian.
UNCLE	His family goes all the way back to King Kamehameha.
ICHIRO	Like our family goes all the way back to the first emperor of Japan, huh?
UNCLE	Baka!
KAMA	[*To Tsuyu.*] He's going to have bachi.
TSUYU	Punished for saying we're related to the Emperor?
KAMA	The Emperor was not an Okinawan.
ICHIRO	[*Offers Uncle sake.*] Here. [*Uncle glares at him, shaking his head.*] Okay. Okay. [*Toasting.*] Here's to King Kamehameha. [*Sips.*]
UNCLE	[*Beat.*] The youngest Makaole girl—remember her?
ICHIRO	Lei? She was just a kid those days. Later, when I saw her in Honolulu, she turned out to be a pretty girl.
UNCLE	She went to Honolulu?
ICHIRO	The same year you left for Okinawa. Her brother, Ernest, and I were juniors at the university then. He took me to his Aunty Becky's, where Lei was.
UNCLE	[*Mutters.*] So she went to Honolulu…

Equestrienne

———————— ✤ ————————

*This chinchin umagwaa doll was sold during the
yukkanufii festival (held during the fourth month
of the lunar calendar). The horse is red and has
a white, flowing mane, and when the doll is pulled,
the horse's head bobs slightly. The female rider
is wearing armor and carries a long sword.*

*During the reign of Sho Shin (1477–1526 C.E.),
Princess Kimihae, the supreme priestess of Kume,
was at the battlefront during the campaign to
conquer the Yaemaya Islands. It is possible
the doll represents this woman warrior.*

*Paper-mâché.
Woodblock print by Ozaki Seiji.*

Leilani appears in a muumuu, a big red hibiscus pinned to her long, dark hair, and Ichiro fades. Although still young and pretty, she is no longer a carefree, dream-filled girl. She is now plagued with somber thoughts.

LEILANI	What we gonna do, Yasu?
UNCLE	We marry.
LEILANI	Before you go?
UNCLE	When I come back.
LEILANI	Maybe you no come back.
UNCLE	I come back. I come back.
LEILANI	What I gonna tell Papa? Y'know, me being hapai. [*Indicates pregnancy.*] Take me with you, Yasu. Please. Take me with you.
UNCLE	Okinawa, long boat ride.
LEILANI	I don't care. I just wanna be with you.
UNCLE	No can! You no can go Okinawa with me!
LEILANI	Why? Why no can?
UNCLE	I tell you, I come back. I come back right 'way.
LEILANI	You promise? You promise you'll be right back?
UNCLE	Yakusoku. I promise.
LEILANI	[*Unpinning hibiscus from hair, offering it.*] Whenever you see a hibiscus flower over there, I want you to remember I'm waiting for you over here.
UNCLE	Will remember. A'ways. Leilani laughing; Leilani dancing; Leilani singing; Leilani…
LEILANI	[*Indicating last two petals.*] Leilani waiting, praying…

As she sings first part of "Aloha Oe," lights start dimming. Uncle joins in. They sing duet until BLACKOUT.

Act Two

Scene One

Several minutes later. Even before the lights go up, we hear soft, tender samisen music. As lights rise, Uncle is at headstones playing his samisen dreamily and singing "Me Oto Bune." Kama and Tsuyu are at bench.

TSUYU	That song Yasuichi is singing—it sure reminds me of our own young days. [*Kama avoids looking at her.*] Ah, those days… Remember when we went to our first movie?
KAMA	That silent movie?
TSUYU	The Indians chasing the cowboys; the cowboys chasing the Indians. Then, when the pretty haole girl was being rescued, you moved closer to me in the darkness and touched my hand. [*Touches his hand.*]
KAMA	[*Very casually pushing off her hand.*] Oi, Yasuichi!
TSUYU	Leave him alone, Jisan.
KAMA	[*To Uncle.*] When you go back home, find yourself a nice Okinawan woman.
TSUYU	I'm sure he tried.
KAMA	Oi, Yasuichi! [*Approaches Uncle, who suddenly strikes a chord and stops playing.*]
TSUYU	[*To Kama.*] Come back.
KAMA	[*Returning.*] I guess some people are happy when they're miserable.
TSUYU	Without misery how can you know when you're happy?
KAMA	[*Looks at her.*] You know something, Basan? You've become smarter ever since you came to this side of the world.
TSUYU	[*Returning "compliment."*] Only a great man admits that his wife is smarter than him.
KAMA	[*Reacting.*] I didn't say… Aw…
UNCLE	[*Recites song lyrics.*]
	I sailed out into the sea an eager young man, And returned home a sad old man.
KAMA	There he goes, saying things no one else understands.
TSUYU	He's saying he went out into the world hoping to find happiness.
KAMA	And?
TSUYU	What he found made him wiser—not happier.
UNCLE	[*To headstones. Beat.*] When I was ready to return to Maui, there were no ships sailing back to America. A few months later, Japan attacked Pearl Har-bah. It started a war we never thought would come to Okinawa.

TSUYU	It must have been awful what they went through.
KAMA	Okinawans are survivors, Basan.
TSUYU	We had no choice.
KAMA	Our islands were conquered and occupied by foreigners all the time. But we're still Okinawans.
TSUYU	And still hardheaded and still stubborn.
UNCLE	Now, at last, I have come to take you home…
	Leilani enters Upstage Right. She looks curiously at Uncle. She is no longer the young, impressionable girl of yesteryear, but an attractive, prim lady in her mid-thirties. Statuesque in heels, her dark hair upswept, a hibiscus flower in it, she has on a form-fitting, tropical dress.
KAMA	Akisamiyo. That's the girl. Leilani.
TSUYU	My, she's grown up to be a real churakagi.
LEILANI	[*Beat. To Uncle.*] Yasu? [*Uncle turns tentatively.*] Yasu?
UNCLE	Leilani?
LEILANI	Yes. Lei…Leilani.
UNCLE	[*Rising, then bowing low.*] You come. You come.
LEILANI	I'm sorry I couldn't make it to Papa's yesterday. [*Steps over to headstones; bows respectfully.*]
UNCLE	No pilikia. No pilikia.
LEILANI	How are you?
UNCLE	Fine. Very fine. You?
LEILANI	I'm fine, too.
UNCLE	Long time…
LEILANI	Yes. It's been a long time. [*Looking around.*] Where's Ichiro and Kimi? I thought they'd be here, too.
UNCLE	Ichiro go airport. Wait for Kimiko.
LEILANI	How are they? It's been years since I've seen them.
UNCLE	They okay. Okay. [*Admiringly.*] Leilani no longer Peahi gal; now beautiful young lady.
LEILANI	Thank you. You…haven't changed much.
UNCLE	Aw, makule, old man now.

LEILANI	Your hair—it's still dark.
UNCLE	Yes. Whatever left. [*Looking behind her.*] Emma? She no come?
LEILANI	[*Shaking head.*] I…ah, I didn't tell her.
UNCLE	No?
LEILANI	I…still haven't gotten over…You know, you being back.
UNCLE	Yes. Understand.
LEILANI	When Papa called yesterday…It's been twenty years since you left.
UNCLE	Nineteen.
LEILANI	The year the war started.
TSUYU	It must have been like waiting for a nightmare to end, for Yasuichi, each day the war went on.
UNCLE	Leilani now speak very good English.
LEILANI	Your English, it's improved, too.
UNCLE	GI English. [*Imitates.*] "Hey, Papa-san, hubba-hubba, git going; clean up hootch." "Okay, GI Joe. Okay."
LEILANI	[*Chuckling.*] You were always a fast learner.
UNCLE	"Four score, seven e-yas 'go…"
LEILANI	My god.
UNCLE	Like on'y yesterday.
LEILANI	Many yesterdays ago. [*Beat.*] I'm glad you went to see Papa.
UNCLE	Oh, yeah. Very nice, long talk. You—three children, he say.
LEILANI	Three girls. Emma will be going to the university in September.
UNCLE	Emma go university?
LEILANI	She graduated in the top three in her high school.
UNCLE	Ah, must be smart gal.
KAMA	Of course. She's a Gusuda.
LEILANI	She speaks a little Japanese.
UNCLE	Ah, so.
LEILANI	She picked it up from her friends.
UNCLE	Some friends Okinawan?
LEILANI	Her best friend is Haruko Shimabukuro.

UNCLE	Shimabukuro…
LEILANI	Haruko's mother taught her some Okinawan dances.
KAMA	Hear that, Basan? The girl learned our dances.
TSUYU	She's half Okinawan, remember?
UNCLE	Very sorry, Leilani. Very sorry broke yakusoku.
KAMA	He shouldn't have made it.
TSUYU	It wasn't his fault that he couldn't honor it.
KAMA	A yakusoku is a promise that must be honored no matter what.
LEILANI	That's all in the past, Yasu.
UNCLE	When I go, I know I come back right 'way.
LEILANI	Yasu. Please… [*Beat.*] Papa wasn't sure whether you have a family of your own over there. [*Uncle shakes head.*] Never got married?
UNCLE	A'ways wanna come back Maui. War—no food; no house; no clothes; no nothing.
LEILANI	[*Beat.*] I waited, Yasu. I waited as long as I could.
UNCLE	I ready to come back Maui. Pearl Har-bah… Wanna write letter. How can?
LEILANI	I wanted to write to you, too. But in what? Japanese?
UNCLE	One day, war come Okinawa, too. Nightmare. POW. Speak English to GI. Think more, more Leilani. Leilani okay? And baby…?
LEILANI	[*Beat.*] I didn't tell Papa for a long time. One day, I took a long walk down to the Peahi Cliff. Where you and I used to have our picnics. I stood there looking down at the sea, the waves, the rocks. I was just about to—
UNCLE	No!
LEILANI	That's when I felt our baby moving inside me.
KAMA	That stupid fool! He should've told me.
TSUYU	About him fathering a Kanaka baby?
KAMA	The baby is not a Kanaka!
LEILANI	When I finally told Papa, he shipped me off to Honolulu. Even before the baby was born, Albert—Albert Wu—asked me to marry him. He was Aunty Becky's neighbor. I was sure you had forgotten us!
UNCLE	Never forget! Never!

LEILANI	After the baby was born, we moved to Maui and opened a Chinese restaurant in Kahului.
UNCLE	Yes. Papa say that.
LEILANI	Did he also tell you what I went through all those months waiting?! Huh? Did he?!
UNCLE	I know!
LEILANI	[*Slapping him.*] How can you know?! [*Stunned, Uncle lowers his head.*] Nobody can ever! [*Beat.*] I…thought of you even after I was married.
UNCLE	Ever' time see hibiscus flower, tink of Leilani. "Leilani laughing; Leilani dancing; Leilani singing…"
LEILANI	[*Throwing hibiscus flower at him.*] And waiting! And praying! [*Beat.*] It's best we put all that behind us.
UNCLE	And forget?
LEILANI	And be thankful we're alright.
UNCLE	Emma, too?
LEILANI	Emma, too. [*Beat.*] I…have to go. [*Takes tentative step, then stops.*] Goodbye, Yasu.
UNCLE	Goodbye, Leilani. [*Leilani dashes off, and lights begin dimming. He picks up hibiscus flower, looks at it fondly, then suddenly, painfully, raises it over his head to heave it on the ground.*] Ahh!
	Lights keep dimming until BLACKOUT.

Scene Two

Shortly thereafter. At the beach. Leilani, taking off shoes, crosses anxiously Downstage Right.

EMMA	[*Offstage.*] Mom! Wait for me.
LEILANI	C'mon.
EMMA	[*Follows, taking off her slippers. She has on an aloha shirt and shorts.*] Why are you in such a hurry?
LEILANI	The sun's going to be over the mountains soon, and the tide's coming in fast.
EMMA	The sun's always going over the mountains, and the tide's always coming in or going out. [*Approaching, looks curiously at her mother.*] Something wrong, Mom? You're not feeling good?

LEILANI	I'm fine. Fine…[*Beat.*] I still can't believe you'll be going off to college.
EMMA	I'm only going to UH—not some college in the Mainland.
LEILANI	I just hope you'll always be my Emma Lani.
EMMA	Oh, Mom.
LEILANI	Our neighbor's girl—remember what happened to her?
EMMA	Masako?
LEILANI	After speaking Japanese to her mother all her life, she comes home from college and no longer understands her.
EMMA	That's her. "Sophisticated" Masako. She suddenly understands only proper English. If it makes you feel any better, Mom… [*Speaking pidgin.*] Auwe! I gonna talk pidgin to you whenevah I come home from school.
LEILANI	[*Speaking pidgin.*] Auwe! You gonna talk like that after your father and me—we spend all the kala send you college?
EMMA	Once a Hawaiian, a'ways a Hawaiian.
LEILANI	Just remember that— Look. [*Indicating Upstage Left.*] The SS *Hualalai* is just coming in.
EMMA	Mom. It's been coming in from Honolulu every week.
LEILANI	It's the SS *Waialeale* that comes in every week.
EMMA	The *Hualalai,* the *Waialeale*—what's the difference?
LEILANI	[*Beat.*] I ever told you about my first boat ride to Honolulu?
EMMA	You getting seasick?
LEILANI	The whole night. Terrible.
EMMA	You should've gone over on a canoe like the old Hawaiians used to.
LEILANI	Oh, sure.
EMMA	Or paddled your way over on a surfboard.
LEILANI	Or swam over.
EMMA	Right through the Maui-Molokai channel, the manos escorting you.
LEILANI	Or eating me up.
EMMA	And we wouldn't be here talking like this.

LEILANI	[*Beat.*] Ever wondered why you're different from Kalehua and Maile?
EMMA	Different?
LEILANI	You've all been wonderful children, but—
EMMA	Even sisters have their own personalities.
LEILANI	Yes. Of course. But you, you're— Oh, maybe it's because I wasn't much older than you are now when I had you.
EMMA	Go on. Say it. You get a big kick from people mistaking us for sisters.
LEILANI	What mother wouldn't?
EMMA	I rather have you as my mother, not my sister.
LEILANI	You sure know how to hurt somebody's feelings.
EMMA	Poor Mama…
LEILANI	Ever since you came into my life—
EMMA	Just yours?
LEILANI	Daddy's, too.
EMMA	I couldn't have chosen a better father and mother.
LEILANI	And we couldn't have chosen a better first baby.
EMMA	[*Beat.*] Mom. What is it you really want to tell me?
LEILANI	Tell you?
EMMA	Now, c'mon.
LEILANI	[*Evasively.*] Funny. The boat ride home wasn't all that bad.
EMMA	Mom?
LEILANI	[*Beat.*] It's…about your father.
EMMA	Daddy? Something's wrong with him?!
LEILANI	No. No, he's fine.
EMMA	Then…?
LEILANI	Sweetheart…
EMMA	Uh-oh.
LEILANI	When I was a little younger than you are now…
EMMA	Not those Peahi days again.

LEILANI	Some of those days were the happiest days of my life, sweet-heart.
EMMA	Uh-oh. Twice now: "sweetheart."
LEILANI	You'll always be that to me, dear.
EMMA	Mom?
LEILANI	Your father, he's…
EMMA	You just said…
LEILANI	Your real father.
EMMA	What?!
LEILANI	I always hoped and prayed you'd never have to go through this.
EMMA	Mom?!
LEILANI	Emma, please.
EMMA	Daddy—he's not my father?!
LEILANI	Yes. He is. He always will be. He just isn't…
EMMA	My…real father? [*Leilani shakes head.*] Then who is?!
LEILANI	Sweetheart, please…
EMMA	The Peahi days? [*Leilani nods.*] But…I was born in Honolulu. [*Suddenly realizing, stares at Leilani.*]
LEILANI	Please…Please try to understand…
EMMA	Why are you bringing all this up now?!
LEILANI	He's here.
EMMA	My…?
LEILANI	He came yesterday.
EMMA	From where?
LEILANI	Okinawa.
EMMA	He's Okinawan?
LEILANI	[*Nodding.*] You knew his brother, Mr. Gusuda, who used to come to Grandpa's.
EMMA	He knew all along, Mr. Gusuda?
LEILANI	No one except Grandpa knew.
EMMA	What happened to him—my…

LEILANI	He returned to Okinawa before you were born.
EMMA	And never came back?
LEILANI	He couldn't. The war.
EMMA	Daddy—he knew? And he was still willing to…?
LEILANI	[*Nodding.*] Yasu, your father, he's waiting at—
EMMA	He's not my father!
LEILANI	He's going back in a few days.
EMMA	He shouldn't have come!
LEILANI	He wants to meet you.
EMMA	I don't wanna meet him…
LEILANI	Emma, please…
EMMA	[*Sobbing.*] Mama…
LEILANI	He came all the way…
EMMA	Please. Mama. Don't ask me to. I…can't…I…won't…
LEILANI	[*Holds Emma, and lights begin dimming.*] Alright, dear. Alright.
EMMA	Tell him…[*Dashes off, sobbing. Leilani watches her running off, fights back tears.*]
	Lights keep dimming until BLACKOUT.

Scene Three

An hour later. Kama and Tsuyu are at headstones. Kimiko, in printed tropical dress, is rearranging bouquets of flowers at their graves.

KIMIKO	[*To headstones.*] I won't let them take you away, Otosan, Okasan. I just won't!…And here I thought Uncle just wanted the three of us to get together for a quick reunion. [*As Ichiro approaches her.*] And you, Ichiro, I can't believe you're willing to go along with him.
ICHIRO	Look, there's a big family tomb back in Okinawa…
KIMIKO	[*Glancing toward where Uncle was.*] Where'd he go?
ICHIRO	I think he wants to be alone.
KIMIKO	What makes him so sure Otosan and Okasan want to be moved to Okinawa?
ICHIRO	It's a tradition, Kimi: all family members buried in a family tomb.

KAMA	You should have taught Kimiko some of our traditions.
TSUYU	Eating pig's feet soup three times a day?
KAMA	Why must you always remember the worst of our homeland?
TSUYU	It makes our life here that much better.
ICHIRO	[*Beat.*] What happened, Kimi? Your letters—I know you tried to tell me…
KIMIKO	The doctor warned Otosan. His blood pressure was dangerously high. He should stop drinking.
ICHIRO	Okasan…So soon afterwards.
KIMIKO	It was just a cold in the beginning. It kept getting worse.
ICHIRO	You don't believe Otosan had anything to do with it?
KIMIKO	She lost her will to live, Ichiro.
ICHIRO	She really believed Otosan was coming back for her?
KIMIKO	After hearing him say it over and over?
TSUYU	What took you so long to come and get me?
KAMA	I was hoping Ichiro would be able to see you once more.
TSUYU	Didn't you miss me?
KAMA	I came to get you, didn't I?
KIMIKO	All the people who came to Otosan's funeral came to Okasan's— Japanese and non-Japanese. Mr. Makaole and most of his family were there: Willie, Ernest, Johnny, Lei—
ICHIRO	Lei came, too?
KIMIKO	With her daughter. A cute Chinese-Hawaiian girl.
KAMA	Oi, Kimiko! That girl is your cousin.
TSUYU	I'm sure Yasuichi intends to tell them.
KAMA	He better, baka Okinawan!
ICHIRO	[*To Kimiko.*] The Makaoles—they were the only Hawaiians Otosan liked those days. The rest, to him, were lazy drunkards who did nothing but sing, dance, and raise hell.
KIMIKO	Otosan used to enjoy singing Hawaiian songs and dancing the hula, too.
ICHIRO	Yeah. Whenever drunk. [*Pause.*] You got through UH the year the war ended, right?

KIMIKO	Nineteen forty-five. No more curfews, no more rations, no more gas masks.
KAMA	The American newspapers, the radio, the Maui big-shot haoles— they were all lying.
TSUYU	About Japan losing the war?
KAMA	Japan never lost the war!
TSUYU	The war ended. And Ichiro was alright. That's all that mattered.
KAMA	All Japan needed was more resources.
TSUYU	That's why you sent the Emperor that fifty dollars?
KAMA	That son-nana-gun Okinawan!
TSUYU	The Emperor?!
KAMA	The man I gave the money.
ICHIRO	Otosan and Okasan, they must have been worried by then, you not meeting a "nice" Japanese boy.
KIMIKO	I did.
ICHIRO	Meet a nice Japanese boy?
KIMIKO	It was during my last year at UH. When we got serious, he took me to meet his mother.
ICHIRO	And?
KIMIKO	She was one of those proud and proper Japanese women. She and her husband ran a Japanese school before the war. She made sure I knew that. You should have seen her when I told her about Otosan…[*Imitating.*] "Ah, so, your father is now an Okinawan pig farmer…"
ICHIRO	Oh, boy…
KIMIKO	"There were several Okinawan students in our school. They were fine students. But different from the other students."
ICHIRO	Yeah. Sure. "Different." Nice way of saying Okinawans are hairy like pigs.
KIMIKO	"Think about it very carefully, Kimiko-san. It's always better to marry your own kind. Don't you think so?"
KAMA	Damn proud Naichis! They all started as cane-field workers like us.
TSUYU	I guess we all have to have somebody to look down on.

KAMA	Us Okinawans are at the bottom of the barrel. There's no one to look down on.
TSUYU	Not even the Kanakas?
KAMA	We're not that far down the barrel.
KIMIKO	I kept myself busy after that, teaching music at McKinley, taking graduate classes at UH. Jack was one of my teachers.
ICHIRO	He taught at UH?
KIMIKO	Before that he was a Mormon missionary here in Hawaii. In the Japanese mission, he learned to speak Nihongo. He joined the marines during the war and became an interpreter in the South Pacific.
ICHIRO	He must have been one of the haole interpreters I heard about.
KIMIKO	[*Beat.*] One day, he invited me to his church service.
ICHIRO	You, a Buddhist?
KIMIKO	I made an excuse not to go.
ICHIRO	Then he became a missionary and worked on you, eh?
KIMIKO	When he invited me again, I thought, What do I have to lose? [*Beat.*] The moment I stepped into the church, I felt I belonged there. There were all kinds of people: Hawaiians, Chinese, Japanese, Portuguese…All singing together. Remember those days? The haoles?
ICHIRO	Yeah, them haoles. They the bosses; us the laborers.
KIMIKO	In that church, the haoles were sharing hymn books with non-haoles.
ICHIRO	[*Beat.*] Otosan—what did he say about you wanting to marry Jack?
KAMA	Damn jack-u ass haole!
TSUYU	He spoke Japanese.
KAMA	Nice boy, that jack-u ass haole.
KIMIKO	You should have seen Otosan in his brand-new suit, walking me down the aisle that day. And Okasan in her brand-new dress, looking so beautiful, standing there watching us.
KAMA	Yeah, that sure was a great day alright.
TSUYU	I was worried you might start dancing hula and shaking your okole at that Mor-moon party.

KAMA	How can you get drunk drinking orange juice and 7-Up?
KIMIKO	I told Colleen all about her Okinawan grandpa and grandma, their pioneering spirit, their sacrifices…
ICHIRO	She understood?
KIMIKO	She listened. [*Beat.*] Someday, when she's old enough, I'm going to tell her that I want to be buried on Maui. Next to Otosan and Okasan.
ICHIRO	What about Jack?
KIMIKO	I'm sure he'd like to be buried here, too. He's always saying how happy he was living in Hawaii.
KAMA	I guess we won't be moving back home.
TSUYU	Home is here, Jisan. Where our children were born and raised. Besides, when I think of the long boat ride back…
KAMA	Oi, Basan. This is 1960. You don't ride boats anymore; you fly.
TSUYU	All the way to Okinawa? On an airplane?
KAMA	How else can you fly?
TSUYU	By getting drunk like you used to.
ICHIRO	[*As Uncle returns.*] Where'd you go, Uncle?
UNCLE	Went for a walk…They don't have a bathroom here.
KIMIKO	You'd think they would have one by now.
ICHIRO	I'll mention it to the governor.
KIMIKO	Aw…
ICHIRO	Hey, the governor of Hawaii—he's no longer appointed by the president.
KIMIKO	That's what statehood is all about. Otosan and Okasan, if they had lived just a few more years, they could have become citizens and voted like everyone else. They had so much to look forward to.
ICHIRO	Yeah. After all they went through.
KIMIKO	It took me a long time getting over it. You know, coming back to Maui from Honolulu, driving over to the old house, not finding them there.
ICHIRO	I should've come home right afterwards.
KIMIKO	There was nothing you could do. [*Beat.*] It was hardest for me when I came here to say goodbye before moving to Utah.

	Uncle must understand. If he takes Otosan and Okasan back to Okinawa, Maui will no longer be our home.
KAMA	Oi, Kimiko! Ichiro!
TSUYU	I keep telling you, Jisan. They can't hear you.
KAMA	They should know that Yasuichi came back to Maui not just for our ashes.
TSUYU	Maybe, if we concentrate hard enough, they'll get the message.
KAMA	You think so?
TSUYU	Start concentrating. [*Closing their eyes and sitting stiffly, they go into a trance.*]
ICHIRO	C'mon. Let's go get a bite.
TSUYU	[*To Kama.*] You're not supposed to be thinking of food!
KAMA	I started smelling noodles.
KIMIKO	How about some good-old Maui noodles?
ICHIRO	Sounds great. [*Approaching Uncle.*] Uncle, let's go.
UNCLE	Where?
ICHIRO	Kau kau.
UNCLE	I want to spend a few more minutes with your father and mother.
KIMIKO	Uncle, I didn't mean to be disrespectful…I just want you to understand…
UNCLE	Go! Go!
ICHIRO	Well, okay then. We're gonna go down the road to Aloha Saimin.
KIMIKO	If that place is still there.
ICHIRO	We'll be back for you in a few minutes.
	They exit. Alone, Uncle, agitated, reflects on what transpired with Leilani and then Kimiko. He steps toward gravestones, about to vent his frustration.
TSUYU	Poor Yasuichi…He won't be able to see his daughter. And Kimiko won't let him take our ashes to Okinawa.
KAMA	Oi, Yasuichi! Bury the past. Go back home. Forget Hawaii.
UNCLE	[*Lights begin dimming. Unable to restrain himself.*] Yakamashi!!!
	Lights keep dimming until BLACKOUT.

Scene Four

Moments later. The sun has set beyond the West Maui Mountains, and shadows of peaks are cast on the graves and surroundings. Chirping of birds, barking of dogs, and early nocturnal sounds of tropical crickets.

UNCLE   [*Exploding.*] I should have married Leilani and refused to go to Okinawa with Tokujiro's ashes! Never mind what you would say. Never mind what all the Okinawans on Maui would say, me marrying a Kanaka girl. Anta no kanke denai!

TSUYU   We could have told everyone she was Okinawan.

KAMA   And try to pass her off as one of us?

TSUYU   Some of us are darker than her.

UNCLE   [*To headstones.*] Now…My daughter, my own daughter…I won't be able to meet her.

             Emma, hesitantly, enters Downstage Right. She has on a colorful muumuu and sandals and is carrying a lei. Picking up Uncle's samisen, she crosses Downstage Right.

EMMA   Hi…

UNCLE   Hi…

EMMA   [*Looks around.*] Ah…Excuse me. [*Beat.*] I'm Emma. [*Uncle studies her.*] I'm Emma.

UNCLE   Emma? [*Emma nods.*] My Emma? [*Bows, then speaks gratefully.*] You come. You come.

TSUYU   She's very pretty.

KAMA   Yes, she sure is. She'd be even prettier if she was full Okinawan.

UNCLE   [*Looking behind her.*] Mama…? No come?

EMMA   I drove over myself. I'm sorry I didn't come earlier.

UNCLE   Oh, no pilikia.

EMMA   When Mama told me…Something like that happens to others—not me.

UNCLE   Understand.

EMMA   I needed to be alone. Try and let everything sink in. [*Beat.*] I went to the restaurant. I told Daddy that I just found out. About me. He held me a long time. Like he used to when I was a little girl. [*Beat.*] He said I should go and meet you.

UNCLE   Oh?

EMMA	I might not have another chance, he said.
TSUYU	Poor girl. Finding out, so suddenly, who she really is.
KAMA	Not girl, Basan. Emma. One of us.
UNCLE	[*Beat.*] Wanna come back Maui long time 'go.
EMMA	All these years, there were some things Mama and Daddy never talked about. How they met…When they got married…How come I was born in Honolulu…It didn't matter. It still doesn't matter. Daddy will always be "Daddy."
UNCLE	Understand.
EMMA	You suddenly coming into my life isn't going to change that.
UNCLE	Understand. Understand.
EMMA	[*Tearfully.*] You keep saying that! How could you understand what I'm going through?! Why did you have to come back? Why couldn't you have just left things…[*Shoving Uncle.*] You shouldn't have come back! [*Uncle, recovering, wipes away tears.*] I…didn't mean that…I'm sorry.
TSUYU	It's always the children who suffer most.
KAMA	If he had only told me.
TSUYU	You would have approved the marriage?
KAMA	I wouldn't have stopped it.
EMMA	[*Stepping away.*] I shouldn't have come here…
UNCLE	[*Stopping her.*] No pilikia, Emma. Everyting okay. Okay.
EMMA	Everything's happened so suddenly…
UNCLE	Yes…Yes, so many tings…All one time.
EMMA	I…still feel it's happening to someone else. [*Taking off lei.*] I didn't have enough time to make you a big special one.
UNCLE	[*Looks at lei fondly, breaks down. On his knees.*] Very nice. Tank you. Tank you.
EMMA	[*Kneeling, too, places lei around his neck.*] You're leaving in a few days?
	Nodding, Uncle rises and helps Emma up. They cling to each other.
UNCLE	Like dream, holding you.
EMMA	Can't you stay a little longer?

UNCLE	Maybe next time. English not too good. But you write me; I write you.
EMMA	Yes. Of course.
UNCLE	Maybe, someday, you come Okinawa. Visit tomb of grandfather and grandmother.
EMMA	I'd like that. You'll be coming back again, won't you?
UNCLE	Yes. Whenever can.
LEILANI	[*Entering, concerned.*] Sweetheart…
EMMA	Oh! Hi, Mom.
LEILANI	Are you alright?
EMMA	Yes. Yes, I'm fine.
LEILANI	Daddy said…I…just wanted to make sure.
EMMA	I'm fine, Mom. Really.
UNCLE	Very fine. Very fine.
	Kimiko and Ichiro enter. Kimiko is carrying a package of soda pop and food. During the ensuing greetings, Uncle remains in the background, ignored.
KIMIKO	Lei—
LEILANI	Kimi!
KIMIKO	My goodness…
LEILANI	It's been so long…[*They embrace, ad libbing. "How are you?" "I'm fine." "You're looking great," etc.*] Hi, Ichiro.
ICHIRO	Hi, Lei. Long time, eh?
LEILANI	[*Embracing.*] Almost twenty years. [*Ad libbing: "How are you?" etc.*] This is Emma, my daughter.
ICHIRO / KIMIKO / EMMA	Hi…
KIMIKO	You were just a little girl when I last saw you—
UNCLE	*Damare!* [*All eyes shift to him.*] Ichiro. Kimiko. I have something to tell you. Emma is my daughter. [*Ichiro and Kimiko do not quite comprehend.*] I am Emma's father.
ICHIRO / KIMIKO	What?!

ICHIRO	Uncle!
KIMIKO	[*Overlapping.*] You're her—
UNCLE	[*Nods emphatically.*] Her mother and me, we…We once shared a wonderful yume. A dream of owning a big pineapple field.
ICHIRO	You and Lei?
UNCLE	[*Indicating Emma.*] She was also a part of our dream.
ICHIRO	Then, she's our—
KIMIKO	[*Overlapping.*] Our cousin?
EMMA	We're cousins?
LEILANI	Mr. Gusuda was their father.
KIMIKO	My word…[*Hugging Emma.*] A Makaole—a cousin of ours.
ICHIRO	[*Chuckling.*] So, Uncle, those Peahi days…
UNCLE	I did more than just play the samisen.
ICHIRO	You sure did.
EMMA	I have cousins in Okinawa, too?
UNCLE	Many. Many.
ICHIRO	Half the island. They'll all be glad to meet you.
UNCLE	Ichiro.
ICHIRO	Yeah, Uncle?
UNCLE	I want you to do something for me someday.
ICHIRO	Sure. Anything.
UNCLE	When I die, I want you to bury my ashes here.
ICHIRO	Here? Maui?
UNCLE	Next to your father and mother.
ICHIRO	What about the tomb back in Okinawa?
UNCLE	This is where we spent the best years of our lives; this is where we should be buried.
KIMIKO	[*Gratefully steps over to Uncle, raises arms to hug him.*] Uncle… [*Reconsiders and steps back, bows respectfully.*]
UNCLE	[*Slaps her arm teasingly.*] You nuga…[*Chuckling, hugs her.*]
KAMA	Like us, he became a Hawaiian.

TSUYU	You're not an Okinawan anymore?
UNCLE	Well, then…
ICHIRO	No more ashes problems.
UNCLE	And I got to meet my Emma. This calls for a celebration.
ICHIRO	Yeah. Sure. [*Stepping over.*] I brought some food, and there's some more sake left. [*Kimiko opens package and hands out soda pop to Leilani and Emma.*]
UNCLE	I sure need a drink.
ICHIRO	[*To Leilani and Emma.*] Drink?
LEILANI / EMMA	No. No thanks.
ICHIRO	[*To Kimiko.*] Yeah. I know. Mormons don't drink. [*Pours into cup for Uncle, then his own.*]
TSUYU	This turned out to be a happy day after all.
KAMA	Ah, yes. Almost as happy as the day we first met. You in your beautiful kimono…
TSUYU	[*Teasingly.*] And you in your white suit, so handsome, helping me on your white horse. And smelling like a breath of fresh air. [*Gestures that something is smelly.*]
ICHIRO	C'mon, Uncle. Okole maluna.
UNCLE	[*Toasting headstones.*] To your father. And to your mother.
	They all toast and drink.
KAMA	Lucky come Hawaii.
TSUYU	Yes, we sure were lucky to have come to a beautiful place like Hawaii.
UNCLE	[*Picking up samisen, steps up to Leilani and plays Okinawan song "Asadoya Yunta."*] When happy, sing, dance—huh, Leilani? Remember this song? [*Now sings. Leilani acknowledges tearfully. Uncle sings first verse to Leilani, then others join in on next two, including Kama and Tsuyu.*]
KAMA	About time he played that song.
UNCLE	[*Plays "Hatomo Bushi."*] Ichiro! [*Ichiro is encouraged to dance by Kimiko. He encourages Emma to join in.*]
EMMA	C'mon, Mom. The dance I taught you.
LEILANI	It's been so long.

KIMIKO	Go on, Lei…

Emma and Leilani dance together.

ICHIRO	Uncle! Kachashi!

Uncle shifts into a fast number. Emma does a solo. She steps aside for Ichiro, who then steps aside for Leilani. They all continue dancing, having a good time. At appropriate upbeat, simultaneously the music, singing, and dancing suddenly end, followed by quick shouts and BLACKOUT.

Curtain

Voices from Okinawa

Introduction

Thousands of Okinawan immigrants arrived in Hawaii during the early 1900s. They came as contract laborers for the sugarcane plantations. Some of them returned home after fulfilling their contract. Most, however, chose to stay. Kamata and Uto Gusuda were among them. They hoped to return home wealthy someday. That day never came. The elusive rainbow, neither kind nor cruel, was indifferent to them. This is their legacy.

Cast of Characters

Takeshi Arakaki, aged nineteen. Okinawan man. Chauffeur.

Yasunobu Hokama, aged twenty-five. Okinawan man. Barber.

Kama Hutchins, aged twenty-seven. Okinawan–white American man.

Harue Kaneshiro, aged twenty-five. Okinawan woman. Musician.

Hitoshi Kaneshiro, aged twenty-five. Okinawan man. Musician, Harue's husband.

Namiye Matsuda, aged nineteen. Okinawan woman.

Obaa-san, aged ninety-six. Okinawan great-aunt of Kama Hutchins. Yuta (shaman).

Keiko Oshiro, aged twenty-seven. Okinawan woman. Principal of Naha English School.

Act One ### Scene One

Stage is dark. Kama Hutchins steps Downstage Center, and spotlight focuses on him. He is in casual Levis, untucked shirt, and sandals.

KAMA [*Waving.*] Hai sai! [*Bowing low.*] Irasshai! Welcome! Okinawan, Japanese, American. Me? I'm one-quarter Okinawan, three-quarters American. The Okinawan is from my great-grandpa, who migrated to Hawaii during the opening of the twentieth century. The American? My grandmother married an American, and her daughter, my mother, married an American. Then I came, Kama Hutchins.

I'm an English teacher here in Naha, learning more from my students than they from me. Did you know that millions of

American military have come and gone through Okinawa since 1945, sixty years ago, leaving behind offspring with tall noses and round eyes? The influence of Americans is everywhere today: music, language, clothing…On Kokusai Dori, the Broadway of Naha, every other boy and girl is a blonde. Bottle blonde. Even the dogs and cats are blondes.

YASUNOBU   [*Offstage.*] Kama! Hey, Kama!

KAMA   Be right there, Yasunobu! [*To audience.*] The primary language of my students is, of course, Japanese. But they can all read, write, and speak English. How many of us can read, write, and speak Japanese? [*Gesturing.*] Mensooree. C'mon. Meet the future Okinawan ambassadors to America!

Spotlight fades, and stage lights come on. Spring 2005, Monday evening. Small classroom. On the blackboard Upstage Left are the names of students enrolled in the class: Harue Kaneshiro, Hitoshi Kaneshiro, Namiye Matsuda, Takeshi Arakaki, and Yasunobu Hokama. Above the blackboard is a sign: Naha English School. *Entrance is Upstage Right. Downstage Center is a desk with a telephone and a book. Kama is speaking to Yasunobu, who is in Okinawan kariyushi wear (Okinawan aloha shirt), khakis, and zoris. Two other students, dressed casually, have come in and are settled in their chairs.*

KAMA   You're sure it's her, my great-aunt?

YASUNOBU   Gal in Ginoza office say she "Gusuda Nabe" before she marry.

KAMA   That was her maiden name! "Gusuda Nabe."

YASUNOBU   She ninety-six years old.

KAMA   Ninety-six?! Is she…? You know. Alert?

YASUNOBU   Still very young; not yet one hundred.

KAMA   I'd sure like to meet her.

YASUNOBU   We go up tomorrow. Gal in Ginoza office say Obaa-san speak English.

KAMA   She speaks English?!

YASUNOBU   GI English. One time, she work in GI kitchen. Y'know, maybe hard time for her believe you family.

KAMA   It's all here in this book. [*Shows book on desk.*] Sunrise; Sunset. By my grandma. The photos of all of us are in here. Me, my mom and dad, my grandma and grandpa, and my great-grandpa and great-grandma.

YASUNOBU	I tink, maybe, first time she meet family with blue eyes and tall 'Merican nose.
KAMA	I may be only one-quarter Okinawan, but here [*touches chest*] one hundred percent.
YASUNOBU	How come?
KAMA	I'm one-quarter Okinawan?
YASUNOBU	Here one hundred percent [*touches chest*].
KAMA	Well…I've always heard about Great-grandpa and Great-grandma. Their hard life in Okinawa and their long journey to Hawaii. I decided to write my thesis about them. What village did they come from? What made them leave their homeland? What happened to their families back in Okinawa?
YASUNOBU	Your papa, what kind 'Merican?
KAMA	He's part everything you can think of.
YASUNOBU	Your name. For real? "Kama"?
KAMA	My dad's idea. He wanted me to be proud of Great-grandpa Kamata. You know how he learned to read and write Japanese and English, my great-grandpa? By studying with his young daughter, my grandma, when she started school. A, B, C, D, E, F, G. Ah, Ii, Uu, Eh, Oh… [*Two more students, also dressed casually, settle in their seats.*] Looks like everyone's here. We better get started. [*Yasunobu sits in his chair. To students.*] Hi, gang. How are you this evening?
STUDENTS	Fine, thank you. How are you?
KAMA	Ah, right…Right…We're gonna do something different starting tonight. I want each of you to come up here and tell us something about yourself. [*Students moan.*] You all learned to read and write English in high school. And, you showed during our one-to-one sessions that you already speak English. Now what you want to do is learn to speak it with confidence. All right. Who's first? [*Another moan.*] C'mon. If you don't want to talk about yourself, talk about friends, family, people you like, people you don't like, just anything. [*Beat.*] Hey, we're all Uchinanchus. Brothers and sisters. [*Students chuckle.*] Namiye? [*She lowers her head.*]
HITOSHI	[*Encouraging.*] Dozo, Namiye-san. Hanashite kudasai.
KAMA	[*Shaking finger.*] Uh-uh. Remember. Only English. No Japanese the moment you step into this room.
HITOSHI	Oh, gomen nasai. Ah, excuse me, sensei.

KAMA	Not "sensei." "Kama." I'm not only your teacher but your friend as well. Yasunobu, how about you? Show them there's nothing to it.
YASUNOBU	[*Stepping up front.*] I say what I want?
KAMA	Just as long as it's in English.
YASUNOBU	Tink Japanese; express English?
KAMA	There you go.
YASUNOBU	I am barber. My barbershop near Kadena Air Base. Most customers GIs. GIs sure talk funny. Always say, "Gotcha." What they got, I don' know. Even when speaking to just-a one man, they say, "Y'all." I come Naha English School so I can speak like 'Mericans in 'Merica; not on'y like GIs in Okinawa. First customer other day. GI father with red-hair boy.

"I hear you're the best barber in town."

"I hear that, too."

"Well, son, looks like we came to the right place."

[*To class.*] Boy, about five, bery quiet. He sit on magazine chair. GI sit in barber chair. Nice soft hair. I can do bery fast.

"So what y'all think?"

"Tink? Tink what?"

"That we should all leave?"

"Not all. Just-a most."

"Y'all have to close up your shop."

"Aw, I go plant rice."

"Yeah. Sure."

[*To class.*] Whenever GI don' know what I talk 'bout, "Yeah. Sure."

"You Okinawans would be livin' in grass huts 'gain if we leave."

Now my turn. "Yeah. Sure."

When I finish with him, he call boy. "C'mon, son."

I start cuttin' boy's hair. GI say to me, "I go shopping. When I come back, I pay for him and me, okay?"

"No pro'lem."

After finish boy, I wait for GI. "Your papa sure takin' long time shoppin'," I say to boy.

"He's not my papa. The man brought me here for a free haircut."

Akisamiyo! [*Class laughs.*] GIs a'ways tinking new idea. "Gotcha."

NAMIYE   They a'ways treatin' us like we stupid children.

TAKESHI   Most GIs, dey okay.

NAMIYE   Sooner they all go away, better.

KAMA   That was very good, Yasunobu. Well told, funny and enter-
           taining.

YASUNOBU   You like dat story? Lemme tell you 'nother one.

KAMA   Another one?

YASUNOBU   Happen same day. I am reading newspaper in barbershop 'bout
           young boy on bicycle hit by GI truck. GI, he say boy never see
           truck coming. Uchinanchus say GI drivin' too fast. When MPs
           take GI 'way, Uchinanchus throw rocks at truck and break win-
           dows and headlights with baseball bats. [*Keiko Oshiro, in dark
           suit and heels, enters quietly and sits in the back. She listens
           intently.*] Later, my MP friend, Sergeant Terry, come to barber-
           shop. He angry like hell. "I've had it, Yas."

           [*To class.*] 'At's what he call me. "Yas."

           "Had to get away from them troublemakers."

           "What troublemakers, Sergeant?"

           "Them goddamn people who threw rocks and beat up our truck
           with baseball bats. They're now picketing our main gate."

           [*Innocently.*] "Oh, yeah?"

           "We made a mistake back in '45, Yas. A big mistake. We should'a
           made all of you Americans. No more 'Yankee go home!'"

           "What if people don' wanna be 'Mericans?"

           "Everybody wanna be Americans."

           "People you fighting over there in oil country, too?"

           "Them Ira-kees?"

           "How long you gonna stay over there?"

           "Until that country's fully recovered."

           "You here in Okinawa sixty years. You no tink we fully
           recovered?"

           "Agreement between Washington and Tokyo. We'll be
           gradually pulling out."

"History of Okinawa. Neve' have nothin' to say in agreement."

"Nothing in the agreement says you all can picket our bases."

"'Merican style."

"You all learned that pretty fast, alright."

"Oh, we enjoy many 'Merican style. Hot-tu dog-gu; ham-ba-ga; taco. And freedom of speech."

"Yeah. And freedom of speech."

I point to Sergeant. "Guess who my sensei?"

"Oh, go ta hell." Translation: end of discussion. Sergeant get up from chair, go to door.

"Back to main gate?"

"Yeah. I better. See how my men are doing."

"I tink I go join picket line."

"What?!"

"I am Okinawan, too."

"What's your sign gonna say?"

"WELCOME AMERICANS! NOT FOREVER!"

"Just remember, I don't know you; you don't know me out there."

"Gotcha, Sergeant."

KAMA	[*Applauding.*] That was great, Yasunobu. Great. Funny, yet meaningful. And timely.
NAMIYE	What happen to driver who hit boy?
YASUNOBU	According to newspaper, he transferred to Hawaii.
NAMIYE	He is free?!
TAKESHI	Cannot believe Commanding General permit this.
NAMIYE	He like other 'Mericans. Tink we all stupid.
TAKESHI	Maybe he don' know nothin' 'bout accident.
KAMA	Hitoshi, you have anything to add?
HITOSHI	Ever since reversion to Japan in 1972, Okinawan law covers everyone, even 'Merican military, if crime outside of base.
KAMA	Then that GI could've been tried in an Okinawan court?
HITOSHI	Hai. 'Merican officer lawyer a'ways one steps 'head of Okinawan police. No driver; no trial.

KAMA	I want the rest of you to do what Yasunobu just did. [*Students moan.*]
TAKESHI	A little Japanese okay?
KAMA	All English.
TAKESHI	Oh, boy.
KAMA	We still have a little time left. Anyone else want to come up? Nobody?
YASUNOBU	Let Namiye tell us why she hate GI so much.
KAMA	Namiye?
NAMIYE	Not ready.
YASUNOBU	[*Gestures to ring.*] Gonna marry GI?
NAMIYE	None of you business!
KAMA	A private matter, Yasunobu.
YASUNOBU	She never tell us not'ing 'bout herself.
KAMA	I'm sure she will when she's ready. Right, Namiye? Okay. On Friday, that's four nights from now, the rest of you will tell us your story. [*Students moan.*] See you all Friday night.
STUDENTS	[*Exiting.*] Goodnight. Sayonara. See you.
YASUNOBU	[*To Kama.*] Tomorrow, okay?
KAMA	Right. Domo arigato gozaimasu.
KEIKO	[*Having endured Yasunobu's speech, marches up to Kama. Speaking with a slight accent.*] Mr. Hutchins! You are completely ignoring our school policy.
KAMA	Ignoring?
KEIKO	The students should be participating in English conversations—not listening to speeches.
KAMA	They'll learn much faster if given a chance to speak to the class and start a discussion.
KEIKO	This is not a speech class! It is not a class encouraging students to join picket lines either.
KAMA	Freedom of expression. As American as apple pie.
KEIKO	This is not America!
KAMA	It teaches the students to speak up. Discuss issues.

KEIKO	Not GI issues!
KAMA	Keiko—Miss Oshiro…The students are beginning to open up. Getting over their shyness of mispronouncing words, of saying things in English they wouldn't have dared say a few days ago.
KEIKO	Proper English is learned by repeating words and sentences over and over.
KAMA	Words and sentences that don't make sense to them?
KEIKO	You were hired to teach standard English—not introduce your own method.
KAMA	You heard Yasunobu. He was great.
KEIKO	Can he retain everything he said?
KAMA	He will if he repeats words and sentences over and over?
KEIKO	The board of directors of this school is interested in only one thing: progress of the students. They are expecting an evaluation report on you next month.
KAMA	Shape up or ship out, eh?
KEIKO	My report will be unbiased.
KAMA	Look. I need this job. Not just for the money; for my visa, too.
KEIKO	You still have a month.
KAMA	I have the students repeat words and sentences, and I get to stick around. Otherwise, sayonara, eh?
	Lights begin to dim.
KEIKO	We are only interested in—
KAMA	Yeah. Progress.
	Lights keep dimming until BLACKOUT.

Scene Two

Ginoza Village. Next day. Kama, Yasunobu, and Obaa-san are sitting on the goza-matted floor of Obaa-san's tiny living room. On the table before them are a container of sake and three sake cups. Against the wall is an obutsudan altar and beside it a crystal ball, osenko sticks, ojuzu beads, and a ceremonial white robe. On the floor, before the altar, is a chikonki, an old hand-winding phonograph. Obaa-san, in faded kimono, her hair upswept into a bun, is trying to keep from staring at Kama across the low table. Although nearly a centenarian, she is alert and independent, her only idiosyncrasy bursts of hand-covered laughter. Parentheses in the dialogue indicate when characters are speaking in Japanese.

Shirota . Voices from Okinawa   101

OBAA-SAN	[*Gesturing at Kama.*] (If he did not have those funny blue eyes and long bird's nose, he would really look like Kamata.)
YASUNOBU	She say you have nice eyes, nice nose.
OBAA-SAN	[*Pouring sake into cups.*] (Eh, Yasunobu-san. Drink. Drink.) Eh, Kama. [*Gestures to Kama to drink.*]
KAMA	Awamori?
OBAA-SAN	Iie. Home-made. Numbah one. Kanpai!
	They lift their cups in toast, then sip.
YASUNOBU	(Ahh…It is good, Obaa-san. Very good.)
OBAA-SAN	Eh, Kama. Good-u? You like-u?
KAMA	Very good, Obaa-san. Number one. This [*points to cup*] your secret for long life?
OBAA-SAN	Hai. Hai. Tink young. Feel young.
YASUNOBU	So, ne?
OBAA-SAN	Also, eat rotsa seaweed, fish, tofu. And natto.
KAMA	Natto?
YASUNOBU	Stink beans.
KAMA	They keep you young?
YASUNOBU	If stink don' kill you first.
OBAA-SAN	Natto make you feel, you know…[*Whispering to Yasunobu.*] Sexy.
YASUNOBU	Aw, Obaa-san.
OBAA-SAN	(At one time, I was the number-one gal in all Ginoza.)
YASUNOBU	She, one time, queen of Ginoza.
KAMA	I'm not surprised.
OBAA-SAN	(My hair was completely black, and there was not one wrinkle on my face.)
YASUNOBU	Not one wrinkle on her face.
OBAA-SAN	(And all my teeth were my own.)
YASUNOBU	Her teeth all her own.
OBAA-SAN	[*Baring teeth.*] (These belong to Dr. Nakama. I borrowed them this morning.) [*Laughs.*]
YASUNOBU	She know we coming, she borrowed teeth from dentist.

KAMA	Oh, Obaa-san. You're so funny.
OBAA-SAN	Life a'ways funny, Kama.
KAMA	So, ne?
OBAA-SAN	[*Pouring.*] Eh, Kama. Drink.
KAMA	Domo arigato gozaimasu, Obaa-san.
OBAA-SAN	Ah, good Nihongo.
KAMA	Hai. Sukoshi hanashimasu.
OBAA-SAN	Kanpai!
KAMA	Kanpai!
YASUNOBU	I better not drink anymore. Long drive back.
OBAA-SAN	Stay. Stay here.
YASUNOBU	Domo arigato, Obaa-san. (I have to get up early to go to work.)
OBAA-SAN	[*To Kama.*] Get old, bery good. No work in rice field; no dig potato; no worry nothin'.
KAMA	Who lives here with you?
OBAA-SAN	Just-a me.
KAMA	You do your own cooking? Laundry? Shopping?
OBAA-SAN	Young son, he come sometimes.
KAMA	You have a young son?!
OBAA-SAN	Just-a eighty.
KAMA	Just…eighty?
OBAA-SAN	[*Sips. Getting drunker, she studies Kama again.*] Hai. You, Kamata, same-u same-u.
KAMA	Wan-ne Uchinanchu yan do.
	Yasunobu joins Obaa-san in laughter.
OBAA-SAN	Akisamiyo! Wife talk Uchinaguchi, too?
YASUNOBU	(He's not married, Obaa-san.)
OBAA-SAN	Not married?! [*Reaches for Kama's hand.*] Nice-looking boy not yet married? [*Rubs his hand between her palms in prayerful gesture.*]
YASUNOBU	She yuta.
KAMA	She's been to Utah?

Handball

———————— ❊ ————————

*In Naha, the maai (handball) was a popular toy given
to girls during the yukkanufii festival (held during the
fourth month of the lunar calendar). It was usually
embroidered with heavy threads of red, green, purple,
and white to create butterfly, crane, and turtle designs.
The art of embroidering maai was once popular among
girls throughout Japan, but it is little practiced now.*

*Playing with handballs at New Year's is still a popular
tradition, however, and appears to be quite old, judging
from its mention in* Chuzan denshinroku (Record of
transmitted facts of Chuzan), *published in 1721.*

*Thread.
Woodblock print by Ozaki Seiji.*

YASUNOBU	She can see tings long before happenin': typhoon, fire, tsunami…
KAMA	A real psychic, eh?
YASUNOBU	Oh, yeah. She can side-kick [*kicks*] anything. She can even talk to people on the other side.
KAMA	Communicates with the dead?! What do they talk about?
YASUNOBU	Dey happy? Sad? Lonely?
KAMA	And, if they are lonely?
YASUNOBU	She match 'em with man or woman who also lonely.
KAMA	And start a romance?
YASUNOBU	I am sure even on other side dey enjoy sex.
OBAA-SAN	[*Moaning.*] Hai. Hai. Wakarimashita. [*To Kama.*] This churakagi gal. Numbah one. [*Kama looks over at Yasunobu.*]
YASUNOBU	You have galfriend?
KAMA	Girlfriend?
YASUNOBU	Must be sensei.
KAMA	Keiko Oshiro?!
YASUNOBU	Okinawan women like dat. She likes you, she show she don' like you.
OBAA-SAN	Eh, Kama. Gal not yet go bed with man.
YASUNOBU	She virgin.
KAMA	I'm not surprised.
OBAA-SAN	She ripe pineapple.
YASUNOBU	Ready for picking.
OBAA-SAN	[*Prayerfully.*] Hai. So desu ne? Eh, Kama. She bossy sometimes, but—
KAMA	Sometimes?!
YASUNOBU	Okinawan women like dat. She no care for you, she bery nice. She care for you, she bery bossy.
KAMA	She must really care for me, that woman.
OBAA-SAN	[*Picks up opened package on floor, ambles over to obutsudan, and places package before the altar. Puts on her ceremonial white robe, wraps the ojuzu beads around her wrists, burns osenko sticks, and*

	plants them in urn. Presses her hands together in gassho prayer.] (Eh, Kamata. Your great-grandson is a very nice boy.) [*Indicating package.*] 'Merican coffee. 'Merican cho-co-late-o.
YASUNOBU	[*To Kama.*] She tell great-grandpa you bery nice boy.
OBAA-SAN	(He looks American, but he is proud to be one of us. A true Uchinanchu.)
YASUNOBU	[*To Kama.*] You true Okinawan.
OBAA-SAN	(This girl, Oshiro Keiko, I must tell her not to let Kama get away.)
YASUNOBU	[*To Kama.*] She must tell sensei not to miss chance of catching you.
KAMA	She's saying that to Great-grandpa? Without talking to me first?
OBAA-SAN	Eh, Kama. [*Gestures to him.*]
YASUNOBU	She wants you burn senko and pray with her.
KAMA	Sure. Glad to.
OBAA-SAN	[*As Kama kneels beside her.*] Burn senko. [*Kama does. She gestures to him to place the osenko stick in urn. Kama does.*] Wanna talk to Ojii-san?
KAMA	Well...[*Prayerfully.*] Ojii-san, will Keiko Oshiro always be bossy?
OBAA-SAN	[*Prayerfully.*] Kamata? [*Then to Kama.*] He say, "No shinpai. More bossy, more rove."
KAMA	Same as "If she likes me, she shows she don't like me"?
OBAA-SAN	You learn bery fast. [*They return to table. To Yasunobu.*] (This boy...He is like his great-grandfather.)
KAMA	How old was she when Great-grandpa left for Hawaii?
YASUNOBU	Obaa-san?
OBAA-SAN	Just-a five—1914.
KAMA	You never saw him after that?
OBAA-SAN	Never...
KAMA	Any letters?
OBAA-SAN	Him, me—no can read, write. On'y rater, we can.
KAMA	You had two other brothers: Chokichi and Shinnichi. What happened to them?

OBAA-SAN	Die long time 'go. On'y me still livin' in Okinawa after dat. With friend help, Kamata send for picture wife. Pretty soon, work ten-hours day; seven-days week in sugarcane field. Ever' month send home $25: $10 for land; $15 for ohaka tomb. Ohaka numbah one in all Ginoza. [*Beat.*] One day, man come home from Hawaii. Bring big box from Kamata. Chikonki.
KAMA	Grandma mentions it in her book. A chikonki phonograph.
OBAA-SAN	[*Steps over and winds phonograph. Fast, scratchy kachashi music bursts forth. Obaa-san starts dancing unsteadily.*] Come, Kama. Come.
KAMA	Okay, Obaa-san. Okay. [*Laughing, joins Obaa-san, trying to follow her.*]
OBAA-SAN	Bery good-u, Kama. Bery good. Sah! Sah! Sah!
YASUNOBU	[*Joining in.*] Sah! Sah! Sah!
OBAA-SAN	[*They keep dancing, having a good time, till Obaa-san, exhausted, turns off the chikonki. To Kama.*] You Uchinanchu. Honto Uchinanchu.
KAMA	I've got to learn that dance.
YASUNOBU	Kachashi. Ever'body dance at parties.
OBAA-SAN	I take chikonki other village. Ever'body enjoy. Never hear music come out from box before.
KAMA	No radios?
OBAA-SAN	No ele-tri-city.
YASUNOBU	Tottemo kuro shimashita ne, Obaa-san.
OBAA-SAN	Taihen deshita. Sweet potato, sweet potato ever' day. Sometimes, just sometimes, rice.
KAMA	Whatever you ate those days must have been very good. Look at you. You don't look a day over… sixty.
OBAA-SAN	Sixty?!
KAMA	Fifty.
OBAA-SAN	Can fine 'nother husband?
KAMA	Many more.
OBAA-SAN	Only three more left now.
KAMA	Husbands?!
OBAA-SAN	Eat, drink… and…

YASUNOBU	And sex?!
OBAA-SAN	And sleep.
YASUNOBU	Yes. Of course. Gotta have rotsa of sleep.
OBAA-SAN	[*Takes another sip. Then another. Fighting back sobs, reaches for Kama's hand.*] Eh, Kamata…(Why didn't you come home like you promised? I waited and waited for you to come home.)
YASUNOBU	Obaa-san. Obaa-san. (That was a long time ago.)
OBAA-SAN	Yesterday. Just yesterday.
YASUNOBU	He came back, Obaa-san. Look. Kamata came back.
KAMA	[*Going along.*] Yes. I came back.
OBAA-SAN	(All the money you sent, remember? We bought the land you wanted. Out there. The sugarcane field.)
	Kama looks at Yasunobu.
YASUNOBU	All the money you send, she buy land. Sugarcane field out there—to you, "Kamata."
KAMA	All that?!
OBAA-SAN	(The money from the field kept me alive during my poor days.)
YASUNOBU	[*To Kama.*] Cane-field money keep her living.
OBAA-SAN	(Even today, it is the best sugarcane field in all Ginoza.)
YASUNOBU	[*To Kama.*] Best field in all Ginoza. [*Beat.*] (Obaa-san. It is getting late. We must be going.)
OBAA-SAN	(Going? Going where? Kamata just came home.)
YASUNOBU	(We have a long drive back to Naha.)
OBAA-SAN	Naha? [*Snapping out of it.*] Oh, yes. Naha. [*Laughs.*] You came from Naha.
KAMA	We will be back, Obaa-san. [*Takes a card from his wallet.*] My meishi. Just in case you want to telephone or visit me at our English school.
OBAA-SAN	Eh, Kama, must come back soon. You chonan.
KAMA	Me, chonan? I'm an American.
OBAA-SAN	Still.
KAMA	Even though I wasn't born here?
OBAA-SAN	Oldest boy of oldest boy. Land now all belong you.

KAMA	Me?! All that land?!
OBAA-SAN	No other boy in Gusuda Kamata family.
KAMA	But the title to the land…?
OBAA-SAN	Okinawan tra-di-tion. Chonan can do what he want.
KAMA	Even sell it?
OBAA-SAN	If wanna.
YASUNOBU	(Obaa-san, are you sure?!)
OBAA-SAN	All belong to chonan.
YASUNOBU	[*To Kama.*] Many tsubos. All yours. Maybe, more than five acres out there.
OBAA-SAN	Army a'ways send Nikkei GI. Interpreter.
KAMA	To buy the land?
OBAA-SAN	Lease.
YASUNOBU	Many landowners near army base get millions for lease.
KAMA	Dollars?!
YASUNOBU	Yens. But still can buy many Toyotas. (Obaa-san, what does the army plan to do with the land?)
OBAA-SAN	Build garage. For tanks, trucks, big guns.
YASUNOBU	Uh-oh.
OBAA-SAN	Nikkei GI a'ways wanna know where chonan.
YASUNOBU	(Tell him you don't know, Obaa-san.)
OBAA-SAN	[*To Kama.*] Don' wanna lease?
YASUNOBU	Better not.
KAMA	Why not?
YASUNOBU	Too many GIs.
KAMA	They'll bring in outside money.
	Lights begin dimming.
YASUNOBU	Just for mama-sans and young gals.
	Lights keep dimming until BLACKOUT.

Scene Three

Following Friday night. Empty classroom. Kama and Keiko enter, speaking loudly.

KEIKO   You, of course, knew nothing about it.

KAMA   Being chonan?

KEIKO   And the land.

KAMA   All news to me.

KEIKO   [*Sarcastically.*] You came here just to teach English.

KAMA   And to do my Ph.D. research on immigration.

KEIKO   [*Sarcastically.*] You're not returning home after selling your land?

KAMA   That's what Yasunobu told you?

KEIKO   Aren't you?

KAMA   I'm only going to lease it.

KEIKO   Lease, sell—what's the difference? More army camps, more abused young girls.

KAMA   There's the police. The MPs.

KEIKO   Who's always blaming the girls.

KAMA   Not when those three marines raped that girl.

KEIKO   She was just twelve years old!

KAMA   [*Beat.*] Look, that land in Ginoza—

KEIKO   I spent many summers in Ginoza. With my grandparents. That land is the most beautiful and peaceful place up there. Why can't you let your obaa-san keep planting sugarcane?

KAMA   She will. When I release everything to her—to my family.

KEIKO   Ten years from now? Twenty? Fifty?

KAMA   I'll be through with my research long before then.

KEIKO   So you did know about the land and being a chonan!

KAMA   It was a windfall, for Chrissake!

KEIKO   Ha!

KAMA   Look. The people I spoke to today, they said that except for a few changes everything will remain the same.

KEIKO   Like "a few changes" they made all over Okinawa: runways, hangars, barracks, long chain-link fences…

KAMA	I won't sign the lease unless I'm assured Obaa-san is—
KEIKO	Who'd you talk to? The public relations people?
KAMA	A Nikkei sergeant in charge of the leasing department. He speaks not only Nihongo but Uchinaguchi, too.
KEIKO	And loves the Okinawan people, right?
KAMA	He's married to one.
KEIKO	That makes him one of us?
KAMA	Far better than just another American.
KEIKO	Like you?
KAMA	I'm one of you, for Chrissake!
KEIKO	Oh, sure.
KAMA	You went to school in the States. Whattahell you got against Americans anyway?!
KEIKO	[*Imitates harshly.*] "Oh, you're from Okinawa. Ever worked at the Dragon Bar in Koza?"
KAMA	Aw, c'mon.
KEIKO	It happened whenever I met an ex-GI who'd been stationed here.
KAMA	Even up in Berkeley?
KEIKO	[*Imitating.*] "Oh. You were a college student there." It was hard even for him to believe that some of us did go to college here.
KAMA	What happened to him? Okay. Okay. None of my business.
KEIKO	You want to know?
KAMA	Sure. Why not?
KEIKO	He was a graduate student like me when I met him. Once, a pilot at Kadena Air Base.
KAMA	An ex-officer. Good taste.
KEIKO	He was from across the bay. San Francisco. He used to take me to karaoke bars in the bay area. Until he found out I did not really enjoy going to those places. He finally took me to meet his family. They lived in a big home up on the hills. His grand-father was there that night. A former marine.
	"Okinawans still eat bats and cats?" he asked right after we met.
	"Bats? Cats?"

"That's what they were eating when we landed there in '45. Bats, cats, snakes, even rats…"

"The people were starving," I tried to explain.

"Those tombs and caves—you still live in them?"

"Things have changed since the war, Mr. Richards."

I looked over at Ernie. He kept sitting next to his grandfather, not saying a word. I noticed then that he was like his grandfather—arrogant, proud, superior. Like most Americans, so sure of himself.

KAMA	Like most Americans?
KEIKO	The Okinawan in you makes you a little less arrogant.
KAMA	[*Bowing.*] Domo.
KEIKO	He tried to apologize for his grandfather the next day.
KAMA	You kept seeing him?
KEIKO	Once more.
KAMA	To tell him he was arrogant and proud like his grandfather?
KEIKO	To return the ring.
KAMA	You were willing to marry him? That jerk!…Okay. So he wasn't a complete jerk.

Yasunobu and Takeshi enter, speaking Japanese, then abruptly switch to English.

KEIKO	Before studying Okinawan immigration, you should learn Okinawan history: 1879 to 2005.
KAMA	Eighteen seventy-nine? When Emperor Meiji took over Okinawa?
KEIKO	And made us second-class Japanese.
KAMA	Not today.
KEIKO	A little improvement; not much.
KAMA	Okinawans proved they were loyal Japanese during the war.
KEIKO	At a great price.
KAMA	General Ushijima should have surrendered. Stopped all the killing.
KEIKO	He was ordered to fight to the last man.
KAMA	Almost to the last Okinawan, too, I read.

KEIKO	Some killed by Japanese soldiers.
KAMA	By their own soldiers?
KEIKO	That's why many Okinawans don't believe in the national anthem anymore.
KAMA	But they still consider themselves Japanese?
KEIKO	Okinawans. They are the ones preserving our dances, our songs, our dialect…
KAMA	At least Americans did not try to destroy your culture.
KEIKO	They destroyed enough.
KAMA	Americans are guests here now—not conquerors.
KEIKO	Would you enjoy having unwelcome guests in your home?
	Hitoshi, Harue, and Namiye enter.
KAMA	They're all here. I better get started.
KEIKO	More speeches?
KAMA	I have a month to prove my method works, remember?
STUDENTS	[*To Keiko, bowing.*] Konbanwa, sensei.
KEIKO	Konbanwa. [*Steps to back of room.*]
KAMA	Hi, gang.
STUDENTS	Hi, Kama.
KAMA	Okay. Let's get started. Who's ready tonight? C'mon. You've had four nights to prepare. Hitoshi?
HITOSHI	Not tonight, Kama.
KAMA	Namiye?
NAMIYE	Not ready, sensei—ah, Kama.
KAMA	Next Friday?
NAMIYE	Maybe.
KAMA	That leaves just you tonight, Takeshi.
TAKESHI	[*Hesitates, then steps up front.*] First time, talkin' like tis. I am houseboy for Mrs. Hampton, wife of General.
HITOSHI	Commanding General's wife?
YASUNOBU	Makes you feel big shot, eh?

NAMIYE	If you with officer, big respect. If with 'nother GI, you nothing.
YASUNOBU	You have officer friend?
NAMIYE	Several at our church.
YASUNOBU	No GIs?
NAMIYE	Few.
KAMA	Any more comments? No? Go on, Takeshi.
TAKESHI	I was newspaper boy when General and Mrs. Hampton first come Okinawa. Mrs. Hampton, she a'ways wanna talk to me. 'Bout school, family, newspaper job. I am a'ways in hurry. Must go next house. And my English worse than now. Then, I rea-ah-rize…[*To Kama.*] Right word?
KAMA	"Realized," Takeshi. "Realized."
TAKESHI	[*Beat.*] Then I…find out, Mrs. Hampton, she bery lonely. She got no children. The General a'ways bery busy; no time for her. I become like son she no have. When I am sixteen, General must transfer to Hawaii. He wanna take me. But my papa say no. General and Mrs. Hampton, they go talk to Papa. Papa, he finally say, "Okay." But I must return soon and continue Japanese school. Hawaii bery nice place. General and Mrs. Hampton, they have special house, Waikiki Beach. Mrs. Hampton and me, we go walkin' in sand all time. One day, she tell me, General returnin' Okinawa one more time. Then he retire, and move back to farm in Indiana. When we come back Okinawa, I live with them. They now my 'Merican father and mother.
HITOSHI	Okay with Papa?
TAKESHI	As long as I go Japanese school. Mrs. Hampton now tell me I can continue high school in Indiana. Prepare for mir-i-tary school. She say best I learn more English now, here in Okinawa.
HARUE	Rike us?
TAKESHI	Papa tell me if I wanna go mir-i-tary school…
KAMA	It's "military," Takeshi. "Military."
TAKESHI	Papa tell me if I wanna go…army school, go Japanese army school. I tell him, in Japan, very hard get in. In 'Merica General Hampton can a'most get-ran-tee…[*To Kama.*] Right word?
KAMA	It's "guarantee."
TAKESHI	General can a'most make sure I get in. Ap-pre-ka-tion ask if I am 'Merican citizen. General say, "No pro'lem. I have con-nec-

tion in Wa-shing-ton." But becomin' 'Merican means I must give up being Japanese.

YASUNOBU   You don' wanna become 'Merican?

TAKESHI   I am Nipponjin!

HITOSHI   [*Applauding.*] Hai! Hai! Kimi wa Nipponjin da!

KEIKO   [*Applauding also.*] Of course. You are Nipponjin.

TAKESHI   Whenever I see 'Merican flag, I am bery happy to have many 'Merican friends. Whenever I see Japanese flag, I am bery proud to be Japanese.

KAMA   That was a very good speech, Takeshi. Very sincere, very warm, and very honest.

YASUNOBU   What you gonna say to General and Mrs. Hampton?

TAKESHI   I will tell 'em they a'ways my 'Merican father and mother.

KEIKO   And you're always their Okinawan son.

KAMA   Great ending to a great story. Any other comments? No? Okay. Let's call it a night. Monday will be Hitoshi's or Harue's turn.

HITOSHI   We together.

YASUNOBU   How come you together?

HITOSHI   "Hitoshi-Haruc Show."

KAMA   If it's an act, I guess it's all right.

    Telephone in Keiko's office rings.

KEIKO   Excuse me. [*Rushes out Downstage Left.*]

YASUNOBU   What 'bout Namiye? When she gonna tell us her story?

KAMA   You might be ready Monday night, too, Namiye?

NAMIYE   I don' think so, sensei—ah, Kama.

KAMA   Friday night?

NAMIYE   Maybe.

YASUNOBU   Come next Friday, she gonna say, "Not yet ready, sensei…"

NAMIYE   My story not funny rike yours!

KEIKO   [*Reappearing. To Kama.*] The phone call is for you.

KAMA   Me?

KEIKO   A lady.

YASUNOBU	[*Teasing.*] A galfriend?
KAMA	Must be Obaa-san. She's the only one who knows I'm here. [*Rushes out Downstage Right. Stage lights fade.*]

Spotlight gradually focuses on Obaa-san Downstage. She has on her ceremonial white robe and ojuzu beads around her wrists, and holds an osenko stick in prayerful gesture.

OBAA-SAN	Dark clouds over sugarcane field, Kama. Den angry lightning, strong wind, loud thunder. Cane-field leaves, dey scared; dey stop dancing in wind; dey cry. Dark clouds den move over house. House shakes; windows rattle; doors bang open, shut. All bad sign. [*Lights start dimming.*] Must come Ginoza righ' 'way, Kama. Pray together to your great-grandpa. Great-grandpa, he know what to do.

Lights keep dimming until BLACKOUT.

Act Two *Scene One*

Next morning. Stage is dark. Spotlight focuses on Keiko Downstage Left.

KEIKO	[*Enraptured.*] Ah, Ginoza. The most beautiful and peaceful place in all Okinawa: the shiny blue sea, the friendly green hill-sides, and the soft, gentle breeze. And Obaa-san, so warm, so kind, so wise. Just imagine! In a few more years, she'll be one hundred years old. Her mind is still as clear as the blue stream running near her home. And her legs and hands—they are as strong as when she used to work in the sugarcane fields. When she burns osenko at the obutsudan, the smell of the osenko purifies her thoughts and transports her to the world where her ancestors have gone. Where the unreal becomes real; the abnormal, normal; the uncommon, common. She had a long talk with the sugarcane leaves and her home last night, she said. The leaves felt a little better. But her home was still worried. The dark clouds kept coming back.
OBAA-SAN	[*Offstage.*] Keiko-san! Keiko-san!
KEIKO	Hai, Obaa-san.

As she walks, spotlight dims and stage lights come on in Obaa-san's living room. Keiko joins Obaa-san, Kama, and Yasunobu at obutsudan. Kama and Yasunobu step back after burning osenko. Keiko burns an osenko stick, places it in the urn, and, bowing, steps back to let Obaa-san proceed. Obaa-san prays silently.

KAMA	[*Whispering to Yasunobu.*] How many times do we have to go through this?

YASUNOBU	Once for sugarcane leaves; once for house; once for great-grandpa.
KEIKO	Shhh.
KAMA	[*Whispering.*] You believe in ancestral worship, too?
KEIKO	I believe our ancestors are always around us.
KAMA	[*Looking around.*] Where?
KEIKO	Same place where your Jesus is.
YASUNOBU	You believe in Jesus; we believe in our ancestors.
KEIKO	We get together with our ancestors once a year and spend three days with them.
KAMA	Three days?
YASUNOBU	First day, welcome; second day, enjoy together; third day, sayonara.
KEIKO	You don't believe in the anniversary of the dead?
KAMA	I believe in the anniversary of birth.
OBAA-SAN	[*To obutsudan.*] "Kamata. Kamata…"
YASUNOBU	Sayonara to great-grandpa.
OBAA-SAN	[*Gathering everyone together.*] Come. Come. We sing to sugar-cane field and house. Kamata say, make 'em happy. Sing nice children song. "Yuyake Koyake."
KAMA	"Yuyake Koyake"? My grandma used to sing it to me when I was little.
EVERYONE	*Forming a semi-circle, holding hands, and facing window Downstage Center, they start singing.*
	Yuyake koyake de hi ga kurete Yama no otera no kane ga naru Otete tsunai de minna kaero Karasu to issho ni kaerimasho.
OBAA-SAN	[*Stepping toward window, looks out.*] See. See. Sugarcane leaves, dey happy now. Dey dancin', singin', laughin'.
KAMA	[*To Yasunobu.*] You hear them, too?
YASUNOBU	I hear rattling of windows. They happy.
KAMA	[*Listens.*] I don't hear anything.
YASUNOBU	You not yet hundred percent Okinawan.

OBAA-SAN	[*To Kama.*] Your Kamata ojii-san, he say watch out dat Nikkei GI.
KAMA	Sergeant Shizuoka?
OBAA-SAN	He Japanee, not Uchinanchu.
KAMA	He's doing his duty, Obaa-san.
OBAA-SAN	Take land, house away from Uchinanchus?
KAMA	I'll share the money with you.
OBAA-SAN	No wan' share money; wan' share sugarcane field and this house.
KAMA	The lease agreement will say you can keep living here.
OBAA-SAN	Yakusoku must a'ways be honored. You tell Nikkei GI.
KAMA	"Yakusoku"?
OBAA-SAN	Hai, I promise you; hai, you promise me.
KAMA	Okay. I'll tell him that.
OBAA-SAN	Tell 'Merican boss, too.
KAMA	Okay.
OBAA-SAN	Make sure he know bachi, too.
KAMA	"Bachi"?
OBAA-SAN	No honor yakusoku, den big, bad luck.
KAMA	Okay. I'll tell him that, too.
OBAA-SAN	You say, "Okay, okay." You sure you understand?
KAMA	Of course, I do. Great-grandpa, he knows that.
OBAA-SAN	When come to money, he say, a'ways be bery careful.
KAMA	Even with me?
OBAA-SAN	We not talkin' 'bout money, you and me! Come. Come. [*Pours tea into cups.*] To sugarcane leaves, to house.
YASUNOBU	And to great-grandpa.
OBAA-SAN	Hai. To Kamata. Kali!
EVERYONE	Kali!
OBAA-SAN	[*Beat.*] Keiko-san, wanna kanpai to baby? Husband?
KEIKO	Baby? Husband?

OBAA-SAN	[*Looking at Kama and Yasunobu, feigns shock.*] You not married yet?! [*Holds Keiko's hand, rubbing it against her cheek. Prayerfully.*] A churakagi girl like you not yet married? Kawaiso na...Too bad Kama not all Okinawan. It is better to marry all-Okinawan boy ne, Keiko-san?
KEIKO	Well...Yes. I guess so.
OBAA-SAN	I find nice boy for you.
KEIKO	Obaa-san. Shinpai nai. I'm sure I'll meet a nice boy someday.
OBAA-SAN	Don' wait too long, Keiko-san. You don' want to marry an old Uchinanchu drunkard.
YASUNOBU	Or a GI.
KEIKO	A GI?!
YASUNOBU	Wait any longer, you have no choice. Right, Kama?
KAMA	Well...Yeah. Sure.
OBAA-SAN	Let's hope Keiko-san will find a good husband. Let's also hope Kama will find a nice girl who is willing to marry a not-all Uchinanchu man.
YASUNOBU	[*Stepping toward door.*] We have to be going, Obaa-san. My barbershop—I have to open it for my afternoon customers.
KEIKO	[*Stepping toward door, then bowing.*] Obaa-san, I'm very glad nothing is going to happen to your sugarcane field or your home.
OBAA-SAN	For now ever'thing okay.
KAMA	[*Walking to door with Obaa-san.*] If there is anything else I can do for you, Obaa-san, please call me.
OBAA-SAN	You come here today, pray with me, save my sugarcane field and my home. Ippei nehei deberu.
KAMA	Iie. It is I who is thankful.
OBAA-SAN	[*Confidentially.*] Don' let her over-ripe, Kama.
KAMA	Most of the time, she acts as though I'm not even around.
OBAA-SAN	She is telling you be more manly.
KAMA	More manly?
OBAA-SAN	Gather her in arms and kiss her.
KAMA	[*Lights begin dimming.*] Okinawan girls like to be kissed?

Mask

———————————— ❧ ————————————

This haachiburaa (toy mask) depicts
an uni (devil) or ogre. Five or six designs were
used for masks of this kind. Similar ogre masks were
made of wood in Miyara village on Ishigaki, one of
the Yaeyama Islands. Often, the ogre's teeth
and eyeballs were made from shells.

Papier-mâché.
Woodblock print by Ozaki Seiji.

OBAA-SAN	One good thing dey learn from 'Mericans.

Lights keep dimming until BLACKOUT.

Scene Two

Following Monday evening. Classroom. Hitoshi and Harue Kaneshiro are in Upstage Right corner rehearsing. Hitoshi on guitar; Harue on drums. Namiye, Takeshi, and Yasunobu are settling in their seats.

NAMIYE	[*To Hitoshi and Harue.*] (You are going to sing Okinawan songs?)
HITOSHI	(Just one Okinawan song, "Asato No Yunta.")
HARUE	(We are practicing for our GI nightclub act.)
HITOSHI	(Some GIs have hard time understanding our English.)
KEIKO	[*Entering with Kama.*] What's that good thing Obaa-san said we have learned from Americans? Speaking English?
KAMA	Speaking English?…Oh, yeah. Speaking English. One good thing you have learned from Americans.
KEIKO	[*Looking at students.*] They're all here.
KAMA	[*To class.*] Okay, gang. Let's get started. Hitoshi, Harue, you ready?
HITOSHI	As ready as can be.
HARUE	[*Steps up front. To audience.*] Ladies and gentlemen, presentin' da Hitoshi-Harue Show!
HITOSHI	[*To audience.*] Speakin' English very difficult. Understandin' even more difficult. One thing Okinawans and 'Mericans like: tellin' nice stories.
	Stage lights dim for a moment. When they rise, "Aiko" (played by Harue) is hiding something Downstage Left. "Kazuo" (played by Hitoshi) enters with a lunch pail, a wrinkled bus driver's cap tilted wearily to one side of his head.
KAZUO	[*In a tired voice.*] Aiko. [*She ignores him.*] Aiko! (Where's my beer?!)
AIKO	Today, I understand on'y English.
KAZUO	Nani?!
AIKO	And my name Alice.
KAZUO	[*Studying her.*] You alright? [*Touches her forehead.*] Better go see doctor.

AIKO	You told GI passengers today your name "Kaz"?
KAZUO	What's wrong with "Kazuo"?
AIKO	Don' sound 'Merican.
KAZUO	I am Okinawan. Get me beer!
AIKO	I am not Okinawan housewife; I am happy salesgal at base PX.
KAZUO	And I wanna be happy bus driver when I come home. Get me beer!
AIKO	"Please."
KAZUO	[*Stepping Downstage Left.*] I get it myself.
AIKO	[*Blocking him.*] No!
KAZUO	I cannot even go in kitchen today?
AIKO	Big surprise for you. [*Steps Downstage Left and brings out box of chocolate.*] Present-o!
KAZUO	Drink beer from chocolate-o box?!
AIKO	Rove, romance, many kisses.
KAZUO	You better stop watchin' 'Merican TV.
AIKO	My 'Merican salesgal friend, she say on this day, husband give her extra big kiss. [*Offers lips.*]
KAZUO	We not 'Mericans.
AIKO	We modern Okinawans. [*Offers lips again.*]
KAZUO	Aiko!
AIKO	Alice! You forgot bring me chocolate-o.
KAZUO	[*Offering Aiko's box.*] Here.
AIKO	Kazuo! Not too long 'go you a'ways bring me present-o when you come home. And you a'ways wanna play.
KAZUO	We not young boy, gal no more.
AIKO	How come other Okinawans our age make many children?
KAZUO	Dey don' have TV.
AIKO	[*Offering lips again.*] How about just a little one.
KAZUO	Aiko!
AIKO	Alice! You know what's trouble with you? No imagination.
KAZUO	"I-ma-gi-na-shon"?

AIKO	My 'Merican galfriend and husband, dey a'ways hold each other, say nice words.
KAZUO	Wanna hear nice words?
AIKO	[*Eagerly.*] Just-a rike 'Merican husband?
KAZUO	Get me beer!
AIKO	"Get me beer! Get me beer!" [*Offering cheek.*] C'mon. Be 'Merican.
KAZUO	Damn 'Mericans. Pretty soon, you wan' my hair red, my eyes blue. [*Giving in, about to kiss her cheek, when Aiko turns her cheek and forces Kazuo to kiss her lips.*]
AIKO	Happy Valentine! [*Hugs him.*]
KAZUO	[*Untangling her arms.*] Bakatare…
HITOSHI	[*Beat. Standing before class.*] Ta-da! [*Bows.*]
KAMA	[*Laughing, applauding.*] That was great, Harue, Hitoshi. Entertaining. Funny. And enlightening. [*Looks at wristwatch.*] We still have some time left.
KEIKO	That book written by your grandmother—why don't you tell the class what it is about? I'm sure they would like to know something about an Uchinanchu family in America.
HARUE	Oh, yes. Please. I want to know 'bout Uchinanchu-'Merican family.
NAMIYE	Me, too.
KAMA	Okay with the rest of you?
OTHERS	Yeah. Yeah.
KAMA	[*Reaching for book.*] The book is called *Sunrise; Sunset.* Grandma's way of saying, "When the sun is rising in Okinawa, it is setting in Hawaii." Some of you asked me what happened to the Uchinanchu pioneers who settled in Hawaii. Did most of them return home? Did their dreams of becoming wealthy come true? This might help you understand what most of them went through. The last chapter…it's about Great-grandpa. [*Paraphrasing.*] Great-grandpa is out in the yard, watering the roses, gardenias, and hibiscus. The hibiscus reminds him of Ginoza, where the flowers bloomed big and colorful. He wishes he could go back to Okinawa and see his sister, Nabe.
TAKESHI	He neve' came back?
KAMA	He could not afford it.

HARUE	Kawaiso na. Ah, how sad.
KAMA	[*Paraphrasing.*] Great-grandpa digs into his pocket and brings out a photo that Yukiko—that's my grandma—sent from California today. It is a picture of a hapa-haole baby.
YASUNOBU	"Hapa-haole"?
KAMA	Half-Okinawan, half-American…My mom. The baby has greenish eyes and brown hair. [*Paraphrasing.*] He was against Yukiko marrying a haole.
HITOSHI	Why?
KAMA	From what Grandma said, her father and mother always wanted to return home to Okinawa. They would, of course, bring Grandma with them so she could marry a nice Okinawan boy.
TAKESHI	No nice Okinawan boy in 'Merica?
KAMA	I'm sure there were. But most of Grandma's friends were non-Okinawans. [*Paraphrasing.*] Great-grandpa had no choice. He disowned Grandma. He announced to all the Uchinanchu neighbors and friends that Grandma was no longer his daughter.
NAMIYE	But he accepted her back?
KAMA	Yes. When the baby came. Grandma, after all, was his only child, and now her baby was his only grandchild. [*Paraphrasing.*] As the years go by, Great-grandpa thinks more and more of his home back in Okinawa…
NAMIYE	After all those years, still miss Okinawa very much?
HARUE	Poor Great-grandpa…
KAMA	[*Paraphrasing.*] Whenever he got drunk, which was becoming more often, he would sing old Okinawan songs and cry…
TAKESHI	Once Uchinanchu, a'ways Uchinanchu.
HARUE	You eve' knew Great-grandpa and Great-grandma?
KAMA	They were long gone when I came along.
NAMIYE	Many Uchinanchu-'Merican girls marry…haoles today?
KAMA	Not many.
NAMIYE	GIs! A'ways sayin', "Ever'body in 'Merica bery happy, bery friendly."
KAMA	There are some places in America that don't want outsiders.
NAMIYE	Outsiders? Like Okinawans?

YASUNOBU	So. Your GI boyfriend lie to you, eh?
NAMIYE	My boyfriend not GI!
KAMA	Any other comments? None? Okay. Let's call it a night. Friday night will be Namiye's turn. Right, Namiye?
NAMIYE	I will try be ready.
KAMA	Good. Well…See you all Friday night.
STUDENTS	[*Exiting.*] Good night…See you…Sayonara…
KEIKO	Really? There are places in America that don't like Okinawans?
KAMA	All minorities.
KEIKO	[*Lights begin dimming.*] I never experienced anything like that.
KAMA	You only lived in California.

Lights continue dimming until BLACKOUT.

Scene Three

Classroom. Following Friday night. Kama is watching Keiko writing on a clipboard.

KEIKO	Yasunobu, plus. Hitoshi and Harue, question mark. Takeshi, minus.
KAMA	I thought they were all very good.
KEIKO	Takeshi, too?
KAMA	So. It comes down to Namiye. If her speech proves my method works, I get to keep my job. If not…the students at least had a chance to speak up.
KEIKO	Without learning the fundamentals of good English.
KAMA	Don't you ever let up, for Chrissake?! Forget "fundamentals of good English." Forget you're the principal here. Relax. Go to parties, dances…
KEIKO	For your information, I go to dances every weekend.
KAMA	I mean dancing…[*Does rock 'n' roll movements.*] Not classical Okinawan dances.
KEIKO	[*Demonstrating foxtrot.*] You call this classical Okinawan dance? We practice not only foxtrot but tango, cha-cha, the waltz, too.
KAMA	You?!
KEIKO	[*Brazenly taking a dance stance.*] Come here. Come here! [*Kama goes along.*] Ever did the waltz?

KAMA	Well…Yeah. Sure.
KEIKO	Just humble yourself and follow me. [*Begins dancing and counting.*] One, two, three…One, two, three…
	Kama holds her close. He stumbles and presses her closer. Keiko goes along for a moment, then pushes him away. As they keep dancing, Yasunobu enters. Unnoticed, he stands there at the door, watching. In a few seconds, the rest of the class enters. Kama and Keiko notice the students. They stop.
YASUNOBU	[*Applauding.*] Hey, Kama, sensei. I neve' know you can dance like that.
	The rest of the class joins in applause.
KEIKO	We were…He…asked me to…
KAMA	I asked her to teach me…
KEIKO	The waltz.
YASUNOBU	Lookin' pretty good, you two together.
KAMA	Wanna learn? C'mon. Nothing to it.
YASUNOBU	No way! [*Joining students stepping toward their seats.*] Kama and sensei look good together.
TAKESHI	You tink somethin' going on between them?
HARUE	Nice romance.
KAMA	Okay, gang. Let's settle down.
OBAA-SAN	[*Entering with cane.*] Eh, Kama. Kama!
KAMA	Obaa-san!
YASUNOBU	Obaa-san! (How did you get here?)
OBAA-SAN	(I came on a GI truck.)
YASUNOBU	(You came here with a GI?!)
KEIKO	English, Yasunobu. English.
YASUNOBU	All the way from Ginoza?
OBAA-SAN	He was coming to Naha.
YASUNOBU	Obaa-san! He could've robbed you. Or…
OBAA-SAN	Or attacked me?
YASUNOBU	Well…Yeah.
OBAA-SAN	He say, "Grandma, I wish gals 'round here friendly like you." "If not too old," I tell him, "I love you, too."

KEIKO	You told him that?!
YASUNOBU	Obaa-san! You might not be so lucky next time.
OBAA-SAN	(Next time, I might meet a GI who really wants to attack me?) [*Laughs.*]
KEIKO / YASUNOBU	Obaa-san!
OBAA-SAN	(Yasunobu-san, they're going to burn my sugarcane field and my house.)
YASUNOBU	Who's going to burn your sugarcane field and your house?!
KAMA	What?!
OBAA-SAN	Be ready to move out, he say.
KAMA	Who said that?
OBAA-SAN	The Nikkei GI.
KAMA	Sergeant Shizuoka? He said that?!
OBAA-SAN	Dis morning. He come dis morning.
YASUNOBU	Bas-tard!
OBAA-SAN	Hai. Hai. Numbah one bha-stad-u.
KAMA	Damn that Shizuoka!
OBAA-SAN	Live there all my life, Kama.
KAMA	I know, Obaa-san. I know.
OBAA-SAN	Don' wanna rive other place.
KAMA	I hear you, Obaa-san.
OBAA-SAN	You not listening!
KEIKO	[*Looking at students. To Kama.*] You better get started.
KAMA	Yeah. We better.
YASUNOBU	Obaa-san, come. Sit here.
OBAA-SAN	[*As she is led to chair near Namiye, she looks at Namiye, then at her ring.*] Are you alright?
YASUNOBU	Somethin' wrong with her, Obaa-san?
OBAA-SAN	This gal, she should be happy havin' dat ring.
YASUNOBU	You don' think she happy?
OBAA-SAN	[*To Namiye.*] Daijobu?

NAMIYE	[*Shaking head.*] Daijobu denai desu.
YASUNOBU	Obaa-san, you came all the way here to find out if Namiye is alright?
KAMA	[*To class.*] Okay, gang. Let's get started.
OBAA-SAN	Don' wanna move, Kama!
KAMA	I understand, Obaa-san! I understand!…Namiye. You ready?
NAMIYE	Must? Right now?
YASUNOBU	See. She neve' ready.
NAMIYE	Don' know where to start.
KAMA	Start at the beginning.
YASUNOBU	A'ways best place to start.
OBAA-SAN	Why Kama he no listen?!
YASUNOBU	Later, Obaa-san. Later.
NAMIYE	[*Beat.*] Happen rittle over month 'go. [*Beat.*] I am member of Okinawa City Christian Church. Now tree years. Sensei is Reverend Kimball. [*Beat.*] I went Bible study class alone dat night. Most time, boyfriend, Masao-san, go with me. But Masao-san went home to Kyoto to visit family and announce our marriage. It is rainin' bery hard when I wait at bus stop. Army truck come. Driver ask if I want ride home. I look at driver. I think he is member of church. When I get in, I smell liquor. He is not church member. I try get back out. "Stop! Let me off!" But GI, he drive off very fast. He grab my hand. "We just-a goin' for short ride." We now in dark park. When truck stop, I jump out and run 'way. GI, he catch me. Jump on me. Hold me down. "Please. Please lemme go." GI, he start kissin' me all over. He tear off my blouse. [*Halting, catching her breath.*] I try push him 'way. He too strong. He laugh crazy laugh. "No! No, please! I not dat kind gal." GI, he laugh more crazy laugh. "I church gal." His hands now reachin' more and more. I start screamin'! Punchin'! Scratchin'! When he back 'way and let go rittle, I jump up and run 'way. GI, he chase me. He catch me and throw me hard on grass. [*Catching her breath.*] GI, he wild animal now. I start screamin'. He shut my mouth. He choke me. I can hear myself cryin' out, "Tasukete! Dareka, tasukete!" [*Beat.*] "No!" I try stop him. "No-o-o-o!" [*Everyone is shocked, horrified as Namiye sobs.*] "Otosan…Okasan…"
KEIKO	[*Rushing over.*] Namiye…Oh, Namiye…

KAMA	[*Also rushes up. Puts arms around both Namiye and Keiko.*] Oh, God, Namiye…
TAKESHI	Hard to believe it happen like she say.
OBAA-SAN	When first time I see her, I see much pain in eyes.
TAKESHI	Maybe GI think she teasing him.
KEIKO	Takeshi! Stop blaming her!
OBAA-SAN	Dis GI, not rike my GI friends.
NAMIYE	I start tinkin' 'bout Masao-san. He still wanna marry me? [*Looks at ring and rubs it fondly against her cheek.*]…I don' know how I got home. [*Beat.*] I feel dirty. Inside, outside. I keep takin' ofuro rong time. Still feel dirty. I wash my ears over and over. Still keep hearin' GI breathin' rike wild animal.
YASUNOBU	You report to police? MP?
NAMIYE	What for? Don' know how GI look.
YASUNOBU	Maybe he got scratch marks.
NAMIYE	Tousands of GIs in Okinawa. How can find dat one?
TAKESHI	Why he choose you at bus stop?
NAMIYE	I was only one dere.
KAMA	Masao? Is he back?
NAMIYE	Not yet. He tele-hone from Kyoto. Don' wanna talk to him. Don' wanna talk to nobody. Only cryin' make me feel rittle better. Pretty soon, I have no more tears left. I now go Itoman to family ohaka. I wanna be with Mama, Papa. Pretty soon, I am at high cliff.
HARUE	Oh, no…
NAMIYE	I walk over to edge, look down at rocks and waves way down below.
HARUE	No!
OBAA-SAN	Akisamiyo!
KEIKO	Namiye!
KAMA	Oh, Christ!
HITOSHI	That goddamn GI!
NAMIYE	I ready to let myself go.
HARUE	No, Namiye! No!

NAMIYE	"Nami-chan! Nami-chan!" It is Mama! Then, "Namiye! Namiye!" It is Papa. "Okasan! Otosan!"
KEIKO	[*Arms around Namiye.*] Namiye…Oh, Namiye…
KAMA	[*Arms around Keiko and Namiye.*] Jeesus, Namiye.
NAMIYE	I now know what I must do. I drive back to city. To church. I tell Reverend Kimball ever'thing. Ever'thing! Reverend Kimball, he cry with me. "Since you don' know who soldier is," he say, "there is no way to find him. What is important now is you. You must get over this."
	"How can? How can I get over? GI is a'ways breathing like wild animal in my ears. I keep smelling his liquor."
	"You must keep talking about this, Namiye. Tell ever'body what happened to you."
	"Ever'body?!"
	"Newspapers, too."
	"Newspapers?!"
	"Namiye," say Reverend, "what happened to you happened before. Nothin' has been done 'cause the girls won't talk about it."
	"Dey afraid. Ever'body say, She dat kinda girl."
	"You are not one of those girls."
	"What about Masao-san?"
	"You have to tell him. The sooner the better."
	[*Beat.*] I go home to apartment. I try tele-hone Masao-san. [*Pause.*] I…cannot tell him. I cannot hurt him. If he don' wanna marry me, I cannot blame him. What Japanese man wanna marry GI gal?
KEIKO	[*Embracing her.*] You are no such thing, Namiye.
NAMIYE	But Masao-san…He might…
HARUE	Namiye…He loves you…
NAMIYE	[*Takes out letter.*] I get dis today. I must meet him at airport tomorrow morning. After I tell him…Maybe, he no rove me no more.
TAKESHI	If really happen rike you say…
NAMIYE	He might tink I am now GI honey.

KEIKO	Namiye!
NAMIYE	Why this happen? Why?!
KEIKO	You can't let this destroy you, Namiye.
NAMIYE	I am already destroyed.
TAKESHI	Other GIs, dey never do nothin' like tis.
KAMA	There's always that one rotten apple.
YASUNOBU	Let's make sure no other GI pick up our young gals at bus stops. We tele-hone ever'body. Knock on doors. Spread word in city, town, village. We start picketing military bases. Big sign! TREAT MY SISTER SAME AS YOU TREAT YOUR OWN SISTER!
HARUE	OKINAWAN GALS NOT ALL GI HONEY!
HITOSHI	BE GOOD NEIGHBORS!
OBAA-SAN	My sign [*gesturing*]: MENSOOREE, GOOD GI! SAYONARA, BAD GI!
KEIKO	Count me in!
	Class applauds.
TAKESHI	I will tell General Hampton what happen to Namiye.
KAMA	Great idea, Takeshi.
NAMIYE	Domo arigato, minna-san.
YASUNOBU	We meet here tomorrow morning. Right now, we go make plans.
	Students begin exiting.
OBAA-SAN	[*As Yasunobu is following class out.*] Kama, my sugarcane field, my house… [*Yasunobu stops and gestures to others to go on ahead.*]
KAMA	Obaa-san, you won't have to move far away.
OBAA-SAN	Don' wan' move!
KAMA	The army will build you a new home.
OBAA-SAN	Don' wan' new home!
YASUNOBU	She born in old house; she wanna die in old house.
OBAA-SAN	Great-grandpa, he work many years Hawaii. He buy land, house in Ginoza. Now all yours. What for?
KAMA	The army will be there just for a short time.

OBAA-SAN	They say that sixty years 'go.
KAMA	It's the location of the land. Very important to the army.
OBAA-SAN	Not important to me?
YASUNOBU	What about ohaka, Kama? Next to house.
OBAA-SAN	When army come, burn house, I tie myself to bed.
KAMA	Obaa-san…
YASUNOBU	She mean it, Kama.
KAMA	[*Reconsiders.*] Nobody's gonna burn your sugarcane field or your home, Obaa-san.
YASUNOBU	[*Relieved.*] Kama not gonna sign lease.
	Obaa-san places her hands together in grateful prayer.
KAMA	Next time that damn Nikkei sergeant comes around, kick his butt out.
OBAA-SAN	"Butt-u"?
YASUNOBU	Oshiri.
OBAA-SAN	Oh. Kick ass-u!
YASUNOBU	Ikimasho, Obaa-san. [*They exit.*]
KEIKO	Poor Namiye. Reliving that horrible nightmare.
KAMA	Couldn't stop once she started.
KEIKO	I hope Masao won't change his mind.
KAMA	He might come up with a million reasons not to go through with it.
KEIKO	And one reason he might. [*Writes on clipboard and announces.*] Namiye…big plus.
KAMA	I get to keep teaching my way?
KEIKO	Just don't be a pushy American.
KAMA	Watakushi wa Okinawan-Amerikan desu.
KEIKO	Please remember that.
KAMA	[*Steps into spotlight Downstage Center. To audience.*] Yes. I am an Okinawan-American. I came to Okinawa as a teacher. The teacher became a student. When a typhoon comes lashing across the island, we Americans say, "Another damn typhoon." Okinawans say, "Welcome, typhoon. Please fill our empty

dams." When Okinawans place food offerings at their graves, we Americans say, "You really believe your dead will be able to eat the food?" Okinawans say, "As much as you Americans believe your dead will be able to smell the flowers you place at their graves." We Americans say, "This ends my speech," and will keep on speaking. Okinawans say, "This ends my speech," and will make you think about what was said. [*Lights begin to dim.*] And so, to all of you who feel Okinawan, wish you were one, or have become one: mata mensooree…sayonara… goodbye…

Lights keep dimming until BLACKOUT.

Curtain

History and Okinawans

Okinawans are a very history-conscious people. The small islands that constitute Okinawa have produced many writers—both scholarly and popular—who are deeply conscious of their tradition and culture. Without going back into pre-modern times, we can cite such outstanding scholars as Fuyū Iha, Kanjun Higashionna, Ankō Majikina, Shunchō Higa, and Zenchū Nakahara. The academic and literary products of these and other scholars run into thousands of publications. Even illiterate members of the older generations highly valued and preserved historical knowledge and legends. This predilection for history is undoubtedly a product of the Okinawan historical experience. Then, what is this historical experience?

From the viewpoint of culture, there is no question that Okinawan culture is but a variant of Japanese culture. However, it is quite another thing in regard to its political history. Located geographically in the periphery of the Japanese sphere, Okinawa has been in and out of the Japanese state throughout its history. As the long history of the Okinawa-Japan relationship is scanned, there seems to be a certain pattern. Okinawa may be likened to an offshore reef, which would be submerged and lose its own separate identity in high tide, but which would, in low tide, appear above water to form an independent entity. Whenever the central government in Japan was firm and strong, its influence would be extended, and Okinawa would be included within its borders. However, when that authority was on the wane, Japan's sphere of political influence would shrink, and the peripheral border regions of the Japanese archipelago, such as Okinawa, would become autonomous and independent.

Thus, in the late sixth and seventh centuries, when there emerged an ancient centralized autocratic government in Japan, the Southern Islands (Ryukyu Islands) appeared in the chronicles of Japan. During the seventh and eighth centuries of the Nara and early Heian periods, when the imperial government remained strong, there were frequent contacts between the Imperial Court and the Southern Islands. Islanders presented tributes to the emperor and received court ranks and titles, and some even took up permanent residence in the Japanese capital. In turn, the Court dispatched officials to the Southern Islands. In 735 A.D., the Southern Islands were placed under the jurisdiction of the Dazaifu (Government of Kyūshū) in northern Kyūshū.

When Japan terminated the sending of embassies to China in 839 A.D., the Southern Islands' importance as the way station to China diminished. From the tenth century onward, the central authority in Kyoto gradually declined and paid less and less attention to the Southern Islands. In contrast was the emergence of local political power in Okinawa, as evidenced by the brisk castle-building activities of the tenth century and the appearance in 1187 of King Shunten, Okinawa's first historical ruler. Two hundred years later, in 1372, Ryukyu established a tributary trade relationship with Ming China, and later, trade was expanded to Southeast Asia. Ryukyu enjoyed prosperity as a maritime trading nation while Japan remained under the rule of the weak Muromachi shogunate and in the turmoils of civil war.

However, shortly after Japan was under the strong central authority established by the Tokugawa shogunate in 1603, Ryukyu was forcibly brought within Japan's sphere by the military action taken by the Shimazu daimyo of Satsuma in 1609. For the next three centuries, as a vassal of the Shimazu daimyo (who himself was a vassal of the Tokugawa shogun), Ryukyu was a part of Tokugawa Japan, yet retained its own "king." Tokugawa's nation-wide laws and edicts, such as the requirements for the national census and the anti-Christianity rule, were enforced in Ryukyu as in the rest of Japan. Study of Japanese learning and arts was encouraged for the gentry. Yet, Ryukyu was ordered to maintain the facade of independence *vis-á-vis* China and other foreign nations. When Okinawans went to Japan, they were forced to act like aliens, but when they were in Okinawa, they were to act like Japanese. Yet when Chinese envoys arrived for the investiture of the king, Okinawans had to get rid of everything—ranging from all Japanese coins in circulation in the island to men's undergarments—that might reveal Okinawa's true political status as a vassal to the Shimazu daimyo of Japan.

In 1867 the Tokugawa feudal government was replaced by the new Meiji government. As Meiji Japan was a highly centralized modern state, Ryukyu was stripped of all pretense of independence and of its tributary relationship with China, and in 1879 it was incorporated by Japan as Okinawa Prefecture. All Okinawans were required or even forced to be "Japanese." In the early years of Meiji Japan, Okinawans were "Japanese" in their duties to the state—such as paying taxes and performing military service—but were denied the full benefits of citizenship, such as the franchise or local autonomy. These privileges were given to them only grudgingly and after a long struggle and wait. Still Japanization proceeded inexorably, and by the 1940s, tested by all standards of citizenship, Okinawans were Japanese. In the Battle of Okinawa in 1945, Okinawa, of all the prefectures of Japan, suffered the heaviest casualties. Yet when Japan lost the war—that is, when the central political power of Japan collapsed—Okinawa again found itself detached from Japan. This time, it was placed under the control of the United States.

Box

---·❧·---

*Called umibaku, this type of simple wooden box was
decorated with red, purple, or gold paper pasted on
its surface. The geometrical designs are created with
chiyogami (handmade paper incorporating bright
colors and patterns). Used to store favorite objects,
these boxes were popular as gifts to girls during the
yukkanufii festival (held during the fourth month of
the lunar calendar). At one time, young girls would
place male and female paper dolls in the boxes,
but that custom seems to have died out.*

*Wood and paper.
Woodblock print by Ozaki Seiji.*

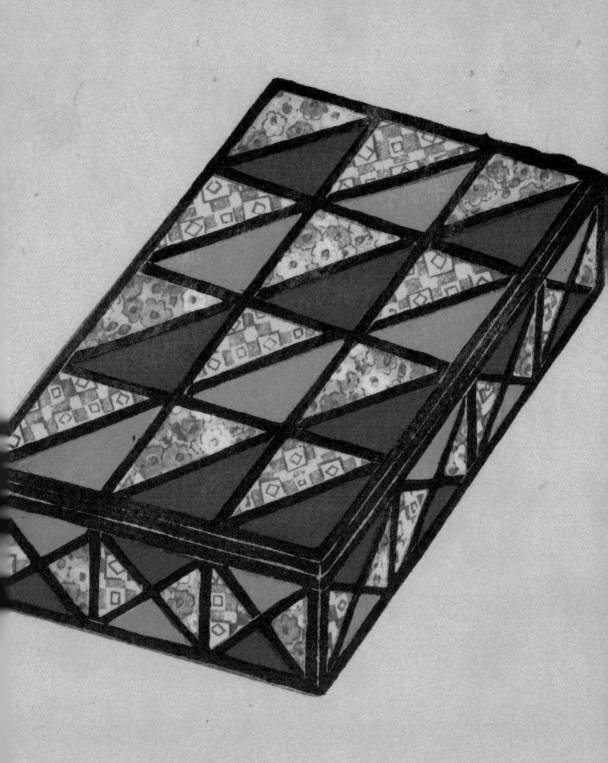

During the twenty-seven years of American occupation, history repeated itself for Okinawans. They were Japanese citizens without the protection of the Japanese constitution, and they lived under the flag of the United States without the protection of the American constitution. They were pressured to denounce their Japanese-ness and to be Americanized, but they could not become fully American. They were supposed to cooperate with the United States to protect democracy against communism, but they found themselves under a military dictatorship that had little regard for their democratic rights. For instance, as Japanese citizens, they demanded the right to educate their children as Japanese, but this right was gained from the U.S. military government only after two vetoes. It was only in 1972, twenty-seven years after the end of the Pacific War and after Japan had become an economic giant with a powerful government, that Okinawa was returned to Japan.

The Okinawan people have been repeatedly victimized by history, so it is their natural impulse to ask, "Why? What have we done to deserve this?"

The forty-thousand-member Okinawan community in Hawai'i began with twenty-six immigrants in 1900. These men were typical of the Okinawan population of the time. Many of them were barely literate and, unfortunately, left little in the way of a written record. There was, however, one letter, written by Matasuke Toyama, younger brother of Kyusuke, on behalf of himself and six others to his brothers, Kyusuke and Buntaro. The letter is dated March 1902, shortly after Matasuke's arrival in Hawai'i. The following is a translation of the original:

> When we first arrived here we knew neither the language nor how to work. Thus we were so worried that we didn't know how to express it. Recently, however, there is no more worry, and even the task of money making is getting more and more interesting day by day.
>
> Laws of the United States are being enforced here so that all of us are now free immigrants and money making is even better. As for the contract work, twenty-six days average [daily wage] comes to three or four or five Japanese yen. Food costs twelve to thirteen yen a month, spending money is about four or five yen, and the rest may be put to savings.
>
> If we stayed in our village as in the past, we would have wasted time by spending two sen for liquor at night, and cutting a load of grass for cattle and horses by the day. To think of it now, what a terrible way it was to waste our life. It is thanks to your wise decision, my brother, that we have by now saved enough money to return home in comfort.
>
> Accordingly, we feel that there is no other land than this which is better suited for making money. To begin with, Buntaro, younger brother, and other relatives and young men of the village who are able and strong in body, must be encouraged to come to this land.

Okinawan immigrants spent all of their adult lives in Hawai'i. Many toiled in the canefields and sugar mills. Others were in the villages and towns catering to the needs of plantation workers. Still others worked in small businesses in Hilo, Waipahu, Wahiawa, and Honolulu. In spite of their initial propensity to make quick money and return home rich, they soon found out that "home" was Hawai'i. It was here, in the simple houses of plantation camps and in the rows of tenement houses in town, that they started their families with their newly arrived picture brides. It is here that they begot their sons and daughters and watched them grow up and go on to fulfill the dreams they once dreamed for themselves. It is here that they saw their sons go off to war in defense of the United States, while the Issei (first-generation Japanese in the United States) remained behind, in agony over their divided loyalty to America and Japan. It was in Hawai'i that they toiled, suffered, grieved, and rejoiced. However, until the Walter McCarran Act went into effect in 1953, these immigrants were aliens in the land which was their home.

Granted there were many happy exceptions, Okinawans found themselves a target of rejection even within the Japanese community of Hawai'i. Being the last arrivals among the Japanese, having come from one of the poorest areas of Japan, speaking an "unintelligible" dialect, and being representative of the distinct culture of Okinawa, they were easily identifiable. Though none of these identifications was, by itself, a mark of inferiority or a cause for derision, the fact was that Okinawans found themselves at the bottom of the pecking order within the Japanese community in Hawai'i. There were many cases of overt discrimination by the Naichi (Japanese from the main islands of Japan) in matters such as marriage. These acts and attitudes deeply wounded the pride of Okinawans. Though largely incurred in the past and healed now, their scars are still discernible to perceptive eyes.

As to how to cope with the situation, one counsel was to mute Okinawanness and to assimilate within the Japanese community. Another was to improve economic standards so that Okinawans would not be looked down upon. Both kinds of counsel were taken seriously. In pre–World War II days, many Okinawans were averse to forming an all-Okinawan organization, fearing it would be misinterpreted as a sign of clannishness and would give more cause for discrimination. Others, however, stubbornly refused to efface their culture, and on the contrary, they perpetuated Okinawan dance and music, thus visibly and loudly proclaiming their Okinawan heritage. Furthermore, their natural desire for economic betterment was spurred on by the urge to catch up with and surpass the Naichi.

Another positive approach was to instill among the Okinawans the confidence and the belief that they were as good as or even better than the Naichi because of Okinawa's unique place in the history and culture of Japan. Professor Fuyū Iha, who visited Hawai'i in 1928, was a perfect spokesman of this counsel. His public lectures drew large crowds everywhere he went. His message was that Okinawans and Japanese both were descendants from the same stock, and therefore Okinawans were not alien or innately inferior; Okinawan culture was in fact indispensable to the understanding of ancient Japan. Thus, in their study of history, Okinawans found a basis for countering prejudice and discrimination. They could take pride in being what they were and at the same time lay claim to membership in the larger Japanese society.

After many years of hardship and struggle, Okinawans in Hawai'i have been able to establish themselves in many fields of endeavor and achieve a measure of success that they can be proud of. This success has gained them full acceptance, not only in the Japanese community, but also in the larger communities of Hawai'i and the United States. It has also given them new confidence, with which they are about to make further advances, proud and certain that they have a contribution to make to the society in which they live.

Grandfather to Grandson:
Perspectives on a Life

Seiyei Wakukawa was a brilliant Japanese American scholar, journalist, and social activist whose life spanned most of the twentieth century. He was born on June 10, 1908, in the small village of Nakijin, located in the Kunigami district of Okinawa. The youngest of seven children, he was two years old when his father died. Seven years later, his mother moved to Hawai'i to be with the children of hers who had immigrated there, and he was left in the care of his relatives in Okinawa.

In 1920, when Wakukawa was twelve, he journeyed by boat and train to Kobe, then on to Hawai'i to join his mother and others in his immediate family. At age eighteen, he graduated with honors from Hawaii Chugakko, a Japanese-language middle school, and two years later he graduated with honors from McKinley High School in Honolulu.

Immediately after graduation, Wakukawa enrolled at the University of Hawai'i, living frugally and supporting himself by working part-time as a translator and reporter at the bilingual newspaper Nippu Jiji *(formerly the* Yamato, *and later the* Hawaii Times*). Despite the burdens the Depression placed on him and his family, he completed his four-year degree in three years, graduating with honors and a perfect academic record in political science and history.*

As an undergraduate, Wakukawa became intensely interested in foreign affairs, particularly after listening to a series of lectures given by the eminent Okinawan scholar Iha Fuyū, a pioneer of Okinawan ethnography and linguistics who was invited to Hawai'i in 1928. At this time, Iha was one of the few Okinawans to have graduated from the prestigious Tokyo Imperial University. In 1911 he had published a landmark study of Okinawa, Ko Ryūkyū (Ancient Ryūkyū). Iha's research had established that Okinawan and Japanese cultures shared common roots and a common heritage. By disseminating this research, he sought to reawaken the self-esteem of Okinawans, who were openly derided—in Hawai'i as well as in Japan's northern islands—as linguistically, culturally, and racially inferior to mainland Japanese. Iha's scholarship affected Wakukawa deeply. Decades later, he said of Iha, "I was tre-

mendously enlightened and came to know Okinawa thanks to my contact with such teachers. It awakened in me an understanding of the native land that bore me…and a sense of devotion."

Two months after graduating from the University of Hawai'i, Wakukawa went to Japan for advanced study at Tokyo Imperial University. His research focused on public administration, Japanese colonial policy toward Taiwan and Korea, and the Japanese farm-tenancy system. Returning to Hawai'i a year later, he became employed in journalism full time.

By 1939, he had left journalism and was supporting himself with several jobs. But much of his energy was given to the establishment of associations devoted to the welfare of Okinawans in Hawai'i, and to the publication of immigrant histories, such as History of Japanese in Hawaii *(1938), written by his brother Ernest. The publication of another book,* The Role of Okinawan Immigrants in the Development of Hawaii, *was aborted by the Japanese attack on Pearl Harbor.*

When the attack came, Wakukawa was running a residential hotel. His brother Katsuzo, six years his elder, was in Washington, D.C., as a Special Attaché of the Japanese Embassy in the United States. It wasn't long before Wakukawa was interrogated by the FBI about his travel to Japan, his large collection of Japanese books, and his brother's employment at the embassy. In 1942, Wakukawa was taken into custody and placed in the Lordsburg Internment Camp in New Mexico. Almost immediately, he wrote a letter directly to President Franklin D. Roosevelt, protesting his internment and asserting that he could be of better service to his country by teaching the Japanese language to Americans. Though he got no formal response, he was released three months later and sent to teach Japanese at the University of Chicago, Columbia, and Harvard. At Harvard, he continued to research Japanese social issues.

In 1947, Wakukawa became director of the Okinawa Relief and Rehabilitation Foundation (Okinawa kyūsai kōsei kai), whose mission was to get humanitarian supplies flowing to Okinawa, and publisher of the newsletter Restoration of Okinawa. Initially, the greatest needs were for food, clothing, and shelter; but as conditions gradually improved, Wakukawa turned his efforts to a campaign for better public education in Okinawa, including education beyond high school. "The reconstruction of Okinawa is not possible," he wrote in the Hawaii Times *on August 11, 1947, "without educating young people at the college level." Over the next three years, he traveled throughout the United States, gathering funds and support for this effort. Three years after his campaign to establish "Okinawa University" was articulated in the* Hawaii Times, *the U.S. Military Government Headquarters opened the University of the Ryukyus, built on the site where Shuri Castle had stood before being demolished in the Battle of Okinawa.*

In 1954, Wakukawa was hired full time by the Hawaii Times, *and in 1970, he became editor-in-chief, working till he retired in 1975. He was appointed an* advisor to the Honolulu staff of the Consulate General of Japan, and he continued to be active in community organizations and was often asked to give talks in Hawai'i and abroad. In 1985, Hawai'i's Japanese community celebrated the centennial of its immigration to the United States, and he participated as a member of the Celebration Committee. In the following years, he donated thousands of volumes from his personal library to the University of the Ryukyus, Meiyo University, and his native Nakijin Village.

Seiyei Wakukawa passed away, at the age of eighty-three, on August 5, 1991. At his funeral, his friend Albert H. Miyasato, president of the Hawaii United Okinawa Association, eulogized him, saying,

> Mr. Wakukawa was literally a genius. His intellectual prowess, his vision, his dreams far exceeded the grasp of his contemporaries....
>
> The legacy he leaves behind is enormous. In that sense he will continue to live on among us. With deep gratitude, we welcome and celebrate this legacy as we say a warm and fond farewell to the one and only Seiyei Wakukawa. Namu Amida Butsu.

The following is an edited version of an exchange between Wakukawa and Layne M. K. Araki, his grandson, conducted in March 1982.

Grandfather to Grandson

I don't recall the Great Depression having changed my everyday life substantially. To begin with, I came from a poor immigrant family. Even before the Depression, the life my kind of people led was near the poverty line.

As for our own household, there were four of us boys living with our mother in a little three-bedroom cottage in the Japanese section of Honolulu. My oldest brother was working in a restaurant, and his monthly earnings were probably in the neighborhood of fifty or sixty dollars a month. Since there were no payroll deductions in those days, he brought home his whole paycheck and turned over about two-thirds of it to Mother, keeping the remainder. Out of his portion, he set aside a certain amount for savings, and the balance he turned over to a stock-market friend to be invested in securities. Of all the Wakukawa brothers, he alone had expertise in money, and was successful throughout his life in managing his financial affairs.

The other three boys, including myself, were in schools during most of the Depression. But we all worked throughout those years. The summer I graduated from grammar school, I started to work as a part-time office helper for twenty dollars a month at the Japanese Chamber of Commerce in Honolulu. Before that, for about three years, I cleaned the office of a savings company every day after school, including Saturdays, for seven dollars a month. For a time, I contracted to clean three offices at seven dollars a month for each. I was a peewee entrepreneur before I knew what the word *entrepreneur* meant.

My next-oldest brother was the least fortunate of the boys when it came to getting a formal American education. While he had a reasonably good Japanese education, it was not until he was well into his twenties that he enrolled for a formal American education. While he was working his way through high school in Los Angeles, he was also giving financial help to his older brother, who was attending college in Ohio, then in New York. His long hours of work at the produce market finally took their toll, and when he was just about to enter the University of Southern California, he came down with a severe case of pleurisy. The Depression was at its height. Ill health and depleted means compelled him to cut short a life-long ambition of acquiring a college education and a profession. Returning to Honolulu, he found the job situation as tight as in Los Angeles. After meandering among odd jobs for a year or so, however, he was offered a teaching position in one of the Japanese-language schools. Here he remained until "the infamy" at Pearl Harbor shattered his teaching career, forcing him to go into business for himself. This was just as well because his business thrived and prospered thanks to his pleasing personality. But long-lasting happiness was not to be his. His promising new career was cut short by an early death at the age of fifty-two.

My other brother was the most fortunate of all. When the walls of Wall Street came tumbling down, he was in his sophomore year at the University of Hawaii, having worked each year of his American education—a span of about twelve years. He worked the first two years as a domestic helper and soda fountain attendant. The remaining years, he supported his education by teaching at Japanese-language schools in Hawaii; when he was on the mainland, he worked weekends, Christmas, and summer vacations. In the summer of 1932, when he finished his university education with a master's from Columbia and returned home, Hawaii was in the throes of the Depression. However, luck was with him. In only a few months, he landed a job as an instructor at his old alma mater, by then the only Japanese-language high school in Hawaii.

At home, living conditions were not as rosy as all that. For one thing, our three-bedroom cottage was overcrowded with many uninvited guests. At one time there were more than twelve people living in a building with no more than five hundred square feet of floor space. Besides the five members of our family, there were old friends who had recently moved to Honolulu from neighboring islands and who deposited themselves with the understanding that this was to be a temporary arrangement until they found jobs. But jobs were not to be found. Moreover, those who found jobs would not move out for fear that they would lose their jobs at any time. Then there were those who felt the arrangement was too comfortable to leave, my mother cooking for them and even occasionally doing their laundry.

The even greater reason for all these guests to stay was the congenial family atmosphere that prevailed, and the sheltering but firm hand that my mother extended to every young man away from home, making these homeless young people reluctant to move to the dark, soulless cubicles of the tenement houses.

So the house was forever crowded throughout the Depression years. Sometimes a room was used in two shifts: during the day by the night-shift workers and at night by the day-shift workers. There were even times when temporary occupants spilled over into the little living room, when tables and chairs had to be moved to the corners to make room for two or three people to lie down. Here was a picture in miniature of what the Depression had brought to many a family. Privacy was a non-existent concept in the world of the deprived.

My everyday life was very simple. During my college days, I used to get up about six o'clock every morning. After the morning chores—which I had to attend to before anyone other than Mother got up because the one bathroom in the house would become crowded—I would gulp down my breakfast of a glass of milk, but never coffee or chocolate, and a piece of white toast. About twice a week, one boiled egg and some orange slices were added. Then with about half a dozen books and a loose-leaf folder, I would rush to the electric-car station about seven minutes' walk from home. I would jump onto the first overcrowded tramcar that took me straight to the college campus in Manoa. After compulsory gym in the morning, I attended three classes without any break; I could not take any afternoon courses because of my work at the newspaper. To complete four years' work in three years, I had to overload myself every semester and register for about five or six more credits than the average student carried. To do this every semester, I had to maintain high grades or the dean would not permit it.

While attending college, I was also working part time as a translator-reporter for a bilingual Japanese newspaper. So after finishing class at twelve thirty, I would rush back home via the same tram, then gulp down my lunch of boiled rice, miso soup, and tsukemono [pickled greens], fortified now and then with a dish of steamed or fried fish or an egg scrambled with Irish potato or some sardines fried in shoyu [soy sauce], or pork or beef cooked the Japanese way with about half a dozen different vegetables. Sometimes Mother added a glass of milk, too. Then I would rush to get to the newsroom, where I worked—except on Sundays and legal holidays—from one to four thirty or five P.M.

Back then, we were not paid by the number of hours we worked, but by the number of days, and there was no such thing as overtime pay. Most unskilled workers received a dollar a day for nine or ten hours of work. I was rather fortunate in that I was paid forty dollars a month, working between twenty-two and twenty-five hours a week. When I began my second year of employment at the newspaper, my pay was raised to forty-five dollars. For that extra five dollars, I really worked hard; my editor used to compliment me by saying that I produced as much as or even more than full-time reporters. The speed with which I produced articles was my trademark in the editorial room. In my second year, I was asked to also contribute to the editorial column once a week. That additional work counted toward the five-dollar raise. Toward the end of the Depression years, I became a full-time member of the editorial staff at sixty-nine dollars a month, which was considered pretty good pay in Hawaii's Japanese community.

On my desk in the newsroom, there was usually a copy of the afternoon English-language paper with about half a dozen articles marked by the executive editor for me to translate. Occasionally I was asked to write an original article on an assigned topic or to cover some afternoon event. Eventually I also had to submit editorials once a week. My executive editor was serving as the Honolulu correspondent of the *Kokumin Shimbun,* an influential national daily in Tokyo, and some of the special articles he assigned me to write were sent to Tokyo under his own byline. I didn't discover this trick of the craft until much later, when one of the regular staff reporters showed me copies of the *Kokumin Shimbun.* There on the front pages of the paper were very prominently displayed some of the articles I had written, with nary an editorial change. These were articles I had researched from various American sources on my own time. At least two of them—one dealing with corruption in American college sports and the other discussing Italian dictator Benito Mussolini's Fascist views on woman's place in modern society—were printed in installments, each installment conspicuously blocked and attractively illustrated with cartoon drawings. I had originally written these in the hope the editor would publish them in our own paper under my byline. When they didn't show up in the paper, I concluded they had ended up in the editor's wastebasket.

Because of the heavy load of work at the newspaper, I hardly ever got back home before five thirty. After bath and supper, I would settle down for my schoolwork. Since every room was fully occupied, I had screened off a portion of the front porch and turned it into a little nook for my study. Here I set a desk with an old Underwood typewriter on it, a chair, and a three-shelf bookrack. My lamp was connected to an extension cord plugged into the ceiling-light fixture in the adjacent bedroom. There was space large enough to place a stool or two to accommodate a visiting friend or two. On clear summer nights, after reading and writing into the wee hours of the morning, I would lay out a small shikibuton [a thick, fluffy Japanese quilt or mattress] on the floor from under the desk to the end of the den. I would lie down and get a few winks of sleep before an alarm clock rushed me to the bathroom still half asleep. This space was a cell all my own—a study, a library, a drawing room, a sanctuary, a berth, a salon, and a refuge all put together. I spent practically all my time in here when I was at home. I dreamed dreams in here for many years.

There was hardly a day when I failed to bring home armfuls of library books to consult for my term papers. Commenting on these papers, the head of the history and political science department of the university once said, "You are the only real student on the campus that I know." Naively encouraged by such compliments, I took more and more to books and completely ignored other amenities of college life. During my three undergraduate years, I attended not a single social function and went to a sports event just once: to see what football was all about. I didn't know the use of the season ticket. I used to give mine away to anybody who asked for it. Not until my last year did I learn these tickets were trafficked for fabulous sums. To this day, I am a wallflower, a sports illiterate, a card-game ignoramus, and an awkward companion—all because I hoped to fulfill a professor's image of a "real student." But to this day, I haven't regretted it, either.

Once secluded in my burrow, I would plunge into my work, always with a box of Hershey's kisses within reach. I am not certain now, but I believe a five-pound box of kisses could be had for less than two dollars. My love of kisses—and incidentally, the only kisses I knew until I was well into my twenties—was so widely known among my friends that one of them gave me boxes at Christmas for more than fifty years, long after I had passed on the addiction to my grandchildren. Hershey supplied me with all the energy I needed to stay up late every night, reading and writing. During weekend holidays or school vacations, there were times when I put in close to fifty hours at a stretch, without a wink of sleep, on reports and term papers. Overexertion, compounded by nutritional deficiency perhaps, and a congenital heart leak, sometimes took their toll. While waiting to transfer to another streetcar one day, I blacked out and scared the daylights out of a female classmate who was standing nearby. After regaining consciousness, I made it home somehow. I didn't say a word to Mother about the incident. After a short rest in bed and a light lunch, I went to work and attended to my usual chores.

Although in many ways I was fortunate compared to others during the Depression, I could not entirely escape the economic hardships of the time. For example, at college I was elected to two prominent national honor societies, but I could not accept membership because I could not afford the eight- or ten-dollar initiation fees. Neither could I afford to attend the graduation banquet, nor afford to buy a copy of the school annual the year I graduated. It was not until some half a century later that I managed to pick up a copy of the annual at a garage sale.

After graduation, I studied for one year at Tokyo Imperial University. I spent a great deal of my time researching the international ramifications of the deepening economic crisis. The result was a long dissertation on Japanese imperialism. Apparently, the content was prescient, as it suggested the possibility of the Japanese military going to war against the United States. The late Gregg M. Sinclair, my former professor at the University of Hawaii and university president soon after the outbreak of the war, took the trouble to recommend the dissertation to one of America's most respected publishing houses. But the idea of pursuing its publication was dropped for reasons of my own. A few years later, in the midst of the war, Dr. Sinclair wrote me:

> I suppose a good deal of the material that you were working on five or eight years ago is not so timely now and perhaps not publishable. If you had published the material at that time, you might have prepared America for what it has had to endure since December 7. Certainly you had more information on what the real leaders of Japan were thinking and doing than anybody else I know of. Might not some of it be revamped even now?

When I returned to Hawaii and resumed journalism as a career, I was giving much thought to why economic systems periodically collapse, the growing military rivalry between the United States and Japan, and the escalating danger of war in the Pacific. The executive editor and the publisher of the newspaper where I worked were men of conservative persuasion, and were enthusiastic supporters of Japan's military adventurism. My criticism of the existing economic anarchy and my occasional editorial diatribes on both Japanese and American military actions did not sit well with them. I could not help feeling an air of constant strain and tension in the office. So I set up two businesses on the side: a bookshop and a grocery store. I had not an iota of experience with either of these kinds of enterprises. I set up one business in order to provide work for an unemployed friend, but he deserted the venture when he found a job with the government. For me, this was the prelude to my leaving journalism as a career, though it took me several more years to finally muster up enough courage to cut the Gordian knot.

For a period of years, as part of my overall study of Japanese imperialism, I also spent considerable time and energy researching Japan's agrarian problem. Part of this study was published in 1946, right after the war, as a sixty-page chapter in the book *Japan's Prospect,* from Harvard University Press; excerpts from it were included in a college textbook, *Imperial Japan, 1800–1945* [Pantheon's Asia Library series, The Japan Reader, edited by Jon Livingston, Joe Moore, and Felicia Oldfather]. When my article appeared in three installments in the *Far Eastern Survey* of the Institute of Pacific Relations in New York, I was informed that it was being put to good use at General MacArthur's headquarters in carrying out postwar Japan's agrarian reform.

In some ways, then, the work I did under the compulsion of the Depression was not altogether in vain.

This pattern of my life did not change much even after the Depression and I had left school and gone to work full-time as an editor. Life's schedule became more flexible, to be sure. Some old addictions were discarded and new ones were added. Some old friends faded away and new ones appeared on the scene. Ideas and perspectives went through an inevitable metamorphosis. Short-term and long-term objectives, mental and physical states, views and convictions had to be reassessed and readjusted. But my love of learning and progress; my fondness for the simple, unaffected things and ways of life; my concerns for peace and human brotherhood; my interest in the liberation of the human mind from superstition and inertia; my disdain of power and position derived from wealth, birth, and manipulation—these remained constant and immovable. So did my material possessions, and my social status. My ways of life persisted. I was no richer than before. I was as poor as the church mouse. I continued to live in an overcrowded house, continued to eat the same kind of food, continued to wear the same kind of clothing, and continued to do the same kind of work as before. But I never lost hope. I continued to study and think with the same enthusiasm.

The Gift: An Interview
with June Hiroko Arakawa

By the 1920s, many first-generation Okinawan immigrants in Hawai'i were faced with the problem of how to provide both a Japanese education and an American one for their Hawai'i-born children. Parents would usually send their children to Japanese-language school in Hawai'i. In addition, some would send one or more of them to Okinawa or mainland Japan for *Nihon ryugaku;* that is, "studying in Japan." It was also not unusual for many first-generation Okinawan immigrants to send their children for *kuchiberashi;* that is, "to reduce the number of mouths to feed." In Okinawa, children could live with grandparents inexpensively; parents could remain in Hawai'i meanwhile, working to earn money for their own return.

The Nisei children (whether Japanese or Okinawan) who were educated in Japan and who later returned to Hawai'i were referred to as Kibei Nisei. Often they had problems assimilating back into the community after returning from Japan, especially if they had been sent to Okinawa or mainland Japan at an early age and had lived there for most of their youth. During the 1920s and 1930s, approximately three thousand Okinawan Kibei who had grown up in Okinawa returned to Hawai'i. Many Kibei Nisei who returned to the Islands in the late 1930s and early 1940s—when rumors of war in the Pacific were spreading—were suspected of being pro-Japanese and therefore disloyal to the United States. It was presumed that, during their time in Japan, they had been indoctrinated in the militarism associated with emperor worship.

Some Okinawan Kibei used their experiences living in Okinawa or mainland Japan to help the local Okinawan community develop a sense of pride in its distinct cultural heritage, and bridge differences among the Japanese in Hawai'i.

What follows is a profile of June Hiroko Arakawa, an Okinawan Kibei Nisei who became well known in Hawai'i for her kindness and contributions to the Okinawan community. I met Mrs. Arakawa when I arrived in Hawai'i in 2004 as an Obuchi Scholarship student from Okinawa. She was seventy-nine years old at the time and still an active leader in the Okinawan community. She welcomed me into her home, and I interviewed her several times over the next few years as I did research for my master's degree in sociology at the University of Hawai'i. Mrs. Arakawa had collected many documents, and she often sent me articles related to my research. Our last conversation was in mid-July 2008, approximately six weeks before she passed away, at age eighty-four. Because she was frail, she asked me to come to her home to conduct the following interview, presented in an edited form. We spoke in both English and Japanese. She seemed to know that she did not have much longer to live and that it was important to preserve the stories of Kibei Nisei like herself for the sake of the community she loved. Having cleared a small space amidst the many piles of books, we sat at a table off the kitchen.

"My name is June Hiroko Arakawa," she began. "My maiden name was Arakaki. I was the second daughter of Kyo and Tsuyo Arakaki. My older sister, the first daughter, died when she was twelve years old, so it seemed that I became the eldest daughter.

"I was born on June 7, 1924, in the middle of Honolulu, where Fort Street is, and raised in that area, where the YMCA is now located.

"My mother's father was an immigrant. He worked for twenty-two years on the island of Maui. He said that when he was ready to go back to Okinawa, he did not have any money to buy *omiyage* [gifts], so he decided to take one of his grandchildren. And I don't know why, but I was the one he selected. I was only five years old and had entered kindergarten. But I just went with him to Okinawa, where I was cared for by my grandmother and grandfather.

"Soon afterwards, when my aunty from Tokyo came down to Okinawa, she suggested that if I was going to start school, I should go to Tokyo. So I went back with her and entered school there. We were living in the area then known as Koishigawa, and is now Bunkyoku.

"In the summer of my second year, my mother came from Hawai'i with my brother and sister to attend a funeral in Okinawa, I think. That's when I found out I was a Hawai'i girl, not a Japanese girl. I told my mother that I really wanted to go back to Hawai'i—you know, to be with family. So, with my mother and two brothers and two sisters, I came back.

"By then, I was already eight years old. I was placed in the first grade in elementary school. My teacher told me to skip another grade, to be in a class with children my age, but I decided not to. I was kind of satisfied with where I was. I had nice, good teachers at that school. I also went to Japanese school, where I was placed in the third grade. Following elementary school, I went to Central Intermediate. I was in the same typing class with former governor George Ariyoshi. The teacher, Mrs. Miyamoto, arranged us alphabetically—Arakaki, Ariyoshi—so we sat next to each other. Another classmate was George Akita, who later was a professor at the University of Hawai'i. He was very intelligent. We had many good students.

"After I finished intermediate school, I insisted on Kamehameha Day—June 11, 1941—that, no matter what, I wanted to go back to Japan to study. My mother was worried. She said that, according to my uncle in Okinawa, a war was looming, so maybe I shouldn't go. But I said no, and so I went.

"I got on the ship *Katsuta Maru* and left Honolulu in very good spirits. My friends and family were there. At the same time, I felt really bad about leaving my youngest sister, Nancy Masako. She was a tiny girl, and I remember seeing her looking at me through a small space between my friends. She called to me, 'Hiroko *nesan* [older sister]! Hiroko *nesan!*' That was the last time I saw her alive."

Mrs. Arakawa stopped speaking, and I turned off the tape recorder to comfort her. She cried, remembering that her departure for Japan took place only months before the bombing of Pearl Harbor, in December 1941. It was a difficult time in her life. She wrote about it in a 1986 article for the *Pacific Press* newspaper. Many of the details in the following account also appeared in that article.

"When I reached Yokohama, it was June, and it was a very gloomy day. It kind of reflected the years I was going to spend in Japan. When we were on the ship, people who worked on it were telling us that war was looming in the Pacific.

"For Hawai'i, the war began on December 7, but in Japan, where I was now in school, the attack was on December 8, Monday. Our radio was broken, so I did not hear the news until I went to class that morning. My schoolmates at Ozuma Girls High School told me that war had erupted in the Pacific. Using the loudspeaker, the principal told us to assemble in the auditorium. She then read the proclamation by the Emperor, which told us of the war with Britain and America. When I heard that Pearl Harbor had been attacked, I was really worried about my family, who lived in Honolulu, not too far away. I thought the whole of Oahu was devastated. I couldn't help the tears that rolled down my cheeks. All my classmates were happy to hear of the tremendous victory, and joyful shouts rang out among them. I was the only one crying. I think it was difficult for my classmates to understand my mixed feelings. Under these circumstances, it was especially difficult for my two siblings and me to live away from our parents in a foreign country.

"As the war continued, there were fewer daily necessities in the stores, and even the farmers stopped selling farm products. After the American military conquered Saipan and other nearby islands in 1944, there were air raids on Tokyo practically every day. On May 23, we had our first bad experience. The house in back of ours was in flames even before the siren went off. Our neighbors, who had experienced other air raids, just ran away. My siblings and I stayed behind, trying to extinguish the fire that was started by the bombs. I told my brother to throw a futon on it. Then we used water

Kite Toy

— ❧ —

*Paper is pasted over bamboo
to make this butterfly-shaped toy.
When a kite is aloft, the butterfly is threaded
onto the string; it ascends, strikes the kite, and releases
bits of colorful paper, which gaily flutter down.*

*Bamboo, paper.
Woodblock print by Ozaki Seiji.*

that we brought from the well in a bucket, but it was of no use. If the wall with the exit burned, we would be stuck like rats in a trap. We decided to give up and try to escape. The funny thing is that my brother was carrying a pot of rice and my sister the empty bucket when we ran from the fire. I took our important papers, like our bank account book.

"We had been living in Harajuku, right behind the Togo Shrine. After losing our home, we stayed in our friend's home in Sendagaya, Shibuya. A hapai woman who lived next door was going to move to a safer place, but she died during an air raid the next day. My siblings and I escaped to a nearby temple, which had a graveyard. I prayed, お墓の人どうか見守ってください。[Please, whoever is in this grave, protect us.] Then we saw a plane zigzagging in the sky, so my sister, Alice, and I ran to a safer place. My brother, Henry, had disappeared. As soon as Alice and I hurried through the temple gate, it burned to the ground behind us. We then ran toward Yoyogi Park. Many people were there, looking for lost family members and calling out their names. I was worried about my brother. When daylight came, I went out looking for him. A large area was in flames, and the smoke made the sun very hazy. We lost everything we had tried to save during the air raids because we could not run while carrying anything. Finally around noon, I found Henry in a bomb shelter outside the temple grounds. He had been hurt by the firebombs dropped by a B-29. My brother はね。足をやられて、左の足をやられて、歩けなかったから這って逃げたっていうのね。お寺の外の防空壕に入っていたの。防空壕にいても煙があるから大変でしょ。でも我慢したんでしょうね。[My brother had injured his left leg. He could not walk, so he crawled and escaped. He stayed in an air-raid shelter. It must have been very hard for him, but he endured.] A nearby military regiment put him on a makeshift stretcher and took him to a military doctor. The doctor gave Henry's injured foot a good cleaning and then gave him a tetanus shot. With a borrowed cart, I was able to transfer my brother from Sendagaya to Shinjuku Railroad Hospital. Later, he was transferred by truck to Meguro Naval Kyosai Hospital. I had been working in the Navy Department, and dependents were allowed into the hospital. My brother was hospitalized for about three months, and luckily, his foot was spared amputation. With crutches, he was able to walk again. For this, I credit the military doctor who first treated my brother.

"In the middle of August 1945, we were told that the Emperor was going to say something over the radio. It was his message announcing Japan's surrender. Everybody was crying and afraid. Because we didn't know what the Americans were going to do to us, we were told to stay indoors. By this time, we were at the very end of our resources, with no place to sleep, no food, and no clothing. Everyone was suffering a lot. I saw many war orphans who had escaped from orphanages because they were being mistreated. Once, I saw a terribly disheveled woman in tattered clothing, oblivious to the stares of people around her. She seemed to be the only survivor in her family. When I was working for the Forty-second General Hospital in Tokyo, I saw other desperate people. Then, when St. Luke International Hospital in Tsukiji was taken over by the U.S. military, I saw women hiding pots behind their backs and waiting by the kitchen area where all the leftover food was taken. They were collecting the scraps to eat.

"I later met a Nisei soldier who told me what had happened to Nancy, my eight-year-old sister. She had been attending Japanese Sunday school in Hawai'i on December 7. An anti-aircraft bomb from Punchbowl fell on the school grounds, and some of the shrapnel killed Nancy and injured a boy. I heard that there were many civilian casualties on that day, a fact that few people knew until recently. Many precious, innocent lives were lost.

"Each December 7, my memories are full of such tragedies. I would never again want to experience what I went through during the war years in Japan. We should use all means to avoid war and should pray for peace.

"After the war, I immediately called the American consulate in Yokohama to make an appointment, but I was told I couldn't get one for two years. A military chaplain then asked me about my situation; when I told him, he said he would talk to someone at the consulate. I was able to get my passport in December 1946, one year after the war ended. My siblings, Henry and Alice, were able to return to Hawai'i with me on April 1, 1947. We went by U.S. military transport. As we approached Oahu, the Waianae Range was such a welcome sight that we could not stop the happy tears streaming down our cheeks. Our parents and some of my classmates were there to greet us at the pier. Because April 1 is April Fool's Day, some people did not believe the news that we were coming home.

"Being in Hawai'i again was both happy and sad. Soon after we three children had arrived in Tokyo, our parents had gotten a divorce, in the latter part of 1941. When the war broke out, my father, who had a trucking business, was classified an enemy alien, so he could not go to the waterfront to load his truck or make deliveries to stores and military installations. He lost the business he had worked hard to build up. Then, in 1944, he was interned by the U.S. military at Honouliuli Internment Camp in Ewa. After his release, he started the Venice Taxi service, located next to Venice Café on College Walk. Later he moved to Liliha Street and lived in a one-room building next to his taxi stand. We children were in his custody, but he did not have room for us, so we moved in with our mother. I wanted to continue my schooling because I only had an intermediate-level education in Hawai'i. My classmates were getting married one by one, and it seemed I would be left behind if I went back to school.

"I started to look for a job to support myself, and although I spoke both English and Japanese, my formal education had been limited. I knew the Japanese language well, having attended Chuo Gakuin, known as Central Institute, until the eleventh grade and had completed my high school education in Japan. Later on, I took the General Education Development test and received my high school diploma from Farrington Adult School.

"In 1947, I was working and used to stop by Toyo Shoes, which was owned by Katsumi Hokama. In September, he started the first Okinawan radio program in Honolulu and asked me to help as an announcer. Another announcer was Richard Koja, also a Kibei Nisei. Mr. Hokama began the program in order to raise money for the Okinawan relief effort, so there was no funding to pay us: it was a volunteer job. In fact, he had to solicit advertising to cover the cost of radio time. It was on station KAHU, located along the Ala Wai Canal. After I was hired, I was surprised to learn, the station received two letters asking why Okinawans had been hired. Before the war, I had experienced Japanese prejudice, but I could not believe that prejudice towards Okinawans still existed. Because of this incident, I was determined to work hard as an announcer. As a radio announcer, I had the opportunity to become familiar with Okinawan classical and folk music. It was a learning experience for me. I met many shamisen sensei: Ryokin Nakama, Yeikichi Miyagi, Seiko Ikehara, Kanyei Izumigawa, and others.

"In 1950, I was hired as a Japanese announcer at KULA radio station, located on Kapiolani Boulevard. All the announcers at that time were local Nisei or Kibei Nisei. On Saturday nights, KULA had a program called *Chop Suey Melody,* which was very popular, and that's how I met my future husband, Tomu, who was a singer for one of the orchestras.

"The Korean War started in June 1950, and Tomu and I were married in September. After we married, I worked for Goldtone Photo Studio as an office clerk. When my boys—Thomas Takeshi and John Takeo—started American school, I also sent them to Tachikawa Japanese Language School on Piikoi and Rycroft Streets. Sae Tachikawa, the principal of the school, asked me if I could teach Japanese because a teacher had recently left. I accepted and taught first and seventh grade for four years. Later, when my sons attended Maryknoll, the school asked for parent volunteers in various areas. I decided to help the school librarian, Sister Mary Paula. Because of my volunteer work, I ended up taking care of the Maryknoll School library for twenty-two years, after the sister returned to New York. I was not a professional librarian and my pay was small, but the principal, teachers, and staff supported and guided me in my work.

"When I retired from Maryknoll School, they gave me a retirement party at Tripler Military Hospital Officers Club. They even invited my husband. I was very much touched by the teachers and staff of Maryknoll School, who gave me so much support and encouragement even though I was never a professional librarian.

"Then I taught two years at Manoa Japanese Language School and later went back to Tachikawa Japanese Language School, teaching until it closed down. Finally, I left the work force to volunteer at the Hawaii Okinawa Center. I became involved in the Hawaii United Okinawa Association when the late Masato Kamisato became president. In 1970, he asked me to serve as a recording secretary. He opened the door for women, and I became the first woman officer of HUOA. Later, from 1993 to 1994, Jane Serikaku served as the first woman president."

Mrs. Arakawa, however, was more than a dedicated volunteer at the Hawaii Okinawa Center. She worked there for seventeen years, and among her accomplishments was the launching of the Okinawan Festival, which is now one of the most successful ethnic celebrations in Hawai'i, attracting over fifty thousand people annually.

"When we started the Okinawan Festival back in the 1970s, it was known as the Cultural Jubilee," she said. "At that time, we wanted to share our culture with the larger community—not only with Okinawans, but with the general public, too. Other ethnic groups participate in this program. I think it is very good that we share with each other. That's how we get to understand each other's lives. Even people from England, Europe, South America, and North America come to the festival. Though they are not Okinawans, they come out because they have the Okinawan spirit and they help us."

Mrs. Arakawa told me that she wanted to leave a message for the younger generations in Okinawa. She said that Mr. Matsuoka, the former governor of Okinawa, had reminded her of the traditional saying "The frog in the well knows nothing of the great ocean." In other words, we don't understand ourselves until we leave our small world and see our community from the outside. "When I meet young Study Abroad students, they say a similar thing," she said. "When they see Okinawa from outside, for the first time, they notice how good Okinawa is, how beautiful the island and the people are. Leaving enables us to appreciate our unique and distinct culture."

When I heard she had fallen ill after our last interview, I wrote her a letter. I expressed my gratitude for how much she had done for me since I first arrived in Hawai'i, for how much she had done for all the Okinawan students, for touching many lives, and for working to preserve the Okinawan culture.

Mrs. Arakawa died on August 27, 2008, in her home in Honolulu. She is survived by her sons Thomas and John, her brothers Henry and David Arakaki, her sister Alice Kishimoto, and a grandchild.

The Dawning of an Okinawan

The sandy, rock-strewn path to the gravesite of my father and mother is up a sharp incline bordered by tangled tropical weeds and sharp thorny bushes. The steep, arduous climb seems to symbolize the hard, grueling lives Otōsan and Okāsan endured so that their children might one day climb up to their graves and appreciate the spectacle of peace and serenity below. Where dry, flammable sugarcane once grew, wavering in the wind, are now groves of sturdy blue-green macadamia trees. And where patches of red-brown mud blighted the meadowlands, now sparkling white homes stand, surrounded by majestic cloud-draped mountain peaks.

Happy, lilting voices of young children down at the St. Anthony High School football field suddenly evoke bittersweet memories of my own childhood, and momentarily distract me from the headstones.

KAMATA SHIROTA, 1888–1950

UTO SHIROTA, 1891–1950

Forty years ago!

It's been forty years, Otōsan, since you and Okāsan left us! Not only in the same year, but also the same month!

Otōsan had left his poverty-stricken, oppressed homeland at the opening of the century, when he was barely eighteen. He had heard of the fortunes that were being made by the first group of twenty-seven young Okinawans who emigrated to Hawaii in 1899, and was determined to seek his fortune there, too. But it was not until 1907 that he finally arrived in Hawaii with a group led by pioneer Kyuzo Toyama, who was a fellow Yambara from the mountains of Ginoza District.

After laboring in the Waipahu canefields on Oahu for a couple of years and not being able to save anything from the one dollar he earned each day, he thought of moving to California, where a group of young Okinawans were working for the railroads. Restrictive emigration laws, however, forbade him from moving to the Mainland. He could either return to Okinawa or remain in Hawaii. He chose to remain in Hawaii, and his dream of amassing a fortune remained just that. A dream.

After another year of slaving in the Waipahu canefields, he moved to Lahaina, Maui. He still earned one dollar a day, and he was getting no closer to building that village castle of his than when he first arrived. In 1911, he paid a matchmaker in Ginoza Village to send him a wife. His young picture bride arrived shortly.

Restless, still determined to return to his homeland wealthy, he moved to Peahi on the eastern slopes of Maui, where, like other Yambaras, he became an independent pineapple grower. Children and more children followed. Eight altogether. Otōsan and Okāsan believed in equality. Four boys; four girls.

I was number six. Hiroshi. Had Otōsan realized the misery that his recalcitrant sixth child would cause him in years to come, he surely would have stopped at number five. Otōsan and Okāsan, however, were a healthy couple, and did not permit mysterious concepts like contraception to interfere with the romantic interludes in their spartan lives.

The next move was to the western slopes of Maui in Kahakuloa, where the pineapples reputedly grew bigger than watermelons. We lived in Kapuna Valley and commuted to the pineapple fields. Our home was built by a co-op of Okinawans. Consisting of several families, the co-op would build a house for a family, then move on to build a house for another family, until all the families were provided with homes built by unskilled, but persevering hands. Each home had its own outhouse and a furo bathhouse.

More than half a century later, our house, built by Otōsan and his fellow Okinawans, would still be standing on its original foundation. It would be owned by a young haole doctor and his wife from New York City, who lived in it for a number of years, then rented it to a haole family from California.

That home, which cost you less than five hundred dollars to build, Otōsan, is now rented for more than that each month! Of course, there is electricity in the house now, also an indoor bathroom with flush toilet. They also have...sorry, I forgot. You wouldn't know what a TV or a microwave oven is. The only modern convenience we had in those days was a small radio. Oh, yes, a tele-hone, too. That's what you called it, remember? Tele-hone. One ring meant the Portuguese family up the river; two rings, us.

Otōsan's younger brother, Uncle Seiyei, a warm and loving man who lived with us, was Otōsan's partner in the pineapple business. I would discover much later why Uncle Seiyei never took trips back to Okinawa to see his wife and child. He had come to Hawaii on someone else's passport. He was an illegal immigrant.

Kau-kau time, or lunch breaks, in the open pineapple fields were the happiest moments for me. I would no longer have to play alone in the dirt and grass or transport myself to imaginary worlds. I would eat delicious bento with everyone—rice, pickled vegetables, fried fish and/or meat—then lie down beside Otōsan for a little moi-moi nap, feeling secure in the crook of his arm. Neither Otōsan nor Uncle Seiyei, however, was around to comfort me when I was first exposed to a world outside the Kapuna Valley Okinawan community.

To supplement his sparse profit from the pineapple fields, Otōsan had begun working for the WPA projects founded by the Roosevelt administration. He would take me with him to his jobs along the roads, and though I never felt intimidated by Otōsan's non-Okinawan fellow workers, my first exposure to a multiethnic, multicultural classroom was frightful.

My English schoolteacher was a hapa-haole woman. She seemed kind, but was quite stern and impatient. While the non-Japanese children stood up confidently and announced in English that their father or mother brought them to school, I rose tearfully and muttered in pidgin English, "My Otōsan, he da one wen' brin' me to school."

If English school was intimidating, Japanese school in the afternoons was painful. I was told—indoctrinated—that we were Japanese and that Okinawa was a prefecture of Japan; therefore, we were Okinawa-ken.

Exposure, however, to the wily Naichi non-Okinawan children in Waihee Village revealed otherwise.

There was virtually complete segregation between the Naichi and Okinawan children in the Japanese-school classrooms and on the playground. The Naichis, not wanting to be plagued by our Okinawan-ness, disassociated themselves from us. When they spoke to us, we were flattered. They flaunted their Naichi-ness by taunting us: "You Okinawan chin-chin buta kau-kau."

And that agonizing, distressing epithet would keep haunting me into adulthood.

You Okinawan chin-chin buta kau-kau!

What the Naichis really meant was this: Okinawans raised and slaughtered pigs; therefore, they could not be much better than the pigs they raised and slaughtered.

Many years later, I would learn that in the Japanese dictionary there is a word, *burakumin,* which refers to the group of social outcasts that tanned hides and butchered animals. Those engaged in such endeavors were perceived to be unclean, and contact with such people was avoided. Perhaps this is the derivation of the Naichi prejudice we all experienced.

"Just don't let them beat you in anything!" That was the only advice Otōsan was capable of giving me and my sisters when we told him of our confrontations. By this time, we had discovered that the Okinawans did not speak Japanese as fluently as the Naichis, that they spoke with a distinct, sometimes unintelligible, accent laden with a sing-song lilt. Moreover, we had discovered that the Okinawan-Japanese they spoke was sprinkled with English and Hawaiian words.

In any given day, Otōsan would be greeted by our Okinawan neighbor, "Oi, Kamata! You ki-yo hoe hana sa-bi-tan?" That short, concise question—consisting of Okinawan, Japanese, English, and Hawaiian words—inquired if Otōsan had worked in the field that day. Under closer scrutiny, however, it was a warm and impassioned greeting expressed by one elder Okinawan to another: "How's things today?"

Although the Naichi kids abused us at school, economically the Okinawans in Kapuna Valley were better off than the Waihee Naichis. We were, in a sense, entrepreneurs. We grew pineapples, taro, and vegetables. We also raised chickens and hogs. We transported our products in cars that we owned. The Naichis in Waihee Village were common laborers in the canefields. Most of them had never even seen the inside of a car.

Yes, indeed, Otōsan: "Don't let them beat you in anything."

Couldn't you have elaborated a little, though? Made us understand why we were picked on? Told us that everyone has a need to feel superior, especially those with little to be smug about?

But how could you, Otōsan? You had enough problems feeding, clothing, and educating us. Complex insights into human behavior were for the educated. You were barely able to read and write. The first time you entered a classroom was when you escorted your first child to school. As he learned to read and write, so did you.

Painful memories of those childhood days were somewhat eased many years later during an autographing session for a book I had written. A man I recognized as having been one of the most belligerent Naichi boys—someone who used to chase me home as I was crying—stepped up and asked me to inscribe his book "For old days."

Then he introduced an attractive woman beside him. "This is my wife," he said, adding, "Her name used to be Shimabukuro."

I savored that momentous occasion. "So, you're one of us now," I said and laughed. We shook hands. Meaningfully. And closed a chapter in both our lives.

Despite the daunting Japanese-school days in Waihee, there were many happy, carefree days growing up in Kapuna Valley. Like Tom Sawyer, we would go fishing and "bare ass" swimming down at the river, and build fires to cook our fish. We would also lie naked on the warm, smooth rocks to dry ourselves and dream of sleeping with some of the pretty girls at school.

There were heroes we looked up to. And none would be bigger or faster or stronger than the Okinawan athletes: Oki Shikina, wrestling; Kiyoshi Nakama, swimming; Richard Chinen, boxing; and the Tamashiro old man, who was the strongest and fastest *hapai ko* man at the Maui County Fair cane-loading contest.

We would often exchange hilarious tales about our "old folks" Okinawan parents so we could feel superior about their shortcomings. And, of course, each retelling was funnier than the previous version. Our favorite went like this. A haole salesman asks, "Mama-san, where is Papa-san?" And Mama-san replies, "Oh, Papa-san, he go away. Pretty soon come home." "Well, I'll be back later," says the haole man. An hour later, the haole man returns and gets the same reply. Two hours later, when the haole man returns and gets the same reply, he says, "Jesus Christ! Wheredahell did Papa-san go?" Quite annoyed by now, Mama-san replies, "Papa-san, he go Okinawa! Pretty soon come home!"

We were always told that Okinawans were hard-working, honest people and that they would never do anything to shame their fellow Okinawans. If a Japanese violated any law, the culprit was never an Okinawan; he was always a Naichi. Once, when an Okinawan boy was caught stealing, we were relieved to learn that his name could be either Okinawan or Naichi.

Okinawans, like the native Hawaiians in Kapuna Valley, needed only a slight excuse to have a party: arrivals, departures; sickness, health; marriages, divorces; birth, death. When Uncle Seiyei finally decided to return to Okinawa, it was both a happy and a sad occasion. He would, at last, be returning home, but we would never see him again. His voluntary return to Okinawa was tantamount to a deportation.

Uncle Seiyei had received word through the Okinawan grapevine that his wife and child were living with another man. That explained the plaintive, heart-rending songs he played on his *shamisen* night after night until Otōsan, sharing his grief, suggested that he return home and straighten out his family affairs. After a huge Okinawan luau attended by hundreds of well-wishers at our home, the party shifted to Kahului Harbor. As the interisland steamer SS *Waialeale* gradually slipped away from the pier and the Maui County Band began playing "Aloha Oe," Uncle Seiyei waved his handkerchief tearfully to us, resigned that he would never see any of us again. Little did he realize that the clashing of world events would prove him wrong.

The farewell party for Uncle Seiyei continued even after we returned home from Kahului Harbor. Otōsan, responsible for arranging Uncle Seiyei's illegal passport, was guilt stricken that Uncle's wife had left him. Trying to lift the spirits of his fellow commiserating Okinawans, Otōsan made light of Uncle Seiyei's predicament. He told a story of a young couple in Okinawa encountering marital problems:

The husband returns home from the fields one day and sees a man jumping out of their bedroom window. He confronts his wife.

"Who was that?!" he screams at her. "Who was that I just saw jumping out of our bedroom window?"

When his wife chooses to remain silent, he keeps screaming at her. *"That was my friend Kiyoshi, right?!* It was Kiyoshi! He was always after you!"

His wife says nothing.

"If it wasn't Kiyoshi, then it must have been my friend Genkichi! He was always in love with you!"

His wife remains stolidly silent.

"If it wasn't my friend Kiyoshi or Genkichi," the husband goes on relentlessly, "then it must have been my friend…Susumu. Right? It was my sneaky friend, Susumu!"

His wife finally looks up at him. "All the time: your friend, your friend," she says scornfully. "I have friends, too!"

Everyone burst out laughing. Otōsan's laughter, however, was filled with half-sobs, and the tears that filled his eyes were not tears of laughter, but of pain and sorrow.

The Depression of the 1930s struck the Territory as it did the rest of the country. Most of the independent Okinawan pineapple growers on Maui went out of business. Many moved back to plantation camps to labor in the canefields or to work in pineapple fields owned by Libby Pineapple Company. Some of the more adventurous moved to Honolulu, where, they had heard, opportunities were better.

One of the families expanded their taro-growing venture and later bought a poi factory in Wailuku. Years later, their son, a boyhood friend, would venture even further in the taro-poi business and become one of Hawaii's most successful poi manufacturers.

Otōsan, through the help of a fellow Yambaru Okinawan, was able to buy a grocery–meat market in Wailuku town. He financed the transaction through *tanomoshi*—a sort of Okinawan neighborhood credit union—and after many years fully repaid the debt.

We now had two homes: the Kapuna Valley house and a small, crowded apartment behind the market. Our farm in Kapuna Valley supplied our market with vegetables, pork, eggs, and chickens. The meat and other groceries were purchased from wholesale vendors.

The move to Wailuku was a social revolution. We were now "big city" folks. Across from our market was a theater, and there were streetlights and brightly lit stores all around us. The walk to school was no longer through canefield-bordered roads, but on crowded sidewalks through town. Our elementary school was so big that each grade was divided into different classrooms. The schoolteachers were mostly haoles who spoke only pure English.

At Waihee School, our teachers were either hapa haoles or native Hawaiians who were more interested in teaching us Hawaiian history and its accompanying songs and folklore than in the regular school curriculum. Not a day went by that we did not begin school with a song or two of old Hawaii. And, during the course of the day, if the teacher felt like singing, we were urged to accompany her. The songs we learned and sang would later become an important part of my life, but they did not help me when I started school in the "big city." I was in the fourth grade and hardly knew arithmetic, history, or geography. I did, however, excel in Hawaiian songs and Hawaiian folklore.

The Japanese Buddhist school was no longer a one-room building. It was as big as the English school in Waihee. The teachers were no-nonsense disciplinarians. *"Kimi wa Nippon-jin da!"* was a militant order of the day— not merely a statement that we were all Japanese. We stood in line and went through a series of military exercises before entering our classrooms. In the classrooms, we were forever reminded, either through the books we read or the stories we were told, that we were Nippon-jin first and foremost. Occasionally we stood up and, either facing toward Japan or turning toward a picture of the emperor on the wall, bowed low with reverence. On Saturdays, the boys learned *judo* and *kendo;* the girls, sewing and Japanese etiquette.

The Okinawan name-calling was not as blatant as it used to be at the Waihee Japanese School. I would learn that our family name, Shirota, was not a typical Okinawan name and that my Naichi friends would assume I was one of them, which made my situation awkward. Whenever I heard unsavory remarks about Okinawans, I had the choice of announcing that I, too, was an Okinawan, or else remaining silent and hoping that I would never be found out. I chose the latter, and would suffer guiltily for it in the years to come.

One of my Naichi friends invited me to join the Christian Church Cub Scouts, which led to my joining the Boy Scouts of America. This event had a profound effect on me. It gave me an opportunity to associate with Naichis who were beyond name-calling, mostly Sansei from educated families. They had been exposed to music, literature, and plays. Some of them were even attending special schools with haoles. They spoke "good English."

Joining the Cub Scouts and Boy Scouts instilled a sense of patriotism in me for the "Red, White, and Blue," "The Star-Spangled Banner," "America the Beautiful," and "Home on the Range." It also made me scornful of feeding pigs and cleaning pigpens. It made me yearn for a life beyond collecting buta kau-kau pig slops. I took my agitation out on the pigs; I kicked them whenever Otōsan wasn't around.

Remember how I would hide low beside you in our buta kau-kau truck as we drove through town, Otōsan? Or how I would look around, praying that none of my Naichi friends would see me, before joining you to pick up the buta kau-kau from the restaurants? Surely, you must have noticed. Why didn't you tell me, Otōsan, that there was nothing wrong with gathering pig slops? That it was honest work?

But again, Otōsan, how could you? You had more pressing problems. You always did. How could you have known of my sudden rise in society—that the fathers of my friends were schoolteachers, insurance salesmen, librarians, and office workers? They were big-shot Naichis—not Okinawan pig raisers!

By this time, of course, your number-one son was attending Waseda University, the Harvard of Japan. You had gotten into debt, not just from sending him there, but also because your business was not as good as you had hoped it would be. No, Otōsan, I shouldn't have expected you to understand what I was going through. I shouldn't have expected you to talk to me the way my friends' fathers talked to them.

The only time you spoke to me was when you were scolding me: "Hiroshi! Go feed the pigs! Hiroshi! Go wash the pigpens!" And what I really wanted, Otōsan, was to be with my friends who went to the library and read books, who repeated stories from the hundreds of books they read and sounded as though they were making up these stories.

You and I—we never sat down and discussed anything, did we, Otōsan? There was, of course, the language barrier. My Japanese was bad and I couldn't speak Okinawan; your English was limited and you couldn't explain much in Japanese. But surely you could have at least told me—in pidgin English—that "growing up" is never easy. That, for some, it is very painful.

I knew very little, if anything, of your own boyhood, Otōsan, your home in Ginoza Village, your father and mother, your brothers and sisters. And I knew absolutely nothing about Okāsan. She always chose not to talk about herself and her family. Why? Even if you and Okāsan did not want to be reminded of your harsh, poverty-stricken days back in Okinawa, it was not enough for either of you to just tell us, "We were very poor…"

Otōsan and Okāsan still belonged in many ways to the old country. Once, when Okāsan was deliriously ill and her fever rose alarmingly, Otōsan sought the help of an Okinawan healer. The healer rubbed her back vigorously with the bark of a banana tree, then commenced to flick his sharp razor blade against her back. Okāsan's back oozed with blood, which presumably was the bad blood that was causing her fever. Okāsan's fever subsided, and Otōsan was forever grateful to the healer. But when he learned of aspirin later on, he stopped seeking the healer's help.

There was yet another kind of healer to whom Otōsan took Okāsan when she was experiencing excruciating headaches. He was an Okinawan psychologist, presumably with a degree from a Yambaru village school of hard knocks. He rang bells and went into spiritual trances for Okāsan's recovery. When Okāsan's headaches persisted, Otōsan took her to another Okinawan psychologist, who suggested that she go on a special duck-soup diet. The ringing of bells and the special duck-soup diet having failed to alleviate Okāsan's headaches, Otōsan desperately sought help from outsiders. One of them was his Portuguese drinking friend, who suggested that Okāsan see an eye doctor. Skeptical but nevertheless heeding his friend's advice, Otōsan took Okāsan to see the town's only optometrist, a young Chinese man. When the optometrist tested her eyes and then fitted her with glasses, Okāsan's headaches immediately disappeared. Otōsan then mentioned the difficulty he was having with his own vision. The optometrist took off Otōsan's old glasses and wiped them clean. My parents walked out of the clinic with a much better perspective on the world around them.

Although Otōsan and I were oceans apart in thoughts and perceptions, we were quite similar in many other respects. I would like to believe that neither Otōsan nor I was really wooden headed, but there is no denying that our being adamant, uncompromising, and hard-headed hurt our deteriorating father-son relationship. We may have marched to the beat of the same drummer, but we headed in opposite directions.

As I grew older, and perhaps smarter, and the beat of the drummer became louder and clearer, I would discover that Otōsan and I had actually been marching in the same direction. Only, I had always been paces behind him. When the beat became gentler and calmer, and Otōsan began to take his last few steps into the waning sunlight, it would be too late for me to acknowledge that many of his words of wisdom still rang in my ears.

Yes, Otōsan, like you always said, "You will have to learn the hard way." What disturbs me now, Otōsan, is not that I had to go on a long, aimless march before learning to march with everyone else, but that I caused you and Okāsan so much trouble. Sometimes one must be dumped into a pile of manure before one can smell it. And, Otōsan, I had my share of dumpings: was caught gambling a number of times, became an alcoholic at a young age, was kicked out of high school, went to jail, ended up in the stockade while in the army. Oh, yes, the smell of manure, when you are neck high in it, can be awful.

Since I hardly knew anything about you and Okāsan, I went to live in Okinawa for a year. I was living in New York City then, and when the chance to work in Okinawa came along, I jumped at it. You and Okāsan were already gone, and I was obsessed: I had to know more about you two. I was out of college by then, and being a little smarter than when I left home, I was becoming proud of my Okinawan-ness. That's another thing, Otōsan. I finished college. Yeah, me: your no-good jackass boy who was going to end up a bum, a *furoshonen*, a gambler.

I visited Ginoza Village, where you had been born, a number of times. I met your sister, who was quite old. She spoke only Okinawan. Not a single word of Nihongo. But, as she held my hand and cried, talking about you, I shared her grief. Words, at that moment, were hardly necessary. We were family.

I visited your brothers, Uncle Seikon and Uncle Seiyei, occasionally. Since both of them had lived in Hawaii, I had no trouble understanding them. They spoke good pidgin English. Poor Uncle Seiyei. His life seemed full of heartaches and setbacks. He had remarried after returning to Okinawa and was apparently happy. Then came the war. I really don't know if he had been in the Japanese army; I didn't ask him. He was, nevertheless, captured by the American forces and ended up a POW in Hawaii, remember? When you heard through the Okinawan grapevine that your brother was a POW in Pearl Harbor, you quickly caught a plane and went to visit him.

Did I ever tell you? A Naichi friend of mine was one of Uncle Seiyei's guards. When I first visited Uncle Seiyei, he said, "Because the guard was your friend, I was treated especially good. Your friend always gave me cigarettes, candy, and extra food. And, I was free to do almost anything I wanted to do."

What I did not tell Uncle Seiyei was that I, too, once guarded Okinawan POWs. I did not tell Otōsan about it either. But, then, Otōsan and I hardly spoke to each other when I returned home from the army. He would always yell, *"Baka!"* and walk away whenever I told him that Japan had lost the war.

I was stationed at Kilauea Military Camp on the Big Island of Hawaii during my first six months in the army. KMC was a rest camp for army personnel, and most of the chores were done by the hundreds of Okinawan POWs who were incarcerated in an adjoining camp. At first, I considered the POWs enemy soldiers and remained aloof, even though the war was already over. When I learned that most, if not all, of the POWs were civilians who had been indiscriminately rounded up by the conquering American forces during the Battle of Okinawa, I viewed them differently. I did not, however, reveal my Okinawan heritage. Disclosing it, I feared, would break the barrier between me, an American soldier on the winning side, and them, who were on the losing side. As long as the POWs considered me a Yamatunchu whose parents came from mainland Japan, I would be able to maintain an air of superiority.

My guard duties included taking a truckload of POWs with a haole driver to clean up an army warehouse near the town of Olaa, several miles away from our camp. I befriended one of the POWs who was affectionately called "Boy-san" by the guards. Boy-san, known for his paintings of snow-capped Mauna Kea overlooking our camp, was only fifteen years old. He had never carried a rifle, let alone fired one, during the Battle of Okinawa. I often took him along to hunt mongoose in the canefields. I shared my carbine rifle with him, and he became quite a good shooter.

After passing through Olaa a couple of times with our truckload of POWs, I realized that the curious people gathered along the roadside were local Uchinanchus. They had somehow discovered that the POWs were their own people. On our way back to camp the third day, the crowd, even bigger then, waved handkerchiefs and called out in Okinawan to the POWs, who, in turn, waved back and called out to the crowd.

The haole driver's eyes met mine. I nodded, and he brought the truck to an abrupt stop. The Uchinanchu women rushed up to the truck, and I could make out that they were inquiring about their families back in devastated Okinawa. Boy-san, sitting up front between the driver and me, kept craning his neck. I opened the door and let him out. The women quickly surrounded him, speaking to him as mothers would to a bewildered son. Some held his hand; others hugged him; some just stood there unable to speak, wiping their eyes.

When Boy-san returned to the truck, he was silent, tears trickling down his face. The driver, I noticed, avoided Boy-san's eyes and started the truck. I discovered that I, too, was avoiding Boy-san's eyes. Our trip back to camp was somber and subdued, unlike our usual drunken, hell-raising singing, laughing, and teasing. As we approached the POW camp gate, Boy-san handed me a ten-dollar bill that one of the women had given him. He asked me to get him a supply of paint brushes, drawing paper, and oil paints from the PX.

I would like to believe that somewhere in Okinawa today a man who had spent a part of his boyhood in a POW camp in Hawaii has enjoyed a measure of success and happiness through his paintings. And, perhaps, remembers a couple of raucous GIs who were not his enemies, but his friends.

In a way, Otōsan, I'm glad I never told you about my guarding Okinawan POWs. You would have scolded me for not inquiring whether any of them were our relatives. What I was even more afraid of was that you would have scolded me for not having released them.

Another period of my army life that I hardly told Otōsan about was the year I spent in Kobe, Japan, as a "Pineapple Soldier" in the Occupation Forces.

When we first marched into Kobe, the Japanese seemed awed to see their fellow Nihon-jins in U.S. Army uniforms. They soon learned that we were Niseis whose country was America. And they, especially the merchants, began greeting us with "Dai Niseis!" or "Honorable Japanese-Americans!"

Before long, we "Pineapple Soldiers" were known as "Baka-Niseis," or crazy, distrustful Niseis. And deservedly so. We flaunted our American-ness on the defeated Japanese and took advantage of them with our limited knowledge of the language. Most of us were only eighteen or nineteen years old, away from home for the first time, and quite rebellious against most things Japanese, presumably because they reminded us of our Japanese schoolteachers who resorted to corporal punishment whenever we misbehaved.

We regarded our fellow Nihon-jins as "gooks," and wondered howdahell these lowly peasants ever thought they could defeat mighty America. We blackmarketed cigarettes and PX goods with the merchants, and were proud that we outsmarted them in the transactions. We ordered the policemen to stop traffic and walked leisurely across busy intersections. We did these things, and much more, as "Dai Niseis" during our Occupation days in the homeland of our parents.

Just before leaving Okinawa, Otōsan, I went to say goodbye to all our relatives. I gave what little money I could afford to some and most of my clothes, including old shoes, to others. I had tried to locate members of Okāsan's family before, but was unsuccessful. Finally, I located Okāsan's half-brother in Katena Village. He and his family had relocated from the Philippines and were struggling, like everyone else, to eke out a living. Okāsan's half-brother, his attractive daughter, and I spent the day on the cool porch of their thatch-roofed home enjoying our limited conversation. He and I got drunk on the gallon of sake I brought and eventually ended up singing old Okinawan songs I remembered you singing when you were

Boat

❖

*With a flag made of chiyogami (handmade,
printed Japanese paper), this toy boat at first does not
appear to be uniquely Ryukyuan; however, the colors
and designs are distinctive. Another type of Okinawan
toy boat is made of leaves from the kuba (fan palm).
The Ryukyuan toy yanbarushin, a third type of
Okinawan boat, is cherished by collectors
in mainland Japan.*

*Wood.
Woodblock print by Ozaki Seiji.*

feeling no pain after a hard day's work. Verbal communication, by then, was not necessary. We were family.

Saying goodbye to Uncle Seiyei was quite painful. He and his family were living in a shack near an American air force base, and when I told him that I was leaving, he opened a bottle of beer. We shared it ceremoniously. Months earlier, Uncle had asked me for a loan so he could buy a truck and start a trucking business, and I had refused him. Now, I was leaving. I could only hope that he believed me when I said I would be needing whatever savings I had to continue my education in America. Which I did.

You will be glad to know, Otōsan, that Uncle Seiyei, your only living brother, has done quite well for himself since I last saw him. He and his wife now live in a big home in Naha, and his son, a bank executive, is providing them with much-deserved luxuries.

As a matter of fact, Otōsan, the Uchina of old that you and Okāsan left is gone. Most of the Uchinanchus back there are doing quite well. Even the Yambaras in your village. They no longer live in grass-thatched shacks, but in concrete houses with indoor bathrooms. Relatives from America who visit them with envelopes containing money are now reciprocated with envelopes containing even bigger sums. It won't be long before our Okinawan relatives will be sending us their old shoes.

An Okinawan Nisei friend of mine whose father you knew, Otōsan, kept refusing to go to Okinawa to settle the estate of his grandparents. He was the chonan—the oldest boy of the oldest boy in his clan. He suspected that his relatives wanted him there so they could "bum some money out of him." Out of respect for his late father, however, he finally decided to go. He was willing to give his "starving" relatives whatever few dollars he was taking along with him.

When my friend got to Okinawa, he was flabbergasted. His cousins were doctors and businessmen who owned big buildings in Naha. At a family council, my friend kept hearing about land, buildings, and money belonging to their clan. He could not, however, figure out what his share would be. (His Japanese is worse than mine, Otōsan.) Finally, unable to take the suspense any longer, my friend turned to one of his cousins who spoke a little English and whispered, "How many Toyotas we talking about anyway?" When his cousin took out a calculator and figured yen in relation to Toyotas, my friend choked on his sushi and andagi. Fifty Toyotas!

Hey, Otōsan, you wouldn't, by chance, own any building or land back in Okinawa, would you? Okay, okay…The only thing you would ever leave for me, you always said, was your liabilities. I might as well tell you, Otōsan… some of the Uchinanchus I met in Okinawa were not…how should I put it? Their morals were not as high as we were always led to believe Uchinanchu morals were. When I mentioned this to Uncle Seiyei, he blamed it on the war and the American Occupation Forces. The Americans, he said, have so much; the Uchinanchus so very little. And the "have-nots" always revert to stealing when they crave what the "haves" won't share with them.

But I wasn't referring to stealing, Otōsan. I was talking about the morals of the young girls. In bars, dance halls, and back rooms. With white Americans, black Americans, and everyone else. You just can't imagine what went on, Otōsan!

How come I know so much about the young girls in those places? I heard about them!

Hey, Otōsan, I know you would have wanted me to marry a nice Okinawan girl when I was back there. I met a girl I was interested in, but she went off and married a haole soldier. You would have liked her. She was beautiful, a real *churakagi*. And, she was a good girl. She had to be. She came from your village. I know. I know. "You jackass, why did you lose her to a haole soldier!"

I was always too smart to listen to you. Remember? I always knew everything there was to know about life. One of the things I can still remember you telling me is, "As long as you don't change, you'll never be able to find a nice girl who will marry you." And now, whenever I meet a nice girl, I can't help thinking something is wrong with her if she's willing to marry someone like me.

The late-afternoon sun is now setting over the West Maui Mountains. The quiet, lonely shadows cast by the macadamia groves in the meadows are growing darker and longer. The birds singing in the nearby trees have made the vast silence around me seem even deeper, their trills echoing serenely in the night air, their wings fluttering to take them to their nests.

I have to leave now, Otōsan, Okāsan. I have to catch a plane to Honolulu, then another one to California, where I now live.

There are lots of Uchinanchus in California, Otōsan. Most of the Issei Uchinanchus came from Hawaii, but there are some who came directly from Japan. Remember your pioneer hero Kyuzo Toyama, who helped you come to Hawaii? His younger brother, Matasuke, who was in the first group of Okinawan immigrants to Hawaii, settled in California shortly afterwards. Matasuke Toyama, however, was not the first Okinawan in California. There were several ahead of him.

Uchinanchus, whether in Hawaii or California, never seem to lose the warmth and respect they have for each other, Otōsan. In California, the Uchinanchus don't get together as often as they do in Hawaii, but whenever we do, the Okinawan-ness of our parents takes over and we become a family.

Speaking of family, Otōsan, do you know that today families gamble together? Oh, yeah. Instead of going on picnics, they go to a place called Las Vegas and gamble.

And you almost disowned me when you found out I gambled!

If you were still around, Otōsan, I would have liked nothing better than to have taken you to Las Vegas. We would have had some fun together. Not

170   *Mānoa . Voices from Okinawa*

just gambling but sitting down and maybe having a few beers. And talking. About anything. And having a few laughs. Just you and me, Otōsan. You used to laugh at me in your harsh, scornful ways, and I at you in my rebellious ways. But we could never laugh together—not during my troubled days anyway.

When my friend took his father to a Las Vegas nightclub, his father almost had a heart attack. *Akisamiyo!* Those naked haole girls kicking their legs in the air! His father asked to be taken to the show again. Just to make sure it wasn't a bad dream. Those shameless girls! They were really naked!

I would have gotten you a special table up front, Otōsan. With bottles of bubbling champagne. And, maybe, have had one of those shameless girls sitting with you.

Aw, c'mon, Otōsan. Nothing wrong with acting high tone now and then.

Yes, Otōsan, life sure has gotten much better for us Uchinanchus. The younger Uchinanchus are not only doctors, lawyers, and professors, but also great athletes, entertainers, artists, and…even struggling writers. One of the greatest baseball players in Japan was a Hawaii Nisei Uchinanchu. Well, actually, he was only one-half Uchinanchu. Just imagine how much greater he would have been if he were full Uchinanchu, eh, Otōsan!

Remember the politicians on Maui? Except for one or two Naichis, they were always haoles, Portuguese, or Pake Chinese. Not a single Uchinanchu. Well, let me tell you…The most powerful labor union leader who tells these politicians what to do on Maui is an Uchinanchu. Not only that, the son of your close Yambaru friend was once a police commissioner. There's even an Uchinanchu judge now!

But that's nothing, Otōsan. In your day, the governor of Hawaii was appointed by the president of the United States, remember? And he was always a haole. Today…

No, Otōsan, the governor of Hawaii is not an Uchinanchu. But his wife is! That's right, Otōsan. The wife of the governor of Hawaii is an Uchinanchu girl! A real *churakagi*. Lots of class. Very gracious.

The governor? He is a Hawaiian. No, I don't think he is related to your Hawaiian friend, Kahalekai, who lives in Waihee. King Kamehameha? Well, yeah, the governor could be a descendant of the king. He looks strong enough to lift the islands on his shoulders, and he's smart. He's a lawyer and an educator. Of course, the smartest thing he ever did was to marry a nice Uchinanchu girl. Right?

I met them, Otōsan. The First Lady of Hawaii and the Governor himself! Yeah, me, the son of buta kau-kau Kamata Shirota actually shook hands with the governor of Hawaii and his wife. Not bad for a jackass who once bummed around the streets of Honolulu, eh?

No. It had nothing to do with politics. It had something to do with…You won't believe me, Otōsan, but I wrote a book; two books, in fact. All right, don't believe me. How else would I meet people like the governor and his wife? No, you don't meet people like them by getting in trouble. They came to see a play I adapted from my first book. And it was performed in a theater next to the governor's mansion.

The title of the book? I called it *Lucky Come Hawaii*. I know, I know. But I'm your son. What's wrong with me stealing an idea from my own father? No, I didn't shame you. In a way, I think I made you famous. Not only in Hawaii, but among thousands of readers all over the country. So, okay? It's all right that I stole the title of my book and my play from what you used to say? Besides, I think the governor and his wife liked the play. I even autographed the copy of the book they bought. Now you believe me?

I really have to leave now if I'm to catch that plane to Honolulu, Otōsan, Okāsan. It seems I'm always coming back home to Maui, then leaving shortly for somewhere. I will always remember the last summer I saw you, Otōsan. I was leaving for the mainland, to attend college, never realizing that I would not see you again. Your last advice to me was, *"Shikkari shite!"* Do your best! And you, Okāsan, somehow you knew we would never see each other again. Tears filled your eyes, and you remained silent. But then, Okāsan, you were never one to say much. You always felt rather than spoke; you always gave rather than received; and through your quiet dignity and loving care, you shared with us your humility, your inner strength and deep understanding.

There are now four generations of us here in America, Otōsan. I would like to believe that you would have been proud of your grandchildren and great-grandchildren. You might have had difficulty understanding them, and they you, but you would have been able to notice a part of you and Okāsan in them. Some of them are hapa haoles. A few, I'm afraid, look more haole than Nihon-jin. They have blue eyes and blond hair. I know, I know. "Akisamiyo! What's happened?"

But then, Otōsan, you would have accepted them like you accepted all the other strange, unexpected things in America. Before long, you would have loved them because you would have noticed the Okinawan in them, in their beautiful smiles, in their warm laughter, and in their young, tender hearts.

Your great-grandchildren already know a little about their haole great-grandparents. Someday, when they are a little older, they will be told about you and Okāsan. They will be told how you journeyed on a donkey from your Yambaru mountain village to Naha Harbor, then climbed aboard a tiny, overcrowded boat and sailed across turbulent waters for weeks before arriving on the shores of an unknown chain of islands called Hawaii. They will be told of your pioneering spirit, your fortitude, your forbearance— and, above all, your sacrifices.

In time, they will know, Otōsan, Okāsan. They will know that you arrived here with nothing more than a dream that your children and your children's children would have a better life than was offered you back in

Okinawa. They will know that your dream, for the most part, became a reality because you persevered, you endured. They will know that through their own perseverance and endurance, they, too, can prevail over the mountains and oceans they will encounter throughout their lives, because their Okinawan great-grandparents prevailed over higher mountains and deeper oceans after settling on these strange, inhospitable shores.

Sayonara, Otōsan, Okāsan.

An Okinawan Nisei in Hawaii

Among other things, I'm an Okinawan, but if you should ask me what it feels like to be an Okinawan Nisei in Hawaii, I would have a hell of a time answering you. But for sure I can tell you I don't feel inferior or superior to others just because my father and mother came from Okinawa of the Ryukyu Islands. I'm glad, of course, that they did, for that made me "Hawaii-born," with all the rights, opportunities, and responsibilities of an American citizen. I don't feel particularly "different" from other Japanese Americans in the Hawaiian Islands. In fact, I don't feel particularly "Okinawan," if that makes any sense. But it wasn't like that in the beginning. No, it wasn't like that for a long time.

I was born years ago in a banana patch deep in a valley in Kahaluu, Oahu, but I don't recall anything of that time or place. My earliest recollections go back to Maunaloa, Molokai, where I spent most of my childhood. It was there on a pineapple plantation in the 1930s that I first became aware that we were Okinawans, supposedly different from and possibly not even Japanese. There were seven of us children then. One more was to come years later. My father was a truck driver, while my mother stayed home to look after us. I was the eldest, the "number one son," who, together with my sister below me, was supposed to set the example for the rest of the kids.

Enclosed by wind-breaking eucalyptus trees and surrounded by miles of pineapple fields cut up into countless gray-green blocks by dusty red roads, our plantation lay on a high, gentle slope of Maunaloa facing Molokai Channel. Oahu—small, low, and gray—was often visible on the far horizon. A dirt road separated Japanese Camp—a group of dark duplex homes arranged in a square—from much larger Filipino Camp, which housed mostly unmarried male Filipino workers.

On the Japanese Camp side of the main road were the public bathhouse, a general store and bakery run by a Chinese, a barbershop, a pool hall, Chinese bachelor's quarters, a movie house, the plantation stables and garage. On the Filipino Camp side were a small hospital, a restaurant, the plantation office, a post office, a boxing and wrestling arena, a mess hall for single Filipino men, and several houses for the plantation lunas, or foremen, public schoolteachers, and a handful of *haole* office workers. The *haole* plantation manager's home—painted white and surrounded by a spacious green lawn abundantly planted with shrubs and trees and enclosed by a white picket fence—sat on a hill overlooking the two camps. The assistant manager, another white man, lived in a small house below his boss. The public elementary school, a red-roofed bungalow, lay at the foot of a long incline in the middle of pineapple fields. Most of the families in Japanese Camp were Naichi Japanese, but there was a goodly number of Okinawan Japanese and a handful of Chinese, a Korean-Hawaiian family, a Filipino-Hawaiian family, and a Portuguese or Spanish family. Although home visits and dinner invitations were usually limited to their own group, on special occasions like New Year's and weddings and funerals, Naichis and Okinawans alike visited each other's homes and participated in each other's celebrations and mournings.

One afternoon—I've forgotten whether it was a Saturday or a Sunday—my sister below me came home crying. She was ten years old and I was twelve. We converged around her quickly—Mother and the rest of us. Father was not around. "What happened?" we asked. "Somebody give you licking?"

"No!" she cried, not looking at us and wiping her eyes with the back of her hands.

"Then why you crying?" we asked.

"Haru called me one Okinawa Big Rope."

"Whatsa matter with her? She got mad at you?" I said.

"Yeah."

"I never do what she like I do."

"What she like you do?"

"I forget, but I never like do 'em, and she get mad and said, 'Okinawa *ken ken buta kau kau.*' She said Okinawans eat pigs and Okinawans eat pig slop."

"That *pilau* bugger!" I said. "Never mind. We fix her up by and by."

After a while, my sister stopped crying. I asked my mother why Naichi people like Haru teased us. "People who tease you like that don't know what they're talking about," she said. "Naichi people and Okinawans are both Japanese. It's only that Naichi people came from Naichi—from places like Hiroshima and Yamaguchi and other prefectures of the main islands of Japan—while Okinawan people came from Okinawa. That's all. It's nothing. Don't let it bother you."

But I wasn't satisfied. "If they don't know what they're talking about, why are they saying things like that?" I asked in Japanese, which was the language spoken between us and our parents. "If Okinawans are also Japanese, why are they teasing us?"

"It's because they're ignorant. Don't listen to them."

I was still bothered. After supper that day, while we were at the table, sitting on the bare floor with our legs bent under us in the Japanese manner, I asked my father whether Okinawans were Japanese.

"Of course, Okinawans are Japanese," he said. "Okinawa is part of Japan. It was an independent country at one time just like Japan. Okinawa had a king. It was a free country for many years, trading with Japan, Korea, China, and other countries in Southeast Asia. Then later Japan—no, it's more correct to say Satsuma, called Kagoshima today—conquered Okinawa, but Okinawa remained more or less free until the last century, when Japan made it a part of the Japanese Empire. Okinawa-*ken* means Okinawa is one of the many prefectures of Japan, just like Hiroshima-*ken* and Yamaguchi-*ken*. So Okinawans are Japanese. Do you understand?"

My father's explanation surprised and pleased me. Nevertheless, I continued, "But aren't Okinawans different? Their language is different. Even we don't understand you when you and mother and the other older Okinawan folk talk Okinawan. The food is different. The music, the dances, and the clothing. And old Okinawan ladies have tattoos on the back of their hands."

"Wait a minute," my father said. "Tattooing was an old practice before Okinawa became a part of Japan. It's not done anymore. In fact, it's illegal. As for the language, people from other parts of Japan wouldn't understand people from Kumamoto Prefecture, for example, and yet Kumamoto-*ken* people are also Japanese. The food and the clothing and the music and the dances are different, too, in different parts of Japan. The people who say Okinawans are not Japanese don't know the history of Japan and Okinawa. You don't have to listen to them."

My father's explanation made me feel better, but this feeling didn't last very long. From time to time things would happen at school, at play, or in the camp to make me feel uneasy. It wasn't that I didn't believe my father, but it hurt to hear Naichi kids chant, "Okinawa *ken ken buta kau kau*," or "Okinawa Big Rope, eat pig slop," even if it was directed at someone else in my presence. We Okinawan kids, however, retorted with our own chant, "Naichi, Naichi, *chi ga nai, chi ga nai*—no more blood, no more blood."

At its worst, that was all it was when we were kids—"talk fight." There was no punching, kicking, biting, scratching, spitting, throwing stones, bottles, or cans, or shooting slingshots, or stabbing or slashing with a knife. And in a few days, we were friends again, Okinawans and Naichis—until the next "talk fight," which did not happen often.

One day, hoping to make some money by shining shoes, my friend Yone Kaneshiro and I walked barefooted into the single-men's section of Filipino Camp, where most of the plantation workers lived. Our newly made shoeshine boxes dangled from shoulder straps along our sides. Yone and I discovered to our surprise that some married men also lived there. They had left their parents and their wives and children in the Philippine Islands, intending to return after making enough money working in the canefields or pineapple fields of Hawaii, but the years had passed and they were still unable to accumulate the money they had dreamed of making. One of them, now a stout man with short black hair and a very brown pockmarked face, stopped me after giving me a quarter—fifteen cents for shining his old shoes and ten cents as tip.

"What your name?"

"What?" I said, scarcely believing the man's generosity and my good fortune.

"What your name?"

"Keimin."

"I mean what your family name?"

"Ige," I said, wondering what he was up to. "And what your name?"

"Domingo. Domingo Dacoscos. Your father—small man—truck driver, eh? That one your father?"

"Yeah." I noticed that he said "father" with a *p* instead of an *f*.

"Your father—hard worker. Good man—that one."

"I think so," I said. I didn't know what else to say.

Then he said, "You Japanee, boy?"

"Yeah."

"No, you not Japanee."

I began to feel uncomfortable, but I didn't sense any insult in his voice or in his look.

"You Okinawa," the man said.

If he knew that, why did he ask, I wondered.

"How you know?" I said cautiously.

"Because you get big eye and plenny hair on your arm and leg. Okinawa people get big eye and plenny hair all over the body."

He had big eyes too, but his arms and legs were hairless.

"Okinawa people nice looking," he said.

"You think so?" I said, pleased and feeling comfortable again. It was okay to continue talking. "But why you say Okinawa people not Japanee? They the same."

"No, not same. Okinawa people not Japanee. Japanee people get small, slant eye. They no more hair on the body like Okinawa."

"You think Okinawa people no good?" I asked, wondering whether it was the right thing to say.

"No, no. I no say that."

"You think Japanee people no good?"

"No, no. I no say that," he said again. "I onny say they different."

"I think they the same. My father say they the same. You like Okinawa people?"

"Yeah, I like Okinawa people. I get plenny Okinawa friend."

"What about Japanee? You like Japanee people?"

"Yeah, I like Japanee people, too. I get plenny Japanee friends. They nice people, too, just like Okinawa people."

I don't know why I said it, but I said, "Just like Filipino people, eh?"

"Yeah, just like Filipino people. Everybody all same. Get good people and get bad people. Everybody must work so can eat and everybody must rest sometime and sleep nighttime."

"Yeah, everybody the same."

When Yone and I left the man, I was all excited and surprised and happy, thinking about what had happened. Making money was the only thing I had expected to get out of working in Filipino Camp—not learning things about Okinawans and Japanese and Filipinos. Shining shoes in Filipino Camp turned out to be a better idea than I had thought.

At our supper table that night, I tried to look at my father's arms as he sat opposite me, but I couldn't see them under his kimono sleeves. "Father," I said, "do you have hair on your arms?"

My father stopped eating and looked at me. "What?"

"Do you have lots of hair on your arms and legs?"

"Not much," he said, pulling up one of his sleeves.

"How come?" I said. "I have more hair on my arms than you. People say Okinawans have lots of hair on their bodies."

"Maybe that's generally true," he said.

"Mother has more hair than you," I said, and my father and mother both laughed.

"All of you are more like your uncle—my brother—in Honolulu. He has lots of hair on his arms and legs."

"Your father is more like a Chinese," my mother said, surprising me. "He might even have some Chinese blood in him."

"That might be true," my father said, laughing. "There were Chinese on Okinawa long ago."

"Is that so?" I said, wondering how come I didn't know all these interesting things.

My father mentioning Chinese on Okinawa made me suddenly want to see Mr. Yuen, the plantation baker who was Chinese. One day I went to see him. He was sitting in the doorway of his bakery, smoking a cigarette and still wearing his usual white apron as I passed by. It was closing time. I stopped before him, at the foot of the wooden steps. My father and I sometimes sawed and split algaroba wood for his oven on weekends.

"Mr. Yuen, I can talk to you?"

He took his cigarette out of his mouth. "Sure," he said, looking at me with a smile. His forehead was wet with sweat.

"You think my father Japanese?" I said, suddenly feeling foolish for asking him because the answer seemed so obvious. I thought he might laugh at me for asking such a stupid question, but he didn't, and his answer surprised me.

"No. Your papa not Japanee. Him Okinawa. Japanee and Okinawa different," he said. "Long time before, Okinawa no belong to Japan. Okinawa had king. King boss of Okinawa. Okinawa not called Okinawa long time before. Chinese call Okinawa Loo Choo. Chinese and Okinawa good friends for long time. They make business. Some Chinese stay in Okinawa, near castle town where king stay. And some Okinawan people stay in China."

"Yeah? This true?" I said, amazed and delighted.

"Yeah. All this true," he said. "Okinawa and China friends for long, long time. Maybe your papa get little bit Chinese blood. Him no more hair. Just like Chinese. Just like me. How come you get plenty hair?" he said, taking hold of my arm, rubbing it, and gently pulling the hair on it. "I think so your papa Chinese and you Okinawan," he said, laughing and letting go of my arm.

He got up, went inside, and returned with two white paper boxes in his hands. "Here, Ige Boy," he said. "This apple pie. You take. You eat with Papa and Mama and brothers and sisters. Tell Papa and Mama Yuen give you this."

I was overjoyed. Pies! What a good man! And so smart. I went up the steps quickly, took the pies, and thanked him for them and for his story and hurried home, urged on by the smell and the warmth of the pies in my hands, and feeling good about the story of the Okinawa Kingdom and the China Empire.

My father and mother shocked us at supper one day when they told us that they had decided to move to Oahu, to Honolulu. My brothers and sisters and I cried out in dismay. We didn't want to move from Maunaloa and leave all our friends. My father and mother sounded kind, saying that they understood how we felt, but after thinking things over they thought that the best thing to do for all of us was to go to a new place and make another start where jobs and educational opportunities were much better. My father said that we had to start thinking about high school and even college pretty soon and that for these things Honolulu was a much better place. We protested in vain. Then I asked my father what he was going to do in Honolulu, and he shocked us a second time.

"Raise pigs," he said and laughed.

"What!" we cried. "Raise pigs?"

My father and mother were laughing good-naturedly at our disbelief.

"But why raise pigs?" I asked.

"Because that's what I can do," my father said. "I don't have the education or training for anything else."

Even in my dismay, that sounded somehow unsettling and sad and strange to my ears. I couldn't think of my father without the education, training, or capability to do other things.

"Why not raise chickens instead?" I said. "You raise lots of chickens now."

"It's decided already. We have a hog farm waiting for us in Waialae in Honolulu. We'll take over as soon as all the arrangements are made. We can raise chickens, too, later on."

I moaned. "Now it's going to be true when Naichi kids say, 'Okinawa *ken ken buta kau kau!*'"

It was bad enough leaving Molokai and our friends behind, but to have *this* to look forward to! "If the Naichi kids tease us now, what can we say, what can we do?"

"You don't have to say or do anything with ignorant people," my father said. "Stay away from them. Just mind your own business, do your own work, and study hard."

Late one dark night in January 1938, one of my father's Okinawan friends drove us on his truck along the several miles of dusty dirt road winding down from Maunaloa to the wooden wharf in Kolo. From there we boarded a small motorboat, which took us farther out to sea, where the interisland steamship *Waialeale* lay waiting in deep water. We were lifted by pineapple skip onto the ship's deck and slept there through the night, covering ourselves with the blankets provided us by the ship's crew. Early the next morning we arrived in the calm, green waters of Honolulu Harbor and Aloha Tower. When we got off the ship, we found that an uncle, my father's brother who had once visited us on Molokai, was already waiting for us. He drove us on his panel truck through downtown Honolulu, already busy with people and traffic, past stores and office buildings several stories high, and through tree-lined streets and residential districts until we came to a farming area called Waialae. My uncle turned off the main street and drove us over a dusty, bumpy dirt road to our destination.

My heart sank not at the sight of our relatives' ancient two-story home, so weather-beaten that no trace of paint remained; not at the rocky road; but at the penetrating stench of pigpens and hogwash that attacked our nostrils. The stench was inescapable. It was everywhere. Only a stiff wind blowing from a direction other than the pigpens brought temporary relief from the terrible odor. Built of concrete walls, floors, and walkways, with a rusting corrugated iron roof slanting in opposite directions, the pigpens sprawled out before our relatives' home. A few small chicken coops and several piles of firewood and empty wooden boxes stood along the sides of the road. Grass and thorny algaroba trees grew in the back of the place despite the rockiness of the land. We all got off the truck and followed our uncle into the old building. I wanted to run inside to get away from the awful smell, but it was no better inside. Sitting on the matted floor in the kitchen and having our first breakfast in Honolulu was like having breakfast in a sea of hogwash. Was this the way Okinawans lived, I wondered.

Within a few weeks we moved to our own hog farm along Kalanianaole Highway. My routine now was to get up at four o'clock every morning with my father and ride out in our old pick-up truck to collect slop from homes and restaurants all over Honolulu, return home, have breakfast, feed the pigs, wash as many of the pigs and pigpens as possible before going to public school, go to Japanese-language school after English school, and then return home for more work on the hog farm. It was hard, dirty, stinking, and humiliating work, but what was worst was the thought that now I was a perfect target for any Naichi boy or girl wanting to tease me, "Okinawa *ken ken buta kau kau.*"

But surprisingly, no one teased me in the way I had expected—not at public school, at the Japanese-language school, in Waialae, or in the streets of Honolulu. I did pretty well academically in both the public schools and the Japanese-language school, holding class and student government positions in both places; and more than held my own in baseball, football, running, wrestling, and *kendo,* or Japanese fencing. And from the first day of school, I had no trouble getting along with Naichi and Okinawan boys and girls or with those who were Chinese, Korean, Filipino, Portuguese, Puerto Rican, Hawaiian, *haole,* or of mixed blood.

In spite of all this, however, I felt keenly uncomfortable—until some time after graduating from high school—about collecting pig slop and emptying and washing five-gallon cans and restaurant garbage barrels around our pick-up truck in the streets of Honolulu. It was strange for me to feel this way since nobody teased me or my brothers and sisters anymore; and I learned that there were some Naichi families that were also raising pigs, which was a big surprise to me. Two of my Naichi friends even asked me to let them work with us so that through the heavy farm work, they could build up the muscles of their bodies. My parents got a big kick out of that and thought that they were wonderful boys. During the several weekends that my friends helped us feed and wash the pigs and clean the pens, I felt as close to them as if they were my brothers.

And yet I couldn't get rid of a feeling of shame deep inside of me because it was undeniably true that we were Okinawans and that we were raising pigs. I couldn't erase from my mind the picture of some people holding their noses and screwing up their faces with a look of disgust as they walked past us dumping slop into the barrels on our pick-up truck and washing the slop cans on the sidewalks or in the streets. No matter how good things looked, I knew that at any time in the classroom, on the playground, or anywhere in Honolulu someone knowing who we were and what we did could make nasty or embarrassing comments about us.

Two things happened during my intermediate-school years that reinforced this truth. One year we had a new student from Okinawa in our ninth-grade class in Japanese school. He had large dark eyes and plenty of hair on his arms and legs. The teacher asked him to stand and read aloud from his reader. Much to my embarrassment, the new student began reading in the sing-song fashion attributed to Okinawans. Afraid that someone might make an insulting remark about Okinawans, I could hardly wait until he had finished reading; but just as I had feared, a voice several seats away from me said softly, "Him from Okinawa," in the middle of his reading. I turned toward the voice and saw one of my Naichi friends grinning all by himself, as he often did even when nothing was funny to the rest of us. After all these years, I notice that he still has this habit. We're still good friends, but even to this day I don't know if he made that remark and grinned over the new student's sing-song style of reading because it sounded funny to him—as it did to me, too, I must admit—or because he felt superior as a Naichi. It wasn't a deeply painful experience, but I can still remember that it made me wince.

The other incident occurred during my ninth-grade year in public school, a year after my promotion to one of the top three sections in the grade. Most of the students were Naichi Japanese. Some were Chinese, *haole,* or of mixed blood, and one was a Puerto Rican or a Black. I was one of two or three Okinawans in the class. I had finished my lunch early and had returned to the classroom, instead of playing with my friends, to review for a social studies examination. There was no one in the classroom when I went in. Then, after a while, I became aware of two students talking, one male, one female. I didn't pay any attention to them at first until suddenly their voices dropped, and the girl said, "He's Okinawan."

"What! How you know?" the boy asked softly.

"From the name, the eyes, and the hair. Okinawans have plenty hair on the arms and legs."

"No kidding!"

I looked up. The girl stopped talking and grinning when she saw me and looked down. The boy had his back toward me. He turned around to look in the direction that she was looking. The grin on his face disappeared abruptly when he saw me staring at him. Both were Naichi. I looked around the classroom. There were no other students in the room. Embarrassed, hurt, and dismayed with my Naichi friend, I did not say anything. He was an outstanding student who was president of the student body government. Later I learned that his father was a Christian minister and that his older brother was a brilliant student at the university. I admired this classmate for his brains, good looks, sense of humor, popularity, and speaking and writing abilities. He wrote an essay on the theme "What America Means to Me" that won a Territory of Hawaii award and a national commendation. I could not believe that anyone who wrote so eloquently about the meaning of America and democracy, about freedom and individual rights, about racial equality and the dignity of man, about white discrimination against black people in America could look down upon Okinawans in Hawaii. Nothing like this incident happened between us again. We remained on friendly terms, and I still respected his abilities, but something important to me was gone from our relationship.

Throughout this period of childhood and youth on Molokai and Oahu and on into the World War II years and beyond, my parents often had their Okinawan friends and relatives from the old-country village of Kin over for dinner at our house. We, in turn, were frequently invited by them to their dinners and weddings and birthday parties. I loved these occasions, for there were always a lot of laughter, happy conversations, and plenty of good food and soda water, as well as beer, whiskey, and *sake*, the Japanese rice wine. The language spoken was Okinawan, though some Japanese was also spoken, and sometimes someone would use a few commonly heard English and Hawaiian words and phrases. In moments like this, the world I lived in was Okinawan, but I did not feel that I was a real part of that world because I didn't know the language. I didn't know what people were talking about, what they were laughing about, mad about, sad about, and serious about. When we were kids, we used to ask our parents to teach us their language, but for some reason they declined, saying that it was enough for us to learn English and Japanese. As a result, my brothers and sisters and I never learned to understand or speak Okinawan. Sure, we knew a few scattered words and phrases, but I'm afraid these probably created more confusion and misunderstanding than intelligence because we had to guess at what our parents were saying. So while I loved the melody and rhythm of Okinawan music and the gracefulness and liveliness of the dances, I didn't know what the songs and dances were all about. It was as if, beyond a level of acquaintanceship between us, our parents and we were strangers in our own home.

But now that I'm a grown man with a family of my own, and I know much more about life and things Okinawan and Japanese than I did before, I feel that the distance between my parents and me has been greatly reduced. I only regret that they didn't see fit to share their language and more of their personal and family background with us when we kids were all growing up. I have a feeling that if they had done that, we all might have been more understanding, more forgiving, and much closer than we were.

The Japanese attack on Pearl Harbor on December 7, 1941, interrupted my high school years and, of course, made enemies of Japan, the birthplace of my alien parents, and the United States, the land of my birth. From the local Okinawan point of view, to be Japanese was nothing to brag about now. The Naichis couldn't very well look down upon us publicly. If they did, we could say, if we wanted to, "You damn Japs!" And if they said, "You're Japs, too!" we could say, "No, we're not. We're Okinawans, like

Straw Horse

---- ⚜ ----

*This horse figure, made principally of straw
and tree bark, captures the unique character-
istics of the Ryukyuan breed of small horses.
The artistry and craftsmanship are particularly fine.
In many other regions of Japan, horse and cow figures
are made out of straw and often used in religious
rituals to bring happiness to children. After the
rituals, the straw figures are given as toys.*

*Straw.
Woodblock print by Ozaki Seiji.*

you always said." But in fact, the Okinawan-Naichi thing was not the big problem anymore, if it ever was. It didn't matter whether we were Okinawan or Naichi. We were all Japanese as far as the rest of the country was concerned. We were all in the same boat. The big problem now was the Japanese-American relationship. Could the Japanese in Hawaii and the other parts of the United States be trusted, or would they be disloyal and side with Japan? The answer on the Mainland was that the Japanese in America could not be trusted. Those in California, Oregon, and Washington were removed from their homes and farms and businesses, and forced into makeshift relocation camps surrounded by barbed wire and guarded by armed soldiers. The answer in Hawaii was that the Japanese—both aliens and citizens—could be trusted. This decision in Hawaii had a calming effect on me and removed most of the nervous uncertainty I felt about our place in the larger community, though I was disturbed by the action against the Japanese on the West Coast.

But it was the blood, guts, and heroism of the 100th Infantry Battalion and the 442nd Regimental Combat Team on the battlefields of Italy and France that allayed, once and for all, the suspicion that the Japanese in the United States were disloyal. These things also gave me a powerful basis for pride and confidence in myself as a Japanese and an American that was not to be shaken again. When the fighting of the Hawaii Nisei on the European front was first reported in our local newspapers, I remember I used to hurry into the privacy of my upstairs study room to read the papers. I didn't want the rest of the family to see the tears of pride and joy that flowed from my eyes or notice that powerful emotions shook my body and squeezed out sobs from somewhere deep inside of me.

At Ohio State University, the many swimming victories of Hawaii-born Keo Nakama in national meets and the football and baseball glories of Wally Yonamine as a high school and professional athlete in Hawaii and Japan filled me with similar pride and happiness. Waves of gladness surged through me when people said of Nakama and Yonamine, "Them guys Okinawans, you know!"

And yet the funny thing was that though I felt confident and secure about being Japanese and American, I didn't quite feel the same way about being Okinawan. The old childhood sense of shame about being Okinawan still persisted in me. It wasn't on the surface all of the time, but it was always ready to show itself when a situation called for it to embarrass me. Strangely, again, it was the same war years that helped me get rid of this hypersensitivity. I recognized that for a long time I did not like to hear or say "Okinawa" or "Okinawan" in public. But during the Battle of Okinawa, toward the end of the war in the Pacific, when American airplanes and warships began to bombard the island with a continuous barrage of bombs and shells and it was mentioned everyday by newspaper and radio newscasters reporting the air, naval, and land assaults on the island, the destruction and capturing of

Japanese positions, and the casualties on both sides, I could not avoid hearing "Okinawa" and "Okinawan." In the beginning, I listened nervously to the radio news, somehow expecting to hear the familiar childhood insults against us and, when they didn't come, to hear some new ones. But nothing happened. There were no taunts, no sneers that associated us with pigs and hairiness and big rope. The announcers said "Okinawa" and "Okinawan" objectively—with respect even, I thought—as they would have said "Hawaiian" or "American." After a while, I noticed that I grew less nervous the more I heard the announcers say the words referring to my ethnicity; in fact, I found myself looking forward to hearing them because I discovered that I was growing stronger and more confident as well. Then one day, I found that I could say these words aloud myself without any feeling of discomfort anymore.

I think it is largely true that the visible success of the Okinawans in Hawaii following the traditional success pattern of immigrants to the United States came after the World War II years, but looking back now nearly thirty-five years after the end of that war, I can say that the war years were the turning point for me as an Okinawan, a Japanese, and an American. For me there is nothing in any one of these parts anymore that is in insolvable conflict with another part, or with the perception I have of myself additionally as a citizen of Hawaii and of the world. Rather than seeing these elements as conflicting parts of me, I see them as enriching and strengthening me in coping with life by providing me with otherwise unavailable choices from three or four cultures. I accept, respect, value, and enjoy each of these parts of me. Immeasurably helpful in this outcome has been a lifetime of fraternization and integration in the imperfect Melting Pot of Hawaii and the nation.

Sparrows of Angel Island: The Experience of a Young Japanese Prisoner of War

The barracks were filled with the bright morning sun. I'd been awake for a while but stayed in bed simply because the white linen sheets felt so clean and pleasant. The room was large and had a high ceiling, and its big windows looked out on the cobalt-blue waters of the bay. Small waves glittered in the sun, and a huge bridge spanned the expanse of water. The Golden Gate Bridge looked mighty and powerful, like America itself.

When the *ding, ding, ding* of a metal triangle sounded outside, we quickly washed and dressed and briskly walked the fifty yards across the compound to a building in the corner. Pfc. Suzuki, an American soldier in his early twenties, stood watching us outside the entrance to the mess hall. When we were all assembled, he said curtly, "Every day from now on, when the triangle sounds at 8 A.M., 12 noon, and 4 P.M. you are to line up here. All of you will take turns on KP duty for a week at a time."

Apart from the KP duty, it was very much like what we had already experienced at the prisoner-of-war camp in Honouliuli, on the Hawaiian island of Oʻahu. The mess hall was simple but very clean. Inside, we picked up a tray and stepped up to a counter where a big Caucasian slapped food onto our tray as we passed by. We served ourselves toast and milk or coffee and sat wherever we wanted. Here on Angel Island the food was a little simpler than at Honouliuli, but it was still good: toast, jam, butter, fried eggs, bacon, cereal, milk, and coffee. That was our first breakfast.

Except for the wire fence around the compound and watchtowers on the corners, American POW camps were not at all like the prison I had been expecting and fearing.

We were all surviving members of the Iron and Blood Loyalist Troop, an impressive name for an unimpressive group of middle-school boys who had volunteered to serve in a support capacity in the Japanese military during the Battle of Okinawa in 1945. I had been a fourth-year student at Naha Commercial Middle School and was to graduate a year early, in March of 1945, because the required five years had been reduced to four. Like most of the capital city of Naha, our school had been reduced to ashes by the American air raid on October 10, 1944, and there was no way to continue schooling. Under these conditions, going to school meant serving in a so-called volunteer labor corps, which built runways and fortifications and dug miles and miles of trenches under the searing Okinawan sun.

In early 1945, with American squadrons just off the coast of Okinawa, air raids became more frequent and intense. At the urging of the government, thousands and thousands of islanders, mostly those too old or too young to be useful to the military, were evacuated by ship to the Japanese mainland in the north, or to Taiwan in the south. Some of those ships were torpedoed by American submarines, and although the military tried to suppress the news, it leaked out through the handfuls of survivors, terrifying the families that remained in Okinawa and contributing to the frenzy created by the war.

One day in late February, shortly before the American invasion of Okinawa, seniors and juniors at our school were told to report to the former site of Shuri Castle—destroyed in the bombing—high on the hill overlooking the blue waters of the East China Sea. It was eight o'clock in the morning. As we stood tensely waiting for our teachers and principal, brisk winter sea breezes stroked our cheeks and we gazed at the charred city of Naha, the once-beautiful capital of Okinawa Prefecture. Nothing was standing or moving. Empty streets crisscrossed the burned sites. We stood at attention when our principal, Mr. Nakasato, appeared. A uniformed, trimly outfitted Japanese army officer wearing a *samurai* sword at his waist was beside him.

At first the officer's speech wasn't much different from many other pep talks we had had to listen to in those tense days just before the American invasion of Okinawa on April 1, 1945. He spoke of the sacred mission of Japan in East Asia, of the insolent Americans and British who dared to thwart it, and of the duty of all of us to crush the foreigners' sinister designs and assuage the anxieties of our Emperor. Concluding his speech, he took a deep breath and shouted, "Those who want to volunteer to fight together at this most critical time of our country, take one step forward!" In precise unison, without even taking a breath, we boldly stepped forward and stood at attention. And that was how we became the Iron and Blood Loyalist Troop.

After stillness reigned on the battlefield of Okinawa, I wondered why I took that step without a second's hesitation. I knew in my heart that I had no strong feelings of loyalty to the Emperor—he was too far away to seem real. But perhaps no other choice was even thinkable. Since December 7, 1941—the day of the attack on Pearl Harbor—we had been prepared for battle. For hours, we sat in Zen meditation to build our Japanese spirit, and we were constantly subjected to intense drills and lectures. *To die on the battlefield is to live in eternal justice. Self-annihilation for the sake of Japan is our highest moral duty. Death in battle and enshrinement in the Yasukuni Temple in Tokyo! Honor! Glory!* We were drunk on the mysteries of such slogans. We believed nothing else.

After our first breakfast on Angel Island, Pfc. Suzuki took me to the kitchen and told the mess sergeant, the big Caucasian who had served us, "This boy speaks some English."

"Oh, you speako English? You wanna be KP honcho?"

"Yes, sir. Thank you, sir."

"OK. You come here. Every morning. Five-thirty. By and by, I show you what you do."

Kitchen duty started right away. Pfc. Suzuki went out and came back with five boys, who also were put on KP duty. Since that was the first morning, there was not much for us to do except wash the dishes and plates and sweep and mop the mess-hall floor. My job was to translate for the mess sergeant and to help him by getting the boys to do such chores as peel potatoes or chop cabbage. I felt proud and willing because I had been the only one out of fifty-three to be selected. Among the senior students, I knew the most English, perhaps because I had attended a commercial middle school where English was a requirement, even during the war. In other schools, such as teacher-training schools, English was regarded as the language of the enemy and the requirement to learn it had been abolished. I also was the only one who had a copy of *Sanseido's Japanese-English Dictionary*, which I had purchased with dollar scrip from the store in the POW camp in Hawai'i. I therefore had picked up some basic vocabulary words and phrases; still, I was keenly aware of the inadequacy of my vocabulary, so I studied whenever I had a chance. I often stayed at the mess hall after lunch and studied there because it was quiet. One day, the sergeant saw me studying and said, "Hey, Honcho, you like study English? I give you good book." And he pulled out a small pocket-sized publication of the U.S. army. It was a book containing popular and useful phrases of daily conversation in both English and Japanese and was very helpful to me because my only other text was the dictionary, which had individual vocabulary entries but no phrases. I thanked the sergeant and studied harder.

The sergeant was a good man. We never found out his name, so we simply called him "Sergeant." He was the only American besides Pfc. Suzuki we came into contact with. I could not guess a Caucasian's age then, but Sergeant was probably in his thirties or forties. He almost always wore a T-shirt and was a heavyset, genial man who just did his job and left us alone. No one ever saw him lose his temper.

In Honolulu Harbor, we had boarded the U.S. military transport ship that would take us to the mainland. We were put in the prisoners' hold with about two dozen older Japanese men: a civilian labor gang that had served the Japanese military in various sectors of the South Pacific. The rest of the ship was crowded with American soldiers returning home from combat in the Pacific. It was late in the afternoon—probably four or five o'clock—when the ship arrived at its destination. As we stood watching from the deck, the Americans got off and were welcomed into the impatient embraces of their wives, children, parents, and relatives, who apparently had been waiting for hours. The military band on the pier kept playing marches, one after another, for hours and hours, until all the soldiers were off the ship. When the pier was finally empty, we were allowed to go ashore: the fifty-three captured members of the Iron and Blood Loyalist Troop.

At the foot of the gangplank, two trucks and a few military policemen waited for us. The MPs shouted "Hubba, hubba!" at us, and accompanied by armed guards, we climbed into the backs of the trucks. The canvas flaps were drawn over us, and the trucks set off. After about five or ten minutes, we stopped and unloaded at a quarantine station. In one bare room and with big armed guards watching, we all stripped naked and, like cattle, were herded into the shower room. Whitish water, probably some disinfectant solution, sprayed down on us from the ceiling, followed by plain cold water.

Among us was a big guy, the survivor of a battle on an island near Australia. He was as tall and big as many Americans, and he had a tattoo on his upper right arm that read "Ōmasa" in Japanese *kanji* (calligraphy). When we students had boarded the ship in Honolulu and found the members of the labor gang in the same hold with us—this man among them—we were frightened. We figured that they were akin to the *yakuza*—a kind of Japanese mafia—so we stayed away from them. But now, this guy was taking a shower next to me. In a corner of the room, a young American MP kept watch over us. When he saw the tattoo, he must have become curious. He stepped over and touched it—or, I should say, he *tried* to touch it. As soon as the MP's arm came near him, the man yelled in Japanese, "What the hell you trying to do!" He then jumped back, holding his left arm in front to defend himself and his right arm in a posture to strike. We were all surprised, but most surprised was the MP. He just stood there, dumbfounded. Then, just as suddenly, the man turned, grabbed a towel, and walked out of the shower room, drying himself and not looking back. And that was the end of the incident. We were all relieved.

Many Japanese prisoners of war, to conceal their identities and avoid shaming themselves and their families, used fictitious names, often taking the name of a historical character known to their countrymen but not to Americans. In the case of "Ōmasa," we knew that was not his name but rather the name of a hero in popular fiction: a *yakuza* who supposedly lived in the nineteenth century.

After we were all processed at the quarantine station, the Japanese labor gang was piled into a truck that disappeared into the city's twilight. It was the last we saw of them. We climbed into the back of another truck. Again the flaps were pulled down, and we rode through the city not knowing where we were. When the truck stopped, we found ourselves at the far end of a long, deserted railway platform. As we got off the truck, we walked single file between two rows of American MPs with rifles in their right hands and their index fingers on the triggers. No one spoke; the air was tense with the raw hostility coming from the MPs. Frightened, we kept absolutely quiet as we walked between those armed human fences leading us to the train parked far from the center of the station.

After we'd all taken seats on the car, a young Nisei in uniform boarded. He stood at the end of the aisle where he could see all of us, and in faltering Japanese introduced himself as Pfc. Suzuki. He said that he would be our interpreter. Most likely he was assigned to this job simply because he was a second-generation Japanese. His Japanese was no more than basic, but because of his face, his white superiors probably assumed that he could understand the language or that he could get along with Japanese POWs better. We soon found out his fondest Japanese phrases: *Shinpai arimasen* (Don't worry) and *Yoku wakarimasen* (I don't understand well), the latter said with a funny American accent toward the end of the sentence and with a shrug of his shoulders, his two hands thrown up in the air. That was Pfc. Suzuki.

After we got on the train, we simply sat there for a long time. The window shades were down. Bored, we pulled the cords and let the shades jump open. Long ago, when it was still very peaceful on Okinawa, whenever I had seen a large ship at anchor in Naha Harbor, I had felt a vague yearning for the strange land of the West that I had read about in novels. Now, by a curious turn of fate, there on the other side of the window was that strange land of Americans, the world I had read about in *The Adventures of Tom Sawyer, Uncle Tom's Cabin,* and *Rip Van Winkle.* It was a world totally different from the one I had known a few months earlier, while struggling to survive in the wet, muddy, mosquito-infested battlefield of Okinawa. I pressed my face to the windowpane. We all were fascinated.

Then Pfc. Suzuki came around and rudely forced us back to reality. *"Dame desu. Dame desu"* (It's not good), he said. He went around pulling all the shades down himself, perhaps because he didn't know enough Japanese to tell us to do it ourselves. We were very unhappy, but none of us was bold enough to challenge him. As soon as he was gone, however, one of the boys could not resist the temptation to raise the shade a few inches and press his face to the narrow aperture. He was immediately joined by the boys beside him. Seeing them get away with this, soon another boy lifted his shade a little, and then another, and another. After a while Pfc. Suzuki returned, and we sprang away from the windows. Without saying anything, he went around and pulled all the shades down again. After playing this game two or three times, he must have tired of it, or perhaps he concluded that it was harmless. In any case, he overlooked what we were doing as long as the shades were not all the way up.

Of course we had no idea what part of town we were in. We knew only that we were in a railway station at dusk and the lights were coming on. We were simply fascinated, watching through our two-inch-high train windows the crowds of Americans walking hither and thither on the train-station platform.

As soon as the train started moving, Pfc. Suzuki came around distributing boxes of K-rations. They seemed a marvel of American civilization. In those small, compact boxes were delicious American meats, eggs, crackers, butter, cheese, and jam. There were even cigarettes and matches. And the boxes were waxed to be moistureproof. Shredded, they would provide excellent fuel, enabling one to heat the cans they had contained. America was rich enough to feed common soldiers this delicious food? We couldn't help comparing these K-rations to the Japanese army's field rations: a bag of crackers with a few sugar candies. In the humid weather of Okinawa, those crackers had quickly become soft, sticky, and moldy. And each of us had had to carry a sockful of rice. Of all foods, rice is the most inappropriate field ration: not only is it heavy, but preparing it requires water and a fire. Eating our morsels of American civilization, we all felt happy and drowsy. The monotonous sound of rails soon worked its magic, putting us to sleep.

When we woke up to the same *clackety-clack* of the rails, warm sun was shining directly on our faces. The train was going at full speed, and all the window shades were up. We were heading southward, and all around us— left and right, front and back—were endless green prairies. Sometimes, because of the lack of any landmarks, the train seemed immobile and the scenery unchanged. We were simply amazed at the vastness surrounding us the way the ocean waters surround Okinawa. I remembered that it was about forty or fifty miles—a two-day trip—from Naha in the south, where I lived, to Motobu in the north, where many of my relatives lived. Whenever I had visited Motobu, it always took days of planning. Fifty miles is fifty miles, but is that distance the same to Americans?

One of us asked Pfc. Suzuki where we were going. Using his favorite phrase, he replied, *"Yoku wakarimasen."* We figured we were somewhere in Washington, but we weren't quite sure if we were south or southeast.

"We may be heading to Montana," one of our group said.

"What do you mean?"

"There are silver mines in Montana. I studied them in our geography class. We're probably being sent to work in the silver mines."

Suddenly we were depressed. We thought we might be sent deep into the earth to mine silver ore, and once underground, we would never see the light of day for the rest of our lives. And our family and friends would never hear of us again. Even the most optimistic of us agreed that we would most likely be sent to a prison somewhere to work as slaves for ten or fifteen years. After all, slave labor was not new to Americans. They would think nothing of exploiting us. As for our countrymen, they would erase all memory of us because we had disgraced Japan: we were prisoners of war—something worse than being dead.

"If we were going to be slaves," someone asked, "how come the Americans are treating us nice?"

"Stupid! Don't you see that we are now property to Americans?" someone else replied. "Nobody would damage his own property. They want us to be healthy and strong. Otherwise, we would be of no value to them."

That shut up everyone. Till then, we had thought Americans were being good to us, but now we saw that they were feeding us the way we had fed pigs just before we slaughtered them.

While we talked, our train continued to race south across the prairies. After traveling for hours, we would spot a few houses on the horizon, then watch them grow bigger as we approached. Passing them, we would continue to watch as they became small again, finally disappearing beyond the horizon. The train sometimes slowed down when we came to a town, but it seldom stopped. Gradually, we decided we were not being taken to the Montana silver mines. Pfc. Suzuki still wouldn't tell us where we were going, but we had another source of information: billboards and signs along the railroad. Some would be welcome signs and would name towns. Others advertised Coca-Cola and other products and included the names of nearby towns. We traveled all day without stopping.

When we woke the next morning, we were in Oregon. The train was going through a long valley, and there were many small towns along the way. Then, without any warning, the train slowed down and came to a complete stop. Outside the window were a train platform and a few buildings but nothing else, not even a small town. Several railroad employees in uniform went to the end of the train, and we assumed they were loading fuel or water. While we were watching, a Caucasian boy, maybe twelve or thirteen years old, passed by. He was eating a popsicle, and although he saw us, he paid us no attention at all. I was surprised that he was dirty and barefoot—and that he looked poor.

For a long time I couldn't stop thinking about that boy, perhaps because of Japanese attitudes toward the West. Ever since Japan became modernized in the late nineteenth century, Europeans and Americans had been our teachers in everything. It was we who struggled to study their languages and their cultures, not the other way around. Like my parents, I had grown up believing Europeans and Americans were somehow innately superior—and this belief was even stronger now that Japan had lost in its challenge of the West. But then I saw that Caucasian boy, poor and dirty!

After a few minutes our train started on its way. We saw in the distance the gentle Cascade Mountains. We went through the fresh, green Willa - mette Valley, sometimes along the highway and sometimes along the clear, sparkling flow of the Willamette River. We passed slowly through the town of Salem, then Albany, Ashland, and Klamath Falls, before crossing into California. Six years later, in 1951, I would return to beautiful Oregon to attend school in Corvallis and then Eugene. But of course, as a prisoner of war in 1945, I had no idea that I would ever see again the landscape that was passing by in front of me.

We passed the second night on the train traveling through northern California. On the third day, we began to get restless, and Pfc. Suzuki also seemed uncomfortable. Luckily, an hour or two after dark, our train passed through brightly lit sections of San Francisco and came to a full stop at a station near the edge of the water. From a deserted pier, we boarded a ferry that took us across the bay. We were met at the landing, and after a short bus ride, we got out in front of a dormitory. Dead tired, we fell asleep as soon as our heads hit the pillows. Thus began our life on Angel Island. It was summer.

Whenever I think back on those days, I recall the following events most vividly. The first was facing the MPs who met our train when it arrived in San Francisco. They formed two lines about three feet apart, each soldier pressed close to the next, his finger on his trigger. None of them said anything. They just stood there, watching our every movement. And we, barely five feet tall and laden with GI duffel bags on our shoulders, walked submissively between these towering human fences. Death seemed to be in the air. We believed that if any one of us had tripped and fallen, he would have been shot dead on the spot. Beyond these double lines of MPs was the darkness of the pier. The lights of San Francisco flickered in the distance.

Did these Americans really hate us? I wondered. Did they really think that fifty-three small, unarmed schoolboys might break the first line of armed MPs and take on the second? Did they think that we were fanatic *kamikaze* (suicide) troopers? I really don't know, but it seems obvious now that they were as frightened of us as we were of them.

A few months earlier, on Okinawa, the last great battlefield of World War II, I had been a radioman assigned to the headquarters of the Tama 44th Composite Division. Because I was with Division Headquarters, it was unlikely that I would ever go to the front. But by the middle of May, Japan's defense line was being pushed further and further back, till finally the entire Tama Division was thrown into the battle. We marched to the front in the darkness of night. Shortly before dawn, we found out that we had unexpectedly come face-to-face with a massive American force. Our commander, a young cadet, became almost hysterical. He drew his *samurai* sword, waved it high over his head, and ordered us to charge forward, shouting, *"Totsugekiiii! Totsugekiiii!"* We could see him standing there in the light of the explosives and were about to charge when our platoon leader, a veteran of the China War, warned us in a low voice, "If you want to die a dog's death, go. If you don't, stay put here with me." We all stayed and survived. A few weeks later, wounded in the left thigh, I was captured in the area of Komesu Village in southern Okinawa.

Japanese propaganda had told us that Americans were devils and beasts who would do horrible things to captives. Women would be raped and men mutilated before being killed. So when I was captured, I had expected the worst. Instead, the marines took me into their own tent, tended to my wound, and even let me eat and sleep there. Because my English was rudimentary, I did not quite understand what they were saying, but I understood enough to know that they were kind and wanted to help me. They helped others as well. It was hard for me to believe, even though I saw it with my own eyes. Why didn't they torture us as we had been told they would? They could see by my uniform that, at the very least, I had been helping to kill Americans. Why, then, weren't they killing us when they had the chance? Or at least torturing us, their prisoners of war?

The second event that I recall most vividly occurred when we were on the military transport ship during the transfer from Hawai'i to Seattle. We were allowed to go up on deck from down in the holds for an hour once a day, in the early afternoon. The deck was crowded with American soldiers, and with no MPs around, we mingled with them. Soon I became friends with a young lieutenant. We spent many hours together. He listened patiently as I spoke in my broken English, and he talked to me about his hopes and dreams in life. He had been a college student when he joined the army, and he planned to return to school upon discharge. He told me over and over that the United States would never harm us and that the war would come to an end soon; when that happened, he said, I should go to college, perhaps in the United States. Above all, he told me, I should not lose hope. He then gave me a piece of paper with his name and address and asked me to write him after returning home.

The soldiers coming home from battle were friendly, but the ones behind the lines, who never saw us before, were hostile. And in my own heart, though there was fear, there was no hatred. Why? It seems to me that fear and hostility were things we had been taught and therefore were artificial, manufactured. It may also be that when one faces death, he is stripped of all his cultural trappings. Thus freed, he realizes that he hates no one. Indeed, why should he? And he knows the guy at the opposite end of the firing line is someone just like himself. I wonder if, reading this, the young officer who befriended and encouraged me would recognize himself. He was the very first person to plant in my head the idea of going to college in the United States.

The third event also took place while we were crossing the Pacific. The ship was plowing through the rough waves of the dark northern sea near Seattle when suddenly sirens wailed full blast and guns fired in all directions. At first we thought we were under attack by Japan. I raced to the deck, looked up at the skies, and scanned the ocean. The entire ship was shaking violently from the repercussions of so many guns being fired. The Americans were in a frenzy, jumping, shouting, yelling, and shooting their rifles into the air and into the water. One of the soldiers shouted excitedly to me, *"Japan surrendered!"* Not thinking I should keep the news to myself, I tumbled down the steep stairs to the hold, shouting, *"Nihonga kihuku shitazo!"* I shouted and screamed with the excitement of the American soldiers.

I don't know what I was expecting, but the response I received was a wave of moans, then absolutely eerie silence. We all had known it was coming—of all the Japanese, we ought to have known because we were the ones who had fought and lost. But no one wanted to admit Japan's defeat because we were also the ones who should have died defending the nation! By surviving we had failed and brought shame on ourselves, our families, and our nation. And now I had violated the taboo on admitting defeat and failure. The silence was awkward and heavy. A member of the labor gang got up and came over to me. Without really looking at me, he said in a low voice, as if talking to himself, "Just because you speak some English, you've stooped to becoming an American dog. Remember, not all nights are moonlit." He walked away. I was frightened: on some dark night he might push me overboard into the cold, rough waters of the North Pacific, and no one would ever know.

It must have been around August 19, 1945, that we began our brief stay on Angel Island. Life there was quite comfortable. It was cool, not hot and humid as on Okinawa. There was no forced labor. We were fed three good meals a day, assigned clean living quarters, and even given some sports equipment. But one thing was missing: a future. Where were we going from here? What would happen to us?

Back at the Honouliuli POW camp, there had been several thousand prisoners from the Battle of Okinawa. One day I was summoned to the camp office. When I got there, I found others like myself: middle-school boys. A young Caucasian naval officer in a crisp, white uniform stepped up on the platform and spoke to us in fluent Japanese. We didn't know who he was; from what I gathered years later, he most likely was an American born in Japan of missionary parents: he had returned to the United States just before the outbreak of the Pacific war, becoming in 1945 a deputy director of the POW camp in Hawai'i and later a professor at Doshisha University in Kyoto. "With the defeat of Japan, the war will come to an end soon. You boys have done your duties well, and there is nothing to be ashamed of. Although Japan will lose the war, it does not mean the end of Japan. Japan will have to be rebuilt. And in this building of a new Japan, young people will be needed more than ever. So that you will be more useful in building the new Japan, we want to send you to the mainland United States to study English and democracy before you return home. You must be prepared to build a new Japan." To be frank, we were neither happy nor unhappy at this news. After all, we were prisoners of war and we had no choice in the matter. We simply accepted it as an order from the authorities and didn't know whether or not to believe it.

However, once we were settled on Angel Island, some of us started wondering what had happened to the promise of sending us to study English and democracy. One day a few others and I approached Pfc. Suzuki and asked him about it. As usual, he said, *"Yoku wakarimasen."* But we persisted, and at last he said that, though he wasn't sure, he thought the original plan was to send us to Camp McCoy in Wisconsin for an education. The war had ended sooner than expected, however, and now, the urgent business of American occupation of Japan took precedence; we would have to wait until a decision was made. His explanation sounded plausible, and we accepted it.

As time passed and we still were not told our fate, we began to notice problems of morale, particularly among the freshmen. Of the fifty-three of us, most were juniors and sophomores, some were freshmen, and four or five were seniors. In Hawai'i, there had been thousands of Okinawans in the prisoner-of-war camp. It was very much as if a complete community had been transplanted, except that it was all male. Some older men had made facsimiles of the *sanshin* (a three-stringed Okinawan musical instrument) out of tin cans, field-cot poles, and canvas, and often at night someone was playing and singing Okinawan songs. Though it was an unusual life, at least there were enough of us for comfort and friendship. And some of the American kitchen staff were of Okinawan descent and therefore friendly to us.

On Angel Island, however, we felt isolated. Though we were very comfortable, nostalgia and anxiety were overtaking us, particularly the younger students, some of whom were only thirteen. During the day, we had no problem keeping ourselves occupied. We ate three meals, talked with friends, and played games. Pfc. Suzuki had brought us sports equipment, including boxing gloves, and in the afternoon, we would gather in the front yard to play baseball or volleyball. None of us knew how to keep score, but we gave it a try anyway. One afternoon, just out of curiosity, a friend and I put on the gloves to see how they'd feel. When the others gathered around us and encouraged us to fight, we half-jokingly started slugging each other. It was one of the funniest experiences I'd ever had. Because my hands were heavy with the gloves, I could not move them as freely as I could in *karate*. And when I got hit, there was not the sharp pain of fist fighting. Instead, it was a heavy thud that made me dizzy and sent me down. My friends had a hearty laugh, and it was laughter like this that kept up our morale.

After supper, when we all went back to the dormitory, it was too early to go to bed, so we often spent this time in bull sessions. Nearly always, we ended up talking about Okinawan food. Someone would say that the best *soba* (noodles) in Okinawa were at Sankakuya Restaurant in downtown

Naha, to which someone else was sure to reply, No, it had to be at the fish-ermen's market in Yonabaru; yet another guy would recommend the *soba* in Nago in the north. Or someone would avow that the famous Yama-gusuku flat *manju* buns in Shuri were so good that he could eat three in a gulp. We would go on and on almost every night, never tiring of talking about food. But when lights-out came at ten o'clock, we often heard the foghorn blowing in San Francisco Bay. Its two notes, high and low, trailed long over the dark waters of the bay. They sounded sad and forlorn. We couldn't see into the darkness, but we thought that there must be a ship leaving or coming into the bay. If it was leaving, could it be going to Oki-nawa? The thought of a ship going across the Pacific made us homesick.

Late one night I heard muffled sobs coming from the bed of one of the thirteen-year-olds. I put my hand on his blanket and said in a low voice so others could not hear, "Don't cry, you fool. You're making me want to cry, too." The sobbing stopped, and stillness returned to the room. I was only sixteen myself, and there were times when I too wanted to cry, but I knew it was my duty as a senior student to be an example to the younger ones.

Gradually a committee of senior students evolved to make decisions concerning the whole group. We decided to instill some discipline in our ranks and, after some discussion, drew up a schedule:

1. Every morning before breakfast we are to assemble at seven o'clock in the front yard and perform a ceremonial bow in the direction of the Imperial Palace in Tokyo.
2. After breakfast, the entire group will be divided into small units to study under the direction of senior students for one hour.
3. After lunch, when we have to vacate our dormitory room for cleaning, everyone will participate in group sports such as baseball, volleyball, and basketball.

The next morning, we rose early and lined up in the front yard like we used to do in school back in Okinawa. Then the senior student in charge for the week shouted, "Attention! Deepest bow to the Imperial Palace. Bow!" We all bowed deeply in the direction of Tokyo, where the Emperor resided. It felt good to be up early and breathe the fresh morning air. I felt as though we had recovered some of the things we had lost.

One afternoon, Pfc. Suzuki brought us the front page of the *San Fran-cisco Chronicle*. The big headline read GENERAL DOHIBARA CHARGED WITH WAR CRIMES. General Dohibara was the commanding general of the Japan-ese expeditionary forces in northern China. We were shocked when Pfc. Suzuki proceeded to read the article aloud, but when he got carried away in his condemnation of General Dohibara, one of the senior students became enraged. The holder of a black belt in *judo*, the student grabbed Pfc. Suzuki by the collar and shouted in Japanese, "*How dare you spread lies about Gen-eral Dohibara!*"

Unable to extricate himself from the *judo* hold, Pfc. Suzuki pleaded—more than ordered—"Let me go! Let me go!" We stood close by, afraid he might pass out. We begged our *judo* friend to let him go. Finally he did. After that, Pfc. Suzuki stayed away for about a week. He was gentler when he came back, and never talked to us about Japanese war criminals again.

And in that manner, time passed. Days became weeks, weeks grew into months. But of all my memories of my stay there, the most unforgettable is the sparrows of Angel Island.

One afternoon, after mess-hall duty, I was sitting by myself on the grass overlooking a gentle slope outside the wire fence surrounding our camp. The slope was sparsely dotted with trees, and the soft, warm sunlight shone through the bright-green leaves. Beyond the slope was the shore of San Francisco Bay, where porpoises were swimming in a line. One by one they dived and came up for air. Their fat, round backs popped up and down in the glittering blue water.

Then, I saw a dozen or so sparrows pecking at the grass on a patch beyond the fence, probably looking for insects. Without thinking, I picked up a small pebble and threw it over the fence. The pebble landed in the middle of the sparrows, rolled a little, and stopped. When I threw the pebble, I had fully expected the sparrows to fly away at once. Instead, they quickly came together, looking for the pebble. Since it was a pebble just like any other, they couldn't find it. So, after pecking here and there a few seconds, they scattered and resumed looking for insects in the grass. Something unbelievable had happened.

All my life in Okinawa—on my way home from school, while with my friends, or out on the street playing—whenever I saw sparrows, I threw pebbles at them. Not really to harm them. Hitting a bird would have taken greater skill than a boy my age possessed. I did it simply to see them quickly fly away in all directions, to become smaller and smaller, and then to disappear in the sky. Many times, the sparrows would fly away when I did no more than make the motion of throwing a pebble. Of course, during the Battle of Okinawa, I hadn't thought of such games. But now, relaxed on the grass, I had thrown the pebble. Why, I wondered, did these sparrows of Angel Island not fly away? They behaved as if I had thrown them some food. Though not a Christian, I suddenly remembered a verse from the Bible: *Which of you, if his son asks for bread, will give him a stone?* Suddenly I realized that these birds were accustomed to being treated kindly. When the pebble I threw landed in their midst, they thought it was a piece of bread, so they came to eat. I then felt ashamed of what I had done. From then on, I took leftover bread from the mess hall and fed it to the sparrows every day. Soon they came to recognize me and to gather near the fence whenever I approached. I have never thrown a pebble at birds or other animals since that day.

This encounter with the sparrows of Angel Island was the beginning of my love for America and its people. It was perhaps a simple sentiment: a recognition that the people who had been kind to these little animals couldn't be bad. After I returned home to Okinawa, I couldn't forget those small birds and the people I had never met, the ones who had been kind to the birds. When I later decided to go to college, I chose the United States, and went to Oregon.

The summer of 1945 became fall, and fall became winter. As the end of the year approached, I grew apprehensive. The holiday season would be particularly tough for us because of memories of happy times spent with friends and family. We had been trying our best to fill the days without talking too much about our future.

By the middle of December, it was chilly and the wind was brisk. One day right after lunch, I was polishing a big stove in the mess hall when Pfc. Suzuki came in the front door. He was out of breath. He looked around, so I called from behind the stove, "Are you looking for me? I'm here."

"Hey, Mike, I've got big news for you. You boys are going home. The day after tomorrow. Go tell everyone!"

I dropped my brush right there and ran outside. I stood on the porch and shouted for everyone to hear: "We are going home! Going home the day after tomorrow!"

Everyone in the yard stopped for a second, then burst out shouting, "Going home! Going home! Going home!" We raced to the dormitory. "We're going home. The day after tomorrow!" It was almost pandemonium, but actually there was nothing to do: our possessions were already in our duffel bags; all we needed to do was to pick them up and walk out the door.

That night we could hardly sleep. We talked and talked till late. We talked about what we might find in Okinawa. We had received no information about what had happened back home since the end of the battle. We were happy to return, but we were also fearful of what we might find there. Where should we go upon landing? Where were our families? Friends? Houses? How would we eat? We had not a single answer.

On the day of departure, we took the same ferry that we had come on, landing at the Presidio. After waiting a few hours, we boarded a ship bound across the Pacific. Our ship passed under the Golden Gate Bridge and out onto the ocean. In contrast to the ships that had carried us from Okinawa to Hawai'i and from Hawai'i to Seattle, this one was rather small, carrying no passengers but us and a few guards. Half a year earlier, on our way to Hawai'i and Seattle, the war was still going on and we were tense. But the war had since come to an end. When the guards went on deck for sentry duty, they left their guns below, and when they made their rounds, they hummed songs and carried the guns upside down.

Our ship headed southward. After about a week, we heard Hawaiian music on the ship's radio, but after two or three days this became more and more faint, then disappeared entirely. We came to an area in the South Pacific where there was absolutely no wind and no waves: the face of the water was as smooth as a mirror, and the only sound between the sky and the water was the ship's own engine. The only waves we could see were in the wake created by the ship's own screws, and even those soon disappeared. Not a single fish in the water either. If ever a sailing ship were to be caught in that sea, it would be impossible to escape. Five or six years later, I came across Samuel T. Coleridge's poem "The Rime of the Ancient Mariner," about a cold northern sea and the blood of an albatross cursing a ship. There was nothing moving, nothing alive in his sea of deathly stillness. Around our ship was the southern sea, but it, too, was a sea of deathly silence. And all of us had seen a great deal of bloodshed recently, so the sense of death hung on us like an albatross. Coleridge's poem brought back to me that eerie stillness in the Pacific. His poem was the product of his imagination; was it also an illusion I saw that December?

The ship changed its course to the northwest and seemed to aim at Japan. There was one main problem: food. On our journeys from Okinawa to Hawai'i and from Hawai'i to Seattle, we had had two meals a day and been satisfied. But because we had become accustomed to three full meals a day on Angel Island, we were unhappy about being fed only twice a day on the return voyage. We boys talked about it and finally decided to appeal to the captain of the guard. Two other senior students and I were chosen as representatives. As we entered the captain's cabin, he was doing some paperwork behind a large desk. He motioned to us to sit down, and we gingerly explained what we wanted. Without interruption, he listened to us, then silently clasped his hands together behind his head as though he were thinking. Finally, he reached into a deep side drawer of his desk and pulled out a recent edition of *Life* magazine. He opened to a double-page photo spread and pushed the magazine across his desk toward us. At the sight of the picture, we froze and fell silent: before us, in black and white, lay a picture of General Wainright and other Allied prisoners of war who had been held in Japanese detention camps. They were nearly skeletons—simply skin and bones. I still don't remember how the three of us retreated from the captain's office. From then on, we never allowed the others to complain.

The Judeo-Christian tradition abhors suicide because it holds that life is given by God, so only He has the right to take it. In America, a prisoner of war is regarded as a soldier who did his best but, unfortunately, was captured by the enemy; he thus has a right to fair treatment and honor. In Japan, the Way of the Samurai has always honored and ritualized death, particularly by one's own hand. Traditionally, it was an honor reserved for warriors and the ruling class. In 1882, this tradition was codified as the

Imperial Edict for Soldiers, which insisted on death before capture. To be a prisoner of war was dishonorable; a man so dishonored no longer existed and therefore had no rights. Why then was I so horrified to see the Allied prisoners of war in a condition of starvation?

As our ship approached Japan, many rumors flew among us. One was that we were to disembark at Yokohama Bay, where Japanese MPs would be waiting for us on the pier. Without saying a word, they would hand each of us a grenade, whose meaning would be clear: "You have been a prisoner of war, a disgrace to your family and the nation. We are sure you know how to use it." When I fought in the Battle of Okinawa in 1945, I was not scared of death at all; but now, I didn't want to die.

When we landed in Okinawa, no Japanese MPs were waiting for us, and we were simply allowed to walk off the ship and go free. For the first few months, I felt awkward meeting old friends and acquaintances—and not meeting others. Whenever I passed the hills and ravines in southern Okinawa, where we had fought and lost, I was reminded of my classmates who died there. Somehow I felt odd for having survived.

Many years later, I got hold of a copy of the alumni directory for Naha Commercial Middle School. For the class of 1945, many of the names were followed by the notation DEAD IN THE BATTLE OF OKINAWA or MISSING IN ACTION IN OKINAWA.

My own name was listed, but was followed by a blank, indicating that my fate was unknown. I mulled over the idea of letting the school know that I was alive and well in Hawai'i. But remembering a classmate who put a pack of dynamite on his back and threw himself underneath an American tank, I decided to leave it alone. For reasons I don't understand, I'm reluctant to draw attention to my existence.

Afterword

For two decades, I have edited a biannual series of volumes under the title *Mānoa: A Pacific Journal of International Writing*. Each volume is published by the University of Hawai'i Press as an original paperback book, and occasionally a volume also appears in hardback form. Oftentimes the publications are compilations of contemporary literature in new English translation from specific places in Asia and the Pacific—places that are not always defined by national borders.

The guiding editorial assumption of *Mānoa* has been that excellent international literature—well wrought and attuned to the multiplicity and mystery of what makes us human—invariably transcends itself, no matter how local its details may be. By literature I mean stories that address the profound concerns of listeners and readers who recognize their own circumstances, and at the same time appreciate a true presentation of the cognitive, moral, and aesthetic variety that comprises the world as a whole. At best, literature carries us—not as tourists or eavesdroppers, but as kin—into the lives and locations of others, to whom we acknowledge a responsibility beyond tribe and nation. Just as in the ecological harmony of plants, animals, and other beings, in the human world every community and relationship matters; none can be subtracted without producing consequences for the whole. Stories reinforce the belief that we live in a complex, polyglot ecology of human experiences; and the ways that we sing, dance, think, and create are the stuff of our shared imaginations, crossing borders and pollinating our better selves to make dignity and justice possible.

In 2008, Professor Katsunori Yamazato of the University of the Ryukyus suggested to me that Okinawan American literature would be appropriate for publication in the *Mānoa* series, where it could appear in the context of other international literature, while also standing on its own.

Clearly, the world has much to learn by reading the best Okinawan literature. Among those lessons, I will mention just two: the ways Okinawans arrange ethical relationships with one another and the world, and the metaphors in Okinawan literature that add to the "word hoard," "story hoard," and "metaphor hoard" of the world's emotional and intellectual resources.

George Kerr notes in *Okinawa: The History of an Island People,* "It is striking that, almost without exception, foreigners who visited Okinawa before 1850 made special note of the Okinawan mildness and kindliness of character" and, he adds, "a general love and aptitude for singing and dancing." As early as the sixteenth century, visitors observed that there were no lethal weapons in Okinawa and the monarchy had no armed forces. Indeed, when Japanese warriors from Satsuma invaded in 1609, they were aware that carrying personal weapons had long been banned. Militarily overmatched, the kingdom was seized by samurai of the Shimazu daimyo from the north. Okinawa remained in a tributary relationship with Satsuma until Commodore Perry arrived in 1853, demanding that Okinawa sign a separate compact with the U.S. Such interference by a number of Western powers hastened the assimilation of the Ryukyu Islands by Japan's Meiji government in 1879.

Despite a history of disputes over their autonomy, Okinawans have maintained a cultural temperament of peace, cooperation, and tolerance—which is not to say passive, uncompetitive, or free of internal conflicts. Today, Okinawans are among the most peace-conscious people in the Japanese prefectures.

At the 1996 Olympic Games in Atlanta, the popular Okinawan musician Kina Shoukichi and his band, Champloose, performed. Their theme was "Lay down your weapons, take up musical instruments" *(Subete no buki wo gakki ni).* A peace advocate and member of the Japanese parliament's House of Councillors, Kina also played at the 2008 Olympic Games in Beijing. His popular music satirically comments on such social issues as cultural identity and the unwelcome presence of U.S. military bases in Okinawa. James E. Roberson discusses Kina's playful, double-edged lyrics in his article "Uchinaa Pop: Place and Identity in Contemporary Okinawan Popular Music." Roberson cites, as an example, the lyrics to "Akisamiyo!" (Oh, No!), from Kina's 1980 album *Blood Line:*

> Hey, Nabi,
> Is Okinawa part of Japan?
> In the past grandpa used to say
> Okinawa, Japan,
> Ryūkyū was part of China
>> *Oh, No! Oh, No!*
>> *Japan, China, America*
>> *They're all mixed up*
>> *and I just don't understand at all*
> Hey, Tara,
> Where is Japan?
> In the past grandma used to say
> It's somewhere way over the mountains
>> [*repeat refrain*]

Hey, Nabi,
Which do you like, Japan or America?
In the past grandpa used to say
Japan is poor and America is rich
    [*repeat refrain*]
Hey, Tara,
Where are our ancestors from?
In the past grandma used to say
Not Japan or America
or China
    [*repeat refrain*]
Oh, No! Oh, No! What should we do?
This small little Okinawa
Why is it always being forced to go
Here and there?
    [*repeat refrain*]

Scholar Shirota Chika has characterized Kina's music as "crystallizing" the Okinawan aspiration for peace in the framework of a distinct cultural spirit. Shirota quotes Kina as saying, in reference to his song "Hana" (Blooming Flowers in the Hearts of All), "I want to keep singing this song with a belief in the music's spirit, which reaches many people's minds and hearts faster than economic systems and deeper than political agendas."

We can see a similar valorizing of a local and universal "homeland of the heart" *(kokoro no furusato)* in Okinawan American literature, and the way this concept is linked to musical expression. The music, dance, and lyrics in Jon Shirota's plays, for example, are not incidental stage business or ornamental interludes. Rather, Shirota uses music and dance to reinforce themes of celebration, healing, and nostalgia. At a crucial moment in *Lucky Come Hawaii,* the vigilant Private Specks gets into a tussle with Kenyei after demanding that Kenyei remove his jacket. When it finally comes off, everyone sees the Imperial Army uniform that Kenyei has put on in hopes of joining the Japanese forces that, he believes, will be occupying Maui soon after the attack on Pearl Harbor. Kama and Kimiko try to keep Kenyei from being arrested by telling Sergeant Weaver and Private Specks that Kenyei is wearing not a Japanese officer's uniform, but a costume for an Okinawan dance. Putting an Okinawan record on the phonograph, Kama urges Kenyei to dance. After a few moments of hesitation, Kenyei starts dancing with Kimiko, and Weaver is encouraged to join in. Soon, all except Specks are clapping or doing a combination of *kachashi* (improvisational folk dancing), jitterbug, and free-form arm waving. When Specks objects, Weaver chides him: "At ease, Specks. At ease. Can't you tell a dancer from an enemy soldier?" The infectiousness of Okinawan music and *kachashi* saves Kenyei from capture and imprisonment—and from his foolish militarism.

In *Leilani's Hibiscus,* the spirits of Kama and Tsuyu emerge from their graves to find Kama's younger brother, Yasuichi, still among the living. Lyrics, singing, and playing of instruments are used by Shirota to move the story's plot along. As the deceased couple begins reminiscing about the past, they observe Yasuichi courting Leilani, a Hawaiian girl, much to Kama's disapproval. At Leilani's urging, Yasuichi sings a Hawaiian song while she plays the ukulele, and their voices merge. "You really becomin' one of us," Leilani says to him. "Even lookin' like us." Shirota's mixing of hula with Okinawan dance—and the Hawaiian love song "Aloha Oe" with the Okinawan "Fishibushi"—enacts the possibility that dance and music can marry two cultures and two peoples through languages of the emotions. The culmination of this wedding occurs at the end, when all the characters unite in joyous dancing and music making.

The structural elements of Okinawan folk music and dance also reflect *kokoro furusato,* as no part dominates, and everyone accepts variation and diversity. The musical structure is heterophonic or polyphonic, in contrast to homophonic; that is, the voice(s) and instrument(s) follow a basic melodic line, but with multiple and simultaneous variations in tempo, rhythm, and other elaborations, often added through improvisation.

Canadian ethnographer and poet Robert Bringhurst explains these musical terms in his essay "Licking the Lips with a Forked Tongue":

Homophonic music…is often played by many instruments or sung by many voices, but all of them are welded harmonically and rhythmically together. A lead voice calls, and all the others move together in a swarm. The sound is *homo*phonic or *sym*phonic. In *poly*phonic music, and in polyphonic speech, the lines are independent. The voices watch out for one another and give each other room, but each one moves through the shared acoustic space at its own speed on its own path. Each, it seems, is doing its own thinking.…

The dawn chorus of songbirds and the evening chorus of frogs are instances of natural polyphony. And then there are those moments when the songbirds and the corvids and the wood frogs and crickets coincide. Polyphony is the sound of the coexistence of species, which is what every ecology, global and local, is all about. It is the music of separate but simultaneous voices in which every voice contributes but no voice is in charge. Is that a political metaphor? Maybe so. But it is a metaphor found in nature, not a fancy I invented. Take that metaphor away, and you will have no life, no world, no species left. No Athens, no Jerusalem, no Paris; no Sierra, no Yosemite, no Yukon.

And no Naha as we know it, no Honolulu—no diverse ecology of human languages, cultures, or knowledge. Singing, dancing, and telling stories simultaneously in multifarious profusion and health—with no voice or culture in charge—sustains balance in a world of vital, intermingled relationships among the human and nonhuman, the local and global, the past and future. The skills necessary for polyphonic listening are rare in many cultures and nations. They require a perceptiveness and appreciation for complex and coexisting rhythms, tempos, tones, harmonies, and melodies—as well as tolerance for dissonant passages. But, with greater familiarity, such listening and its metaphors can be cultivated and appreciated. In the West, polyphony once flourished in the choral singing of medieval Europe and in the fugues of Bach; it was revived in twentieth-century classical music and has always been integral to great jazz. In the East, polyphony flourishes in the living folk music of South Asia, Turkey, Thailand, and Indonesia. And it is popular in some contemporary world music, including Uchinaa Pop.

In Okinawan American literature such as Jon Shirota's, folk music and dance are integral to the polyphonic spirit: a lively "mixing," both literally and metaphorically, of many voices. In this kind of ecology of singing and dancing, no one can be left out, including the American soldiers Specks and Weaver. All are needed in order to tell true stories—and to imagine a world in which everyone participates and celebrates together, the one and many, simultaneously.

Frank Stewart

REFERENCES

Arakaki Makoto. "Hawai'i Uchinanchu and Okinawa: Uchinanchu Spirit and the Formation of a Transnational Identity." In *Okinawan Diaspora,* edited by Ronald Y. Nakasone. Honolulu: University of Hawai'i Press, 2002.

Bringhurst, Robert. *Everywhere Being Is Dancing: Twenty Pieces of Thinking.* Kentville, Nova Scotia: Gasperau Press, 2007.

———. *The Tree of Meaning: Language, Mind and Ecology.* Berkeley, CA: Counterpoint, 2008.

Kerr, George. *Okinawa: The History of an Island People.* Revised Edition. Boston: Tuttle, 2000.

Roberson, James E. "Uchinaa Pop: Place and Identity in Contemporary Okinawan Popular Music." *Critical Asian Studies,* 33:2 (2001), 211–242.

Shirota Chika. "Eissa: Identities and Dances of Okinawan Diasporic Experience." In *Okinawan Diaspora,* edited by Ronald Y. Nakasone. Honolulu: University of Hawai'i Press, 2002.

About the Contributors

Philip K. Ige is a former administrator for the University of Hawai'i and the Hawai'i State Department of Education. He received his doctorate from Columbia University in 1968. One of the first Hawai'i writers to use pidgin English in his writing, he is regarded as a pioneer in Asian American literature.

Mitsugu Sakihara (1928–2001) was born in Okinawa. Drafted into the Japanese army while a teenager, he fought in the 1945 Battle of Okinawa, was wounded, and was taken as a prisoner of war by the United States. After spending the next half year in detention camps in Hawai'i and California, he returned to Okinawa. Later, he attended the University of Oregon, where he received his bachelor's and master's degrees, and the University of Hawai'i, where he received his doctorate and taught for twenty-five years. In 1995, he became president of Hawai'i International College.

Jon Shirota was born on Maui. His father immigrated to Hawai'i from Ginoza Village, Okinawa, in 1907, and his mother immigrated from Kanna Village in 1910. Upon graduating from Brigham Young University in Utah, he worked as a U.S. Treasury agent. In 1963, he was invited to the Handy Writers' Colony, where he completed *Lucky Come Hawaii*, the first of his three published novels. His plays have been produced in Honolulu, Los Angeles, New York, and Tokyo. He has received awards from the Rockefeller Foundation, American College Theater Festival, Los Angeles Actors Theater Festival of One Acts, Japan-U.S. Friendship Commission, and National Endowment for the Arts.

Wesley Iwao Ueunten is an Okinawan Sansei who was born on Kaua'i. He received his doctorate in comparative ethnic studies from the University of California at Berkeley and is assistant professor of Asian studies at San Francisco State University. He has published articles on Okinawan identity and is the co-founder of Genyukai Berkeley, a group that learns, practices, and performs traditional and contemporary Okinawan music.

Katsunori Yamazato received his doctorate from the University of California at Davis and is professor of American literature and culture at the University of the Ryukyus. His books include *Great Earth Sangha: Dialogues between Gary Snyder and Sansei Yamao;* Japanese translations of Snyder's *A Place in Space* and *Mountains and Rivers without End;* and *Post-War Okinawa and America: Fifty Years of Cross-Cultural Contact,* which he co-edited. He is the director of the American

Studies Center of the University of the Ryukyus and director of the Pacific and North/South American Research Project "Human Migration and the Twenty-first Century Global Society."

Kinuko Maehara Yamazato is a doctoral student in sociology at the University of Hawaiʻi. Her article "To Okinawa and Back Again: Life Stories of Okinawan Kibei Nisei in Hawaiʻi" was published in 2007 in *Uchinaanchu Diaspora: Memories, Continuities, and Constructions,* edited by Joyce N. Chinen for *Social Process in Hawaiʻi.*

Permissions and Acknowledgments

PERMISSIONS

"An Okinawan Nisei in Hawaii" by Philip K. Ige first appeared in *Uchinanchu: A History of Okinawans in Hawaii*. Honolulu: Ethnic Studies Oral History Project, Ethnic Studies Program, University of Hawai'i, 1981. Reprinted by permission of the publisher.

"Akisamiyo!" by Kina Shoukichi and Champloose from the album *Blood Line*, Polydor K. K., H25P 20307. 1989 [1980]. Translated by James E. Roberson. Printed by permission of the translator.

"History and Okinawans" by Mitsugu Sakihara first appeared as "Preface" in *Uchinanchu: A History of Okinawans in Hawaii*. Honolulu: Ethnic Studies Oral History Project, Ethnic Studies Program, University of Hawai'i, 1981. Reprinted by permission of the publisher.

"Sparrows of Angel Island" by Mitsugu Sakihara first appeared as "Sparrows of Angel Island: The Experience of a Young Japanese Prisoner of War" in *Mānoa: A Pacific Journal of International Writing* 8:1 (Summer 1996). Printed by permission of the publisher.

"The Dawning of an Okinawan" by Jon Shirota first appeared in *Uchinanchu: A Pictorial Tribute to Okinawans in Hawaii*. Honolulu: EastWest Magazine Co., Ltd., 1990. Reprinted by permission of the author.

Lucky Come Hawaii, *Leilani's Hibiscus*, and *Voices from Okinawa* by Jon Shirota. Printed by permission of the author.

"A Grandfather to His Grandson: A Viewpoint of 'The Great Depression'" by Seiyei Wakukawa appeared in an earlier form in *Seiyei Wakukawa: Building Bridges of Understanding Between America and Japan*. Naha, Okinawa: Niraisha, 2000. Reprinted by permission of Setsuko Wakukawa.

"The Gift: An Interview with June Hiroko Arakawa" by Kinuko Maehara Yamazato. Printed by permission of the author.

ACKNOWLEDGMENTS

Created by Ozaki Seiji, the woodblock prints in this volume depict Okinawan dolls and toys. The prints are reproduced from his book *Ryukyu gangu zufu* (Kasahara Shoni Hoken Kenkyujo, 1936), which is in the Sakamaki/Hawley Collection in Hamilton Library, of the University of Hawai'i. A multitude of Ryukyu/Okinawa materials were destroyed during World War II, so numerous items in the collection are one of a kind. Ozaki's book is one of the more than nine hundred items collected by the late English journalist-scholar Frank Hawley (1906–1961).

Ozaki's captions were translated by Lynette Teruya, Program Coordinator at the Center for Okinawan Studies, of the University of Hawai'i, then edited and abridged for concision; additional help was provided by Kinuko Yamazato. In some cases, Ozaki's 1930s Japanese terms have been modernized and the spelling of Ryukyuan words standardized in accordance with *Okinawan-English Wordbook* by Mitsugu Sakihara (University of Hawai'i Press, 2006). Any errors introduced in the editing and abridgement are the responsibility of *Mānoa*'s general editor.

We also relied on *Okinawan-English Wordbook* to make orthographic changes in some of the pieces in this volume. In other pieces, we decided to retain the variations in spelling used by individual authors; the variations reflect individual preferences and often the printing or orthographic conventions of the time the pieces were originally published.

A final note of thanks to people and institutions in addition to those mentioned by Katsunori Yamazato in the Preface. Each offered indispensable help and expertise in completing this volume: Tokiko Bazzell, Japan Specialist Librarian, Hamilton Library, University of Hawai'i, Mānoa; Robert G. Buss, Executive Director, Hawai'i Council for the Humanities; Joyce Chinen, Professor of Sociology, University of Hawai'i, West O'ahu; Joel Cohn, Chair, Department of Japanese Literature, East Asian Languages and Literatures, University of Hawai'i, Mānoa; Keala Francis; Alice Mak; Warren S. Nishimoto, Director, Center for Oral History, University of Hawai'i, Mānoa; James E. Roberson, Professor of Cultural Anthropology, Tokyo Jogakkan College; Matthew W. Shores; Christine A. Takata, Preservation Specialist, Hamilton Library, University of Hawai'i, Mānoa; Lynette Teruya, Program Coordinator, Center for Okinawan Studies, University of Hawai'i, Mānoa; Wesley Iwao Ueunten, Assistant Professor, Asian American Studies Department, San Francisco State University; Setsuko Wakukawa; and Kinuko Yamazato.

Further Readings

Arasaki, Moriteru. *Profile of Okinawa: 100 Questions and Answers.* Tokyo: Nikkei, 2000.

Chinen, Joyce N., ed. *Uchinaanchu Diaspora: Memories, Continuities, and Constructions. Social Process in Hawai'i,* vol. 42. Honolulu: Department of Sociology, University of Hawai'i at Mānoa. Distributed by University of Hawai'i Press, 2007.

Ethnic Studies Oral History Project and United Okinawan Association of Hawaii, ed. *Uchinanchu: A History of Okinawans in Hawaii.* Honolulu: Ethnic Studies Oral History Project, Ethnic Studies Program, University of Hawai'i. Distributed by University of Hawai'i Press, 1981.

Glacken, Clarence J. *The Great Loochoo: A Study of Okinawan Village Life.* Berkeley: University of California Press, 1955.

Hawaii United Okinawa Association. *To Our Issei...Our Heartfelt Gratitude.* Edited by the Okinawan Centennial Celebration Issei Commemorative Booklet Committee, June H. Arakawa and Henry H. Isara, co-chairs. Honolulu: The Committee, 2000.

Kerr, George H. *Okinawa: The History of an Island People.* Revised edition. Boston: Tuttle, 2000.

Kimura, Yukiko. *Issei: Japanese Immigrants in Hawaii.* Honolulu: University of Hawai'i Press, 1988.

Nakasone, Ronald Y., ed. *Okinawan Diaspora.* Honolulu: University of Hawai'i Press, 2002.

———. *Reflections on the Okinawan Experience: Essays Commemorating 100 Years of Okinawa Immigration.* Fremont, CA: Dharma Cloud, 1996.

Okamura, Jonathan, ed. *The Japanese American Contemporary Experience in Hawai'i. Social Process in Hawai'i,* vol. 41. Honolulu: Department of Sociology, University of Hawai'i at Mānoa. Distributed by University of Hawai'i Press, 2002.

Okinawa Club of America. *History of the Okinawans in North America.* Translated by Ben Kobashigawa. Los Angeles: Asian American Studies Center, University of California, Los Angeles, 1988.

Okinawa Department of Commerce, Industry & Labor. *Ryukyuan Dance.* Naha, Okinawa: Okinawa Prefecture, 1995.

Okinawan Celebration Education Committee. *Uchinaa: Okinawan History and Culture.* Edited by Joyce N. Chinen and Ruth Adaniya. Honolulu: The Committee, 1990.

Ota, Masahide. *Essays on Okinawa Problems.* Gushikawa City, Okinawa: Yui Suppan, 2000.

Robinson, James C. *Okinawa: A People and Their Gods.* Boston: Tuttle, 1969.

Sakamaki, Shunzō. *Ryūkyū: A Bibliographical Guide to Okinawa Studies.* Honolulu: University of Hawai'i Press, 1963.

Sakihara, Mitsugu. Edited by Stewart Curry et al. *Okinawan-English Wordbook: A Short Lexicon of the Okinawan Language with English Definitions and Japanese Cognates.* Honolulu: University of Hawai'i Press, 2006.

Seiyei Wakukawa Memorial Project Committee, ed. *Seiyei Wakukawa: Building Bridges of Understanding Between America and Japan.* Naha, Okinawa: Niraisha, 2000.

Tamura, Eileen. *Americanization, Acculturation, and Ethnic Identity: The Nisei Generation in Hawaii.* Urbana: University of Illinois Press, 1994.

MĀNOA: A PACIFIC JOURNAL OF INTERNATIONAL WRITING

EDITOR   Frank Stewart

MANAGING EDITOR Pat Matsueda

PRODUCTION EDITOR   Brent Fujinaka

ASSOCIATE EDITOR   Brandy Nālani McDougall

DESIGNER AND ART EDITOR   Barbara Pope

STAFF   Sonia Cabrera, Keala Francis Dickhens, Jennifer Larson, Nicole Sawa, Lourena Yco

CORRESPONDING EDITORS AND ADVISORY GROUP   Esther K. Arinaga,
William H. Hamilton, Barry Lopez, W. S. Merwin, Carol Moldaw, Michael Nye,
Naomi Shihab Nye, Joseph O'Mealy, Robert Shapard, Arthur Sze

HTTP://MANOAJOURNAL.HAWAII.EDU
HTTP://WWW.UHPRESS.HAWAII.EDU/JOURNALS/MANOA/

MĀNOA *means, in the Hawaiian language, "vast and deep." It is the name of the valley*
where the University of Hawai'i is situated.

MĀNOA gratefully acknowledges the continuing support of the University of Hawai'i
Administration; the support of the University of Hawai'i College of Languages, Linguistics,
and Literature; and grants from the National Endowment for the Arts and the Hawai'i State
Foundation on Culture and the Arts. Special thanks for support of this volume to the Mānoa
Foundation through funding from the Hawai'i Council for the Humanities.

ISSN 1045-7909
ISBN 13: 978-0-8248-3391-6